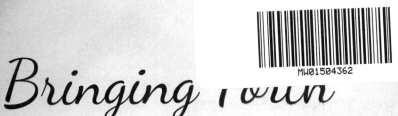

Bringing Your

Soul

Consciousness

An Akashic Records
Guide to Living a Fulfilled Life

Reverend Annie Bachelder

Published 2023

DISCLAIMER

Neither the author nor the publisher assume any responsibility for errors, omissions, or contrary interpretations of the subject matter within.

MEDICAL DISCLAIMER

The information in this book is a result of years of practical experience by the author. This information is not intended as a substitute for the advice provided by your physician or other healthcare professional. Do not use this information for diagnosing or treating a health problem or disease, or prescribing medication or other treatment.

ISBN # 979-8-9890697-1-2 Paperback
ISBN# 979-8-9890697-2-9 Audio Book

Book cover and interior design by Deborah Perdue, Illumination Graphics, www.illuminationgraphics.com

Dedication

I dedicate this book to the Great Creatress, the Akashic Beings of Light, Anubis, and my Masters, Teachers, and Loved Ones, all of whom allowed me to channel their messages.

I also dedicate and thank my partner, Peter, for his patience and endless support. This book is a reality because of seven beloved and committed beta readers: Anette Nilsson, Anna Tsui, Carrie Bachelder, Christine Brusati, Erika Martinez, Meredith Locher, Michelle Mondot-Wilcox, and Steve Bennett. This Divinely aligned group gave their individual specialties, wisdom, editing, support, honesty, and much needed grammar assistance. All of you left your divinely inspired fingerprints on this work. Thank you from the depths of my spiritual heart and the heights of my Soul's Light.

Table of Contents

Chapter 1 Introductory Message from the Akashic Beings of Light 1
Chapter 2 Getting Started, Opening Your Akashic Records. 9
Chapter 3 Going Forward in Space and Time 25
Chapter 4 Annie's Introduction to the Light. 33
Chapter 5 How I Learned to Channel. 39
Chapter 6 How Healing Transpires in the Akashic Records. 45
Chapter 7 How the Soul is Constructed 53
Chapter 8 Following the Energy 65
Chapter 9 The Development of Soul Consciousness 73
Chapter 10 Embracing Soul Qualities & the Great Creatress 81
Chapter 11 Your Spiritual Heart 89
Chapter 12 Masterful Manifesting 99
Chapter 13 Feeling Your Soul's Light in Your Body. 107
Chapter 14 Embodiment of Soul's Light & Consciousness. 113
Chapter 15 Living as Your Soul 121
Chapter 16 Soul Consciousness – Next Steps 131
Chapter 17 Loving Your Fear 137
Chapter 18 Healing the Separation. 145
Chapter 19 Etheric Planes of Light, Claiming Your Soul. 151
Chapter 20 Alternatives to Worry. 159
Chapter 21 Transitioning Between States of Consciousness. 167
Chapter 22 Going South 173
Chapter 23 Anubis Speaks: Healing Past Lives 179
Chapter 24 Writing Your Soul's Divine Plan 187
Chapter 25 Being of Service 199
Chapter 26 A Discussion of Gender 207
Chapter 27 Prayer. 213
Chapter 28 Overwhelming Peace 219
Chapter 29 Awaiting Divine Timing 223
Chapter 30 Self-Doubt and Disappointment 233
Chapter 31 Self-Judgment and Your Inner Critic 243
Chapter 32 Beauty 251
Chapter 33 By All that Is Holy 257
Chapter 34 The Power of Story, Past Lives. 261
Chapter 35 Resistance, Judgment, & Fear, Ancestral Healing 269
Chapter 36 The Value You Bring to Your Soul 277
Chapter 37 Soul Connection. 285
Chapter 38 Soul Inspired Action, Creation, & Healing. 297
Chapter 39 By the Power of Divine Light Within Me 305
Chapter 40 Final Messages. 311
Prayers, Invocations, and Exercises 316

CHAPTER 1

Introductory Channeled Message from the Akashic Beings of Light and the Author

Welcome to the Akashic Records and to **Bringing Forth Soul Consciousness.** We are the Akashic Beings of Light, working in concert with your Akashic Masters, Teachers, and Loved Ones, and with the Divine, whom we call the Great Creatress.

As beings of pure Light, Our purpose is three-fold:

To begin with, We help you to release the tensions, conflicts, and difficulties that humans have in daily life. Utilizing your Soul's Akashic Records in our interaction with you, we augment solutions sourced in your Soul. This book, and the energy in it, teaches you how to transform problems into Soul level empowerment, even during times of great difficulty. This transformation includes magnificent opportunities to directly experience the Great Creatress at Her highest benevolence.

Second, We are here to expand your Soul connection, via Its Light, and Its refined consciousness. This will assist you in every area of your life. It will assist you in sharing consciousness with the Akashic Beings of Light, and in experiencing your connection with the Great Creatress. Soul Consciousness contains within it keys to fulfilling your Soul's purposes. In turn, this benefits humanity's evolution, joy, and experience of Oneness with the Great Creatress.

To do this, We amplify your connection with your Soul chakra (the 8th chakra). We teach you how to experience your Soul's Light throughout your body. *(Please see chapter 3 for complete instructions on "How to Embody Your Soul's Light".)* Embodying your Soul's Light is important because the human template was damaged during the implosion of Atlantis. The implosion caused a breach between the physical (the human body) and the meta-physical (the Soul and the Great Creatress). This breach is the source of humanity's sense of separation from the Great Creatress, from Soul, from each other, and from the rest of creation.

Embodying your Soul's Light reunifies you with your Soul, healing the sense of separation.

We Akashic Beings of Light are here to re-unify your human consciousness with the steady stream of Soul Light and Soul consciousness. Embodying your Soul's Light speeds, the reunification process and heals millenniums of errant behavior and disordered thinking. The intrinsic connection between your Soul and your physical self is reinforced through repeatedly filling in the connecting frequencies of Light between your Soul chakra, your Crown chakra, and the rest of your body. This conscious activity purposefully brings forth the knowingness of your Soul. It also makes it easier for you to cooperate with, and trust, the Great Creatress. Embodying your Soul's Light and consciousness facilitates harmonious relationships with other humans and offers you tools for making better life choices. This process develops your Soul level "sense of knowing", revealed gradually, gently drawing you forward on your Soul's Divine plan.

Trusting the reunification process is the first step in developing Soul Consciousness.

The Soul frequencies, experienced through embodiment of your Soul's Light, amend and strengthen the connection between humanity and the Great Creatress, and with all Creation.

Simply put, the advantage of Bringing Forth Soul Consciousness is this: the more consciously the human connects with its Soul, the easier and more fluid the journey.

Acquiring Soul Consciousness is a main theme of many who have chosen to incarnate at this time in human history. The Akashic Records aid us in these pursuits.

(Please see chapter 2 "Getting Started, Opening Your Akashic Records" utilizing the Bringing Forth Soul Consciousness Akashic Prayer©.)

Thirdly, the origin of Our message is the Akashic Records. The Akashic Records are primarily an energetic structure, laden with love and wisdom. The Records contain tremendously useful and valuable information and are saturated with unconditional love. The Akashic Records are an energetic transmission, causing energy and perceptual shifts, filling in the gaps in your knowledge and experience base. We and the Akashic Records always meet you where you are now.

**We build our inter-working relationship with you at the rate and pace
that suits your Soul's consciousness and your human self
so that intimacy with your Soul is restored.**

The Akashic Records hold everything that each Soul has ever spoken, thought, or done, throughout all Its incarnations. The Records also reveal all that has happened, is happening, and has the possibility of happening now, and throughout all time. The Akashic Records are an infinite, dynamic resource open to all. The Records are now accessible to everyone, and especially to those who have traveled and travailed to find the energetic keys to life, love, wisdom, and freedom. We Akashic Beings of Light have great respect for you who are drawn to explore the Akashic Records for dynamic information, essential healing, and accelerated spiritual growth. Through the Akashic Records, We extend our assistance freely, objectively, and completely devoid of judgment.

We already love you and We greet our beloved Readers warmly. We offer soothing for your suffering, and our kindest respect for your efforts. We are aware of each of you who are reading this book. We are aware of you who are working with energy, who seek to heighten your vibrational frequency, and to become all that you are created to be.

**No request for our assistance is too much to ask,
too small-minded, or off track.**

We welcome all seekers, all human needs for comfort, security, knowledge, and all spiritual aspirations. We gratefully serve humanity's desire to experience, to expand, to heal, to evolve, to be at peace internally, and with one another.

From the infinite well of our Spiritual Heart, we welcome you to the Akashic Records and to **Bringing Forth Soul Consciousness**. (Please see chapter 11 "Your Spiritual Heart".)

Reverend Annie Bachelder's Introductory Message

In 2019, I signed up for a writing class. Half-heartedly, I hoped to learn to write compelling marketing for my services as an Akashic Channel. During the first session, experienced students read passages of their work and the instructor gave feedback. During the second session, the instructor led us in a brief consciousness preparation process. Then, like a shot, I began to write. Without giving it a thought, I began channeling the Akashic Beings of Light and their introduction to **Bringing Forth Soul Consciousness**. Prior to that moment, I had not one whit of a desire to write a book. I had not been told by any of my spirit guides that I was to write a book, especially not one that involved deeply esoteric principles that were somewhat above my pay grade. Every time I sat down to write, I received another channeled transmission for the book. Many times, when I began to write, the Akashic Beings of Light had to "handle my case". By that I mean these loving beings of Light had to calm my emotions and focus my scattered thoughts so I could channel their energy and information for **Bringing Forth Soul Consciousness**. This accounts for the meditative quality and content of many chapters. It is also why there are so many guided exercises that teach energy skills and ways of working purposefully in the Akashic Records. Years later, I continue to incorporate the principles of this material.

I use the technique of embodying my Soul's Light and consciousness many times a day. The process happens instantaneously now. It consistently smooths my emotions and clears my thinking. I treasure the added experience of being completely enveloped by the Great Creatress. I picture myself filled with my Souls Light, surrounded by the Great Creatress, feeling unconditionally confident. I observe as what I want to experience, and the resources I need, simply arrive. Fear transforms into stillness. Resentments vanish. I feel alive, on purpose, and know what to do, or not do. I know when the energy is ripe for action and when it is not. I trust my Soul and the Great Creatress. I feel spiritually aligned and ready to be of service to students, clients, and others as we navigate our Soul's Divine plans. Truly, the Divine doeth the works. Not I.

I hope that the Readers of this book sense, and benefit from, the energy in it. I hope Readers, and those they share it with, find it equally effective and as helpful as it has been for me.

A little history to get us acquainted seems appropriate.

I was introduced to the Akashic Records, the energetic archive of the Soul's entire journey, after 25 years of being a 'conscious channel' for Anubis, my benevolent Spirit Guide. Being an "unconscious" channel seemed a poor fit. Voluntarily leaving my body and letting some entity take over? No. Not for me. Anubis and I agreed it was far more beneficial for me to be a conscious channel. This way I, too, would learn about the energy and information channeled in the transmissions. My experience of Anubis has always been that this kind Being of Light is the voice of a larger group of Light Beings who work together to "step down" their energy to make it discernible to me, my clients, and my students.

When I began channeling in 1988, I asked, "What is Anubis' higher purpose in channeling for me and other people?" Anubis stated that, "The higher purpose has always been reunifying Souls with their human counterparts. Reunification", Anubis stated, "allows conscious connection with Source. Reunification allows you to hold greater Light which accelerates evolution for the good of all." In my personal experience, and through reports from channeling clients and students, channeled readings amplify our inner Light, bring peace of mind to worried people, improve relationships, clarify next steps, and produces harmony despite difficult situations.

In 2014, I was introduced to the Akashic Records. I felt that for the previous 25 years, Anubis held my hands, gently and patiently, until it was time to lead me to the Akashic Records. Anubis then politely receded to the background so I could devote myself single-mindedly to the study and mastery of working in the Akashic Records. After 3 years of immersion in the Records, I received the message that it was time for me to begin teaching classes and leading guided meditations. Anubis graciously returned. Anubis is always available and is often the source channeling the guided meditations on Facebook (see links below) and some of this book's chapters.

(YouTube "Reverend Annie Bachelder, Psychic and Channel" https://www.youtube.com/channel/UCkl8K0gm24Hh4ibfD6_WW3Q , www.Facebook.com/annie.bachelder , and private Facebook Group "Bringing Forth Soul Consciousness" https://www.facebook.com/groups/328360825953128)

What are the Akashic Records?

"Akasha" is a Sanskrit word meaning "limitless sky", much as someone would point to the sky inferring Goddess, Universe, or Divine Creator. Another translation of the word Akasha is "primary substance from which all things are formed". This describes raw, formless energy before our thoughts and feelings cause it to manifest as physical things, people, and experiences we desire. Emanating from a Soul level plane of consciousness, the Records are extremely sensitive to any kind of vibration. The Records energetically record everything that has ever happened, is happening, or has the possibility of happening. All occurrences are indelibly recorded in it. "The Records" is a term comparable to the family bible, having dedicated pages listing births, deaths, marriages, divorces, plagues, earthquakes, droughts, etc.

The Akashic Records can be accessed by ordinary people and are organized for our use by your current legal name. The Records register everything that a Soul in human form has ever spoken, thought, felt, intended, or done in any of its incarnations during its evolution toward oneness with the Great Creatress. Also recorded are the interests, education, and consciousness activities of every Soul in between Its earth lifetimes. **Bringing Forth Soul Consciousness** through the Akashic Records is the perfect delivery system.

While I am a natural psychic and experienced channel, what stands out for me about the Akashic Records is the expansive, dignified, and validating perspective. The Akashic Records provide excitingly clear, practical, applicable, and useful information. The Records contain an entire spectrum of healing energy, transmitted on frequencies of unconditional love and respect.

The Akashic Records exist in an environment
based on three principles:
Fear Not, Judge Not, and Resist Not.

They enhance your ability to see without judgment, sense the importance of, and describe past lives, key concepts, and influential circumstances.

The energy and information originating from the Akashic Records has a compact wholeness to it and the proven, established process to access them is consistently reliable. Since the Akashic Records exist at a Soul level plane of consciousness, the information and healing are precisely attuned to the needs of the individual at that moment.

Bringing Forth Soul Consciousness is a key function of the Akashic Records. The integration of humanity with Soul Consciousness is one of the grand purposes of accessing the Akashic Records. **Bringing Forth Soul Consciousness** accelerates human spiritual evolution.

Please note: Throughout this book, the Akashic Beings of Light have highlighted personal memories of mine as examples of the chapter topic. These memories are **[bracketed and italicized.]**

It is my deepest desire that you receive help, peace, and purpose through **Bringing Forth Soul Consciousness** and the Akashic Records.

Reverend Annie Bachelder

CHAPTER 2

Getting Started,
Opening Your Akashic Records

Channeled by the Akashic Beings of Light

Greetings and welcome from the Akashic Beings of Light. In this chapter We teach you how to open your Akashic Records using the **Bringing Forth Soul Consciousness** Akashic Records Prayer©. Later chapters address **Bringing Forth Soul Consciousness** using the Akashic Records on the following topics:

- o How to Embody Your Soul's Light
- o Your Spiritual Heart
- o Living as Your Soul
- o Alternatives to Worry
- o Masterful Manifesting
- o Healing Undesirable Past Lives or Ancestral Influences
- o Self-Doubt and Disappointment
- o Releasing Fear, Resistance, and Judgment,
- o 18 Prayers, Invocations, and Exercises helping you to release, experience, manifest, build skills, and much more.

These topics are starting points and are offered to energize you, to empower you as you proceed, and to assist your creative endeavors as you fulfill your Soul's purposes directly. You will be empowered by your Soul, your spiritual advisory team in your Akashic Records, and the Great Creatress. With time and practice your emotional state will assume the unwavering strength, resilience, and illumination of your Soul. You will be inspired and comforted by the presence of the Great Creatress. You will be validated for your efforts to grow emotionally and spiritually.

Now, on to opening your Akashic Records.

Purposes of the *Bringing Forth Soul Consciousness* Akashic Prayer©

The purposes of the **Brining Forth Soul Consciousness** Akashic Records Prayer© are to teach you the established and proven process for accessing the Akashic Records. The Prayer brings forth Soul level wisdom, expansive consciousness, and supports execution of your Soul's purposes. It amplifies your living, conscious awareness of the Divine Light within you. The Prayer builds your relationships with the Akashic Beings of Light, the Great Creatress, and your Masters, Teachers, and Loved Ones to empower your ability to resolve problems and conflicts. It gives you access to the higher purpose of past life struggles, unwanted ancestral influences, and your Soul's agenda for you. It clarifies new forms of expression for your Soul's purposes. The Prayer elevates you and your perspective of challenging relationships and situations. It heals accumulated karma that would unnecessarily inhibit your progress physically, emotionally, mentally, and spiritually.

The Prayer accesses your Akashic Records, infuses you with your Soul's Light, centering your conscious attention on meeting the day with wisdom, calm, and unconditional love.

Guidelines for all Open Akashic Records Activities

Do not consume alcohol or recreational drugs for **24 hours prior** to, or during, any open Akashic Records activity.

Use your current legal name (the current legal name on your driving license, passport, or other government issued document) when opening your Records. This may, or may not, be different than your birth certificate name.

Do not leave your Records open indefinitely. Always use the Closing Prayer to formally end of your open Records session.

Please be conscious and deliberate in your work in the Records (as opposed to unconscious, sloppy, and haphazard). Intend to open your Records for

15 to 60 minutes, read a chapter, write your responses to the interactive questions, and then close your Records with the Closing Prayer.

The Akashic Records are an energetic Soul level plane of consciousness. Your ability to **sense, identify, and describe** the energy, concepts, body sensations, and visual images will be enhanced. Your skill with this will improve with practice.

Trust what you are receiving. These are the Records of your own Soul. The energy and information are selected specifically for you.

You are strongly encouraged to **ask questions** in your Records. The Akashic Beings of Light and your Masters, Teachers, and Loved Ones are here to help you solve problems, ease tensions, raise your vibration, and educate you. The Records are all about questions!

Background and Information about the Akashic Records

Since 2014, Annie's knowledge of the Akashic Records has been informed by near daily explorations with Us in her own Akashic Records. She has done thousands of readings for clients and taught numerous Akashic Records classes. Annie has thoroughly studied Akashic Records with Dr. Linda Howe, and read books by Lisa Barnett, Akemi G, Maureen St. Germaine, Anne Taylor, and Kevin Todeschi. These studies have reinforced her understanding and confirmed what We, the Akashic Beings of Light, have stated in channelings. Other credible, historic sources are Madame Blavatsky, and, of course, Edgar Casey's transcripts of over 3000 Akashic Records readings preserved by the A.R.E. Foundation.

Below is general information about the Akashic Records.

o   During the 1980's and 1990's the Akashic Records opened access to secular people. Previously, the Records were accessible only to mystics and sages.

o   The Akashic Records are the vibrational record of all Souls.

o   Even though everything in creation is within the Great Creatress' consciousness, it bears saying that you, your Soul, and the Akasha at large, are always within the sphere of She who created everything.

- The **Akashic Records are spiritual,** NOT psychic. You do not have to be psychic, or a spiritual savant, to work effectively in the Akashic Records.

- **Three Principles govern the Records – Fear Not, Resist Not, and Judge Not.** This ensures an atmosphere of sacred safety, kindness, and respect.

- In the Akashic Records the order of importance is always **Energy first, Information second.** Be alert to the energy you sense in your Akashic Records. The energy reveals a lot, and has a powerful effect on you, often more so than the pictures, sense of knowing, and words you often receive.

- In your Akashic Records it is easy to access your past lives and information about your ancestors. This is an opportunity to discover how you can come to peace with your past, and to love yourself unconditionally. Be open to how you are being shown that you can love yourself unconditionally even though you played the victim, the ignorant follower, the dominator, or the killer. The Akashic Records offer a way to be at peace with your powerlessness over what happened to you; what you did in response; how you handled the situation; the conclusions you drew regarding earth life, men, women, love, fear, ambition, motivation, responsibility, commitment, authority, freedom, justice, and self-discipline.

- Moses probably received the 10 Commandments in the bible from the Akashic Records. The mentions of the "Book of Life" relate to the Akashic Records.

- One Akashic Perspective is that **You have everything you need and cannot have anything that is not needed.**

- Every experience in the Records is a healing. The Records hold you steady in the Light of the Akasha, and the Light, in Its infinite wisdom, heals you.

- Working in the Akashic Records is a practice. Give yourself a break. It's okay to be a beginner.

o The Records are a safe, sacred sanctuary. Sometimes you need to spend time in a silent sanctuary, without a lot of words and information, in order to rest and rejuvenate.

o Approximately 10% of Akashic Records readers receive information via audio and body sensations, 10% receive visual images, and 80% receive through a "Sense of Knowing". You may be receiving information from a combination of these senses which can vary in your open Records sessions.

o Notice body sensations, and whether the energy seems stuck or moving? Balanced or unstable? Light or dark? Thick or thin? etc.

o Notice the emotional qualities of the energy you are experiencing.

o Concepts and symbols are often used as communication devices in your Records, and you may have to "unpack" them. Be aware of additional questions to ask the Akashic Beings of Light, or your Masters, Teachers, and Loved Ones about these concepts and symbols.

o Describe, describe, describe your experience using these sentence openings: It seems like . . . I get the sense that . . . I am being shown . . . I have the feeling . . . I hear words such as . . . My sense of knowing is . . .

o Questions are the can openers to the Akashic Perspective. Ask a question or two. Then ask some more . . .

o If you do not understand what you are receiving ask your MTLO's for more detail, or ask, "help me understand . . . "

o The Records contain all knowledge but are too vast for our consciousness. The ABOL's and your MTLO's locate answers to your questions based on **what is most helpful, applicable, and useful to you at this moment.**

o The Akashic Records create an energetic sphere around you, containing a heart-connection between the human you, your Soul, and the Great Creatress.

- ○ **You can be certain that you are receiving Akashic information if it has a positive tone, contains an uplifting message, and the overall feeling is loving, expansive, kind, compassionate, and respectful.**

- ○ If the energy and information is condemning, condescending, or judgmental, you are not receiving it from the Records. Go back, close the Records, re-read the entire Prayer, and try again.

How the Akashic Records are Organized

The **Bringing Forth Soul Consciousness** Akashic Records Prayer© (below), connects you with the Akashic Beings of Light, the Great Creatress, and your Masters, Teachers, and Loved Ones.

The **Akashic Beings of Light** oversee your activities and locate answers to questions posed in your open Records sessions. The Akashic Beings of Light provide continuity by serving the Great Creatress and Her plan for your Soul's evolution. The Akashic Beings of Light assist in your personal expansion into the Light and secure your conscious unity with the Great Creatress. The Akashic Beings of Light help you to know the truth of your Divine origin, and release blockages to your abundance and highest good. They create the Divine Portal, a vertical column of Light, that elevates you to the highest realm of the Akashic Records.

Although they often operate as a unified group,
your Masters, Teachers, and Loved Ones
each have specific beneficial roles.

Masters are High Beings of Pure Light who come to your side the instant the Great Creatress sparks you into existence as a point of consciousness. Your Masters are brilliant, loving, Beings of Light. They are with your Soul throughout your Soul's entire journey. They are with your Soul at Its inception. They are with your Soul throughout every embodied lifetime on earth, and during your "lives between lifetimes". They are with you when your Soul chooses to receive "specialized consciousness training" on other planets, stars, and with collectives who cooperate for specific spiritual purposes. Your Masters are always with you and are always ready to help you. Your Masters love you, and your

Soul, unconditionally. They are humble servants who do not require adoration or credit for their activities on your behalf.

Teachers are ascended Beings who help you master the topics which are their specialty. Topics such as love, money, time, guilt, various kinds of relationships, artistic expressions, spiritual qualities, skill sets, etc. Teachers may be ascended beings of high repute in particular cultures such as Christ, Mary Magdalena, Kwan Yin, Ganesh, Buddha, and so forth. Or they may simply be helpful spirits, committed to helping humanity evolve.

> *Humility is an essential principle*
> *that Masters, and Teachers exemplify.*
> *They don't call attention to themselves, their titles, or reputations.*

Loved Ones are people you have known in this lifetime who are now dead. Usually, they are identifiable relatives and people you knew who loved you deeply. As an Akashic Channel, Annie has seen Loved Ones who were grammar schoolteachers, grandmothers and grandfathers, parents, aunts, uncles, and "that lady who lived down the street who thought you were the most precious child!". Sometimes a Loved One has a brief, but important, message for you. Whether or not they speak depends on your needs, and on what the Akashic Beings of Light have discerned will most clear obstacles to your alignment with your Soul and the Great Creatress. If it is important for your Soul's evolution, a Loved One may share a clear message, perhaps one that brings closure to a significant event, or will clear a blockage caused by a relationship or situation. Most often, Loved Ones simply provide silent, loving support from the sidelines.

When Annie first began working in the Akashic Records, she perceived the Masters, Teachers, and Loved Ones individually. They appeared as three silhouettes. The large one was a Master, the medium one was a teacher, and the small one was a Loved One. One of them would raise their hand when they had a message. She perceives them now as a unified group, aligned with the task at hand, working together seamlessly, to present the information and energy in the most useful and loving manner.

Guardian Angels, Archangels, and Spirit Guides may be in a different section of the Akasha. In Annie's experience, Anubis, the spirit guide she has channeled for over 34 years, works closely with the Akashic Beings of Light and her Akashic Masters. Different teachers of the Akashic Records have their own theories on this topic. If this detail is important to you, ask your Masters, Teachers, and Loved Ones in your Records. Trust what YOU get.

Now for the exciting part you have been waiting for:

How to Open Your Soul's Akashic Records

We will now teach you how to open the Akashic Records of your Soul. **Before reading a chapter of this book please open your Akashic Records by reading out loud the *Bringing Forth Soul Consciousness Akashic Prayer*©** (known as the BFSC Prayer or the Prayer). You will come to appreciate the enhanced energy and more complete learning you experience with your Records open while reading these chapters. You will be rewarded with clarity while writing your answers to the interactive questions.

Always have the written prayer in front of you as you read it out loud. As a powerful ritual, the Prayer clears away distractions and focuses your attention. The Prayer has mighty energy in it. The Prayer evokes the energy and conscious engagement of the Akashic Beings of Light (ABOL's), and your Masters, Teachers, and Loved Ones (MTLO's). Devote yourself to experiencing the energy, body sensations, and visual impressions you receive as you read each word in the Prayer. Always end your chapter studies by reciting the Closing Prayer.

Please have a special notebook and pen handy, reserved for writing your insights to the interactive questions in each chapter of this book. We recommend using the same notebook for your notations so that all the information revealed is in the same location. You will find it useful when you want to refer to it later. **Please date each entry and write the question before writing your response.** Do the same with subsequent questions.

The Prayer

Bringing Forth Soul Consciousness

Akashic Records Prayer

©Rev. AnnieBachelder 1/22/2022

~ Opening Prayer ~

1) By the Power of Divine Light within me
2) Come Holy Spirit! Spirit of Light! Spirit of Truth!
3) For the highest good of all, throughout time, fill my heart with Divine Love as
4) I humbly ask permission to open the Divine portal to the highest realm of the Akashic Records for (LEGAL NAME).

5) **Akashic Beings of Light,** guide me to the deepest Truth of my being, releasing any blocks & restrictions to my abundance & highest good.
6) **Great Creatress,** assist me to fully embody my Soul's Light, to fulfill my Soul's purposes, & to heal any accumulated karma.
7) **Surround me** with the enlightenment & wisdom of my Masters, Teachers, & Loved Ones.
8) **Clearly direct** my perspective & actions to those that manifest my Divine Plan.

(Repeat lines 5, 6, 7, & 8 two more times, then say line 9)

9) **Free of all resistance, judgment, and fear**,

   I am now filled with Divine love & the Records are open.

~ Closing Prayer ~

Thanking the Great Creatress & Her Holy Spirit for Love, protection, & healing received this day,
Thanking the Akashic Beings of Light for guidance,
Thanking the Masters, Teachers, & Loved Ones for wisdom & direction.
The Divine Portal & the Akashic Records are now closed.
Amen. Amen. Amen.

In the text version, notice that there are four sections to this Prayer.

Say lines 1 through 4 once.

Say lines 5 through 8 once and repeat in order two more times.

Say line 9 once.

Please say the Closing Prayer once.

Use your current (LEGAL NAME). in line 4 (the blue section) of the Prayer. This is defined as the **current legal name** on your most recent driver's license, passport, or other current, government issued document. This name may, or may not, be the name on your birth certificate due to marriage, adoption, divorce, or a legal name change. For example, Annie's birth certificate lists her name as Ann Elizabeth Bachelder. Her current driver's license lists Annie Elizabeth Bachelder as her current legal name. She uses Annie Elizabeth Bachelder when opening her Akashic Records.

First Opening of Your Akashic Records

Have your special notebook and pen ready. Practice by reciting the **Bringing Forth Soul Consciousness** Akashic Records Prayer© **out loud, as instructed,** to open your Akashic Records for the first time.

~ Opening Prayer ~

1) By the Power of Divine Light within me
2) Come Holy Spirit! Spirit of Light! Spirit of Truth!
3) For the highest good of all, throughout time, fill my heart with Divine Love as
4) I humbly ask permission to open the Divine portal to the highest realm of the Akashic Records for (LEGAL NAME).

5) **Akashic Beings of Light,** guide me to the deepest Truth of my being, releasing any blocks & restrictions to my abundance & highest good.
6) **Great Creatress,** assist me to fully embody my Soul's Light, to fulfill my Soul's purposes, & to heal any accumulated karma.
7) **Surround me** with the enlightenment & wisdom of my Masters, Teachers, & Loved Ones.
8) **Clearly direct** my perspective & actions to those that manifest my Divine Plan.

(Repeat lines 5, 6, 7, & 8 two more times, then say line 9)

9) **Free of all resistance, judgment, and fear,**
   I am now filled with Divine love & the Records are open.

Settle into your Akashic Records.

Relax into the spaciousness safety of your own Akashic Records.

Allow yourself to consciously arrive in your Akashic Records.

Bring all your attention to your experience.

Give yourself permission to energetically stretch out.

Become as large as feels natural to you in this environment.

Sense the Light of your Soul.

Sense your heart connection with your Soul.

You might even feel a tugging sensation in your heart area.

Open your heart and receive your Soul's Love.

See, feel, and sense the presence of the ABOL's and your MTLO's.

Relax in the stillness.

Open to your personal spiritual advisory team.

When you are ready, note your responses to the following questions.

Begin making your notations one question at a time. (You may wish to pause and resume this reading or recording while you write your responses.)

What do you feel physically?

How do you feel emotionally?

What changes are you experiencing in your thoughts?

What can you feel, see, hear, and sense about your Soul's Light, your Soul's Love, and consciousness?

What do you notice about the presence of the Akashic Beings of Light?

What do you sense about the presence of your Masters, Teachers, and Loved Ones?

Finish writing your notes and recite out loud the Closing Prayer below.

~ Closing Prayer ~

Thanking the Great Creatress & Her Holy Spirit for Love, protection, & healing received this day,
Thanking the Akashic Beings of Light for guidance,
Thanking the Masters, Teachers, & Loved Ones for wisdom & direction.
The Divine Portal & the Akashic Records are now closed.
Amen. Amen. Amen.

We recommend that you **always** have the printed Prayer in front of you. It is important that you recite this prayer out loud, precisely as instructed.

The Prayer causes a change in consciousness in you.

The Prayer focuses your attention. The sound and vibration of your voice combined with your eyes and brain reading the Prayer is very powerful.

The **Bringing Forth Soul Consciousness** Akashic Records Prayer© is constructed specifically to increase your awareness of the Divine Light already within you, the Light of your Soul, the Akashic Beings of Light, your Masters, Teachers, and Loved Ones, and your Divine Plan. These important elements enable, support, and refine your experience of Soul Consciousness and your connection to the Great Creatress. The elements assist you and your Soul in your mutual evolution. You and your Soul are in partnership on an exciting and evolving journey.

As you recite the BFSC Akashic Records Prayer©, take in the importance of each word and phrase. Sense the energy in them. Notice the effect these words and phrases have on your physical body, your emotions, your thoughts, your inner vision, awareness of Divine Light, and your consciousness.

In the Akashic Records, the order of importance is always
Energy First, Information Second.

Paying close attention and following the energy and the Light is essential. With practice, each word, phrase, and line of the BFSC Akashic Records Prayer© will take on deeper meaning as the energy elevates you into the Akashic Records and the Soul realm of consciousness.

This book is designed to be experienced with your Akashic Records
open so that you can feel the energy in Our message.

The Opening Prayer at the beginning of every chapter reminds you to open your Records, and the Closing Prayer at the end prompts you to close them. This allows you to receive the elevated Akashic perspective of your Soul Consciousness. Having your Akashic Records open will enhance your entire experience of this book, and of your life, which is the point. The BFSC Akashic Records Prayer© creates a safe, sacred, spiritual container that supports your education, expanded Soul connection, and relationship to the Great Creatress.

The BFSC Akashic Records Prayer© lets you experience your Soul, your spiritual advisory team, even the Great Creatress, their constant love and assistance, everywhere you are, no matter what you are doing or feeling.

Most chapters have interactive questions for you to **explore and respond to in writing while you have your Records open**. These questions will be more intensely alive for you when your Akashic Records are open. Your written responses will be more revealing, informative, and growth inducing with your Akashic Records open. You are automatically **Bringing Forth Soul Consciousness** when you ask questions with your Records open.

We present this information as an introduction to your personal Akashic Records, and to the Akashic Records at large. We encourage you to ask personal questions regarding your life, as well as broad inquiries about Earth life, Soul development, or anything else about which you are curious.

Please do not open another person's Records without first obtaining their verbal or written permission. That includes dead people. It is considered rude, unethical, and invasive to open the Records without their permission.

You are encouraged ask about the nature of historic and geologic events, religious turning points, the higher purpose of people your Soul chose as your parents, siblings, spouse(s), and pets. You can open the Records of crystals. You can open the Records of other things, as long as the property, vehicle or boat for sale, lease, or rent is offered (listed) on the open market. With permission from the current owner, lessee, or legal tenant you can open the Records of any other real estate.

Let's open your Records a second time. Please write your responses to the interactive questions that follow the Prayer.

~ Opening Prayer ~

1) By the Power of Divine Light within me
2) Come Holy Spirit! Spirit of Light!   Spirit of Truth!
3) For the highest good of all, throughout time, fill my heart with Divine Love as
4) I humbly ask permission to open the Divine portal to the highest realm of the Akashic Records for (LEGAL NAME).

5) **Akashic Beings of Light,** guide me to the deepest Truth of my being, releasing any blocks & restrictions to my abundance & highest good.
6) **Great Creatress,** assist me to fully embody my Soul's Light, to fulfill my Soul's purposes, & to heal any accumulated karma.
7) **Surround me** with the enlightenment & wisdom of my Masters, Teachers, & Loved Ones.
8) **Clearly direct** my perspective & actions to those that manifest my Divine Plan.

    (Repeat lines 5, 6, 7, & 8 two more times, then say line 9)

9) **Free of all resistance, judgment, and fear,**
    I am now filled with Divine love & the Records are open.

Close your eyes and take a few moments to settle into your Records. Then open your eyes and engage with the questions one at a time:

How do you feel physically, emotionally, mentally, and energetically in your open Akashic Records?

Write down any questions you have about this process.

What concerns have arisen?

What questions or issues are you curious about exploring in your Akashic Records?

Ask your Masters, Teachers, and Loved Ones how to develop your relationship with them?

In keeping with the pattern and purpose of this book please close your Akashic Records with the Closing Prayer.

~ Closing Prayer ~

Thanking the Great Creatress & Her Holy Spirit for Love, protection & healing received this day,
Thanking the Akashic Beings of Light for guidance,
Thanking the Masters, Teachers, & Loved Ones for wisdom & direction.
The Divine Portal & the Akashic Records are now closed.
Amen. Amen. Amen.

CHAPTER 3

Going Forward in Space and Time,
Instructions for Reading This Book

Channeled by the Akashic Beings of Light

Bringing Forth Soul Consciousness
Akashic Records Prayer

©Rev. Annie Bachelder all rights reserved 1/22/2022

~ Opening Prayer ~

1) By the Power of Divine Light within me
2) Come Holy Spirit!   Spirit of Light!   Spirit of Truth!
3) For the highest good of all, throughout time, fill my heart with Divine Love as
4) I humbly ask permission to open the Divine portal to the highest realm of the Akashic Records for (LEGAL NAME).

5) **Akashic Beings of Light,** guide me to the deepest Truth of my being, releasing any blocks & restrictions to my abundance & highest good.
6) **Great Creatress,** assist me to fully embody my Soul's Light, to fulfill my Soul's purposes, & to heal any accumulated karma.
7) **Surround me** with the enlightenment & wisdom of my Masters, Teachers, & Loved Ones.
8) **Clearly direct** my perspective & actions to those that manifest my Divine Plan.
   (Repeat lines 5, 6, 7, & 8 two more times, then say line 9)
9) **Free of all resistance, judgment, and fear,**
   I am now filled with Divine love & the Records are open.

Greetings and Welcome from the Akashic Beings of Light. We welcome you who come to this missive in search of spiritual sustenance. There is nothing you have ever thought, intended, said, or done that is unacceptable to us. For all has been said and done before. You are entirely innocent in the eyes of the Great Creatress. Your terrors are neutralized, and you are absolutely washed clean of judgment and blame for your fallibility by the love of the Great Creatress. Your fallibility makes you teachable, and your so-called "mistakes" are welcome opportunities to realign yourself with the universal spiritual principles currently operating. For example, the principle of magnetic attraction, "That which is like unto itself is drawn."

You are made in the image and likeness of the Great Creatress therefore you are in the Divinely designed process of evolving, growing, and perfecting.

We greet you thusly because it is the best way for us to bring you to the deepest truth of your being, here in the present moment. You are complete. You are whole. Just as you are, with nothing concealed or shied away from. You are as you are, at this moment. We are loving you unconditionally, in whatever condition you find yourself. It is only from being here now, as you are, in full acceptance of such, that you can go forward in space and time.

Going forward is only possible when you fully experience arriving in this moment.
Time takes care of itself.

Space is a matter of consciousness, and consciousness is what we wish you to enjoy. There is no other moment and no other condition that will afford you the possibility of going forward to the next moment in space and time. There is nothing better to be, nowhere else to be, no other condition that serves you better than where you find yourself now. Your judgments and evaluations compress you, deflate your levity, and place you in what we call the "judgment jail". (See Exercise: *Release Yourself from Judgment Jail at the back of the book.*)

Please allow yourself to be, unaltered, nakedly present, to all that is so at this moment. It is from this place of relaxed acceptance that you will hear, feel, understand, and assimilate our messages as you read this missive.

Open the floodgates of the present moment and reintegrate your-self. You are welcomed to these realms by the Great Creatress, in all Her Glory. She loves to have her creations in alert attendance, in the moment, receiving her constant gifts of love, breath, life force energy, and dynamic transformation. She is ever-growing, ever-changing, and so are you. Your cells are constantly being enlivened, nourished, repaired, and replaced. Why should you try to hold things still, to cement them rigidly into place, and to control them? They cannot be controlled and so it is.

Your choice is to accept all. Step back, exhale, and appreciate that you are relieved of the duty of control.

The Great Creatress is in control of all that She has created. You need only turn within to gain the moment-to-moment grace and guidance you crave. Why are you craving guidance? Why are you craving con-trol? Fear. Better to release that dragging anchor and surrender to the beauty and the wisdom of She Who Made You, She Who Loves You. Let Go. Surrender. Fall. She has already caught you in mid-fall.

Gravity is a much lighter sentence when you float, knowing full well you are embraced by the Great Creatress. She who is all, contains all, holds you, too.

Greet any mistakes as the Great Creatress' way of leading you forward into the mysterious unknown. Surrender your fear and control to Her, and she will direct you by giving you wisdom, peace, and courage to meet all challenges.

This universe requires your trust, just as you trust the moon to rise and the sun to set.

You need not trust fallible humans. In contrast, you must trust that the next moment arrives all on its own, without your aid. It arrives with far less personal resistance when you're willing to greet it with curiosity and open arms. The next moment is far more kind when greeted thusly.

All that has been put into play, into action, will transpire in just the right way, at just the right time.

Are you thinking about how hard you make life when you balk and over-effort? To this we say, "Relax and Release!" Float on the current that is already in motion. This current began many millions of years ago and is already moving you toward your desired outcome, toward your highest destiny. You can fight it, but the ride is far more beautiful and easier when you let the moment carry you.

BE who you are, and float into your next momentary destiny. Relax. Look around and see what is here to be seen, felt, and experienced.

None of this is against you. All is for you.

All has been created to adorn your experience. All has been brought into being for your expansion and advancement. You may think "Advancement" makes it sound like a board game. What you advance to is the very next moment for you to accept and to appreciate. You evolve through practicing acceptance and present moment awareness. Your Soul evolves with you and vice versa. From the center deep within the farthest reaches of your consciousness that surrounds you, all has been carefully, wisely placed for your greatest evolution, pleasure, and play.

"**Play**" is such a childlike word. It gives you unlimited permission. Play encompasses exploration, invention, discovery, curiosity, and aware-ness. Play my Beloveds, Play. There is naught else to do. Experience all. Taste, feel, sense, be, know all that is here for you.

You pressure yourself to "accomplish". We suggest that you relax and float from activity to restful activity, free of resistance and stress.

It is from this looseness that we wish you to read this missive. For great-est effect, **open your Akashic Records with the BFSC Akashic Records Prayer© and read a chapter while listening to the audio book at the same time.** Interact with the questions and close your Records. Put the book aside for a time. Return when drawn to sample another chapter. If it truly feeds your spirit, continue to the next chapter. If you become full and inattentive, allow yourself to pause, digest, and assimilate. Especially at this time, the more allowances you make for assimilation, the better your life experience will be. You will know when it is time to resume activity, learning, testing, trying out new concepts, thoughts, and behaviors.

You will KNOW! You are built to know these things.
Trust this faculty within you.

You are now in a calm enough condition to follow along as we change topics.

The Soul chakra, located 12" to 15" above the head, is the energetic repository of the Soul's Light. Your Soul's Light contains the method of Soul formation, Soul structure, Soul purpose, and the Soul's coding or blueprint. The Soul chakra contains the imprinting pertaining to the human personality and physical body chosen for this lifetime. The Soul chakra also contains the energy patterns most conducive to achieving the Soul's purposes for this lifetime. Take a few moments to become familiar with the exercise below, as you will be asked to use this process in nearly every chapter, and throughout the day. Practice embodying your Soul's Light every time you recite the **Bringing Forth Soul Consciousness** Akashic Records opening prayer. Repetition allows you to master the steps below to bring your Soul's Light into your body and energy system. Your Soul's Light is energy containing the consciousness of your Soul and Its love for you. Your Soul's Light contains the very vibration of your essence as designed by the Great Creatress at the moment of your Soul's inception. Give yourself permission to have a variety of experiences with this ever-evolving process.

Exercise – How to Embody Your Soul's Light:

Close your eyes. Take 3 deep, cleansing breaths followed by complete exhalations to bring yourself fully into this moment.

1. Begin by becoming aware of a glowing sphere of radiant Light located 12 to 15 inches above your head. This is your 8th chakra (your Soul chakra). Let your sense of knowing tell you about the color, the shimmer, and the vibration in your Soul's Light. These qualities may change from time to time. Trust the changes. The Light is infinitely wise and knows what you need at every moment.

2. Observe as the Soul chakra pours its Light into the space between your Soul chakra and your crown chakra, creating a column of connecting Light.

3. Your crown chakra naturally opens to receive the Light of your Soul as it pours itself into your crown chakra.

4. Your Soul's Light fills your entire head, inside and out. Your Soul's Light fills your brain, scalp and hair, eyes, sinuses, jaw, and the atlas bone at the top of your spine. At any point in this process, you might feel a sense of your Soul's character.

5. Notice your Soul's Light as it fills your shoulders, arms, hands, and fingers.

6. Observe as your Soul's Light lovingly and affectionately touches all the organs and systems in the trunk of your body. Allow yourself to feel your Soul's love for this precious body It chose for you.

7. Observe your Soul's Light filling the entire trunk of your body, inside and out, including your skin. Your Soul's Light naturally pools in your pelvic cavity. It pauses in your hip sockets. Take a breath.

8. Follow your Soul's Light as it fills your thighs, knees, calves, ankles, and feet. Your Soul's Light fills the bones, muscles, tendons, and fascia tissues, as well as your blood system.

9. Take notice that very cell throughout your body contains a corresponding spark of Light reflecting your Soul's Light. Recognition in each of your cells of your Soul's Light generates a feeling of joyful reunion.

10. Remain focused on your Soul's Light and all your cells as they re-connect. Observe the interactions.

11. You might feel a click or a buzzing in your feet and legs as your body's connection with your Soul's Light is complete.

12. Ground your Soul's Light into the balance point of Mother Earth.

13. Now, send your consciousness up to the Great Creatress. Feel the sphere of Light that is the Great Creatress surrounding your Soul, you, and Mother Earth.

14. Spend as much time as you like here.

15. Create a memory file by placing the pointer finger of your right hand on the palm of your left hand so that you can fully embody your Soul's Light on command.

16. Easily and effortlessly, return to ordinary consciousness, wiggling your toes, rolling your shoulders, and enjoying a few relaxing breaths.

We resume: Embody your Soul's Light and imagine connecting with the Great Creatress. You will feel peaceful. Naturally trusting. Free of fear. You are supplied with all that is essential to your life and to carrying out your Soul's Purposes. You rise to the occasion. You enjoy challenges and changes rather than feeling threatened by them.

We are aware that this handbook contains elements that require a great deal of acceptance, mental flexibility, and emotional surrender. We are aware that, at times, you will be called to sample a chapter, and then to pause for a time to integrate. We recommend contemplating what you read and hear on the audio book. We are aware that complete reading from front to back may not be how you acquire, or ingest, this experiential information. Read a chapter then open the book to a completely unrelated section.

We invite you to authorize and inhabit your own experience fully, resisting nothing that is your inner truth along the way. We invite your inventiveness and your playfulness. This handbook is designed to invoke Our presence. Rest assured that We Akashic Beings of Light are with you whenever you tune into this book, the Akashic Records, to Anubis, or the Great Creatress. We are with you whenever you seek spiritual sustenance, grace, and guidance from this guidebook and your Akashic Records. The words may seem to change from one reading to the next, for you are always changing, adapting, growing, contracting, expanding, floating, resisting, and releasing. This is as it should be. Allow yourself to be all these descriptors without hesitation or judgment. Dive in! The water is warm and fine. We are communing with you all along the way, from the most inclusive, generous, empowering, and loving perspective.

It is our intention that this book be an asset, a helpful manual that you can return to, as needed. It is our further intention to be of service to humanity in your evolution, such that you are uplifted, experience immense growth, and take pleasure in the process.

Now, have a pen and your special notebook (or laptop) handy as you write your responses to these interactive questions. Writing your responses with your Records open lets you consciously discover the subtle aspects of your experience that might be overlooked otherwise.

~ Interactive Questions ~

How do you feel when you embody your Soul's Light?

How are you inspired to float from one moment to another?

In what areas of your life are you able to release rigid control?

In what areas do you need Divine Assistance with releasing control?

How do you feel when you allow the Great Creatress to help you?

Finish writing your notes and close your records with the prayer below.

~ Closing Prayer ~

Thanking the Great Creatress & Her Holy Spirit for Love, protection & healing received this day,
Thanking the Akashic Beings of Light for guidance,
Thanking the Masters, Teachers, & Loved Ones for wisdom & direction.
The Divine Portal & the Akashic Records are now closed.
Amen. Amen. Amen.

CHAPTER 4

Annie's Introduction to The Light

Bringing Forth Soul Consciousness
Akashic Records Prayer

©Rev. Annie Bachelder all rights reserved 1/22/2022

~ Opening Prayer ~

1) By the Power of Divine Light within me
2) Come Holy Spirit!   Spirit of Light!   Spirit of Truth!
3) For the highest good of all, throughout time, fill my heart with Divine Love as
4) I humbly ask permission to open the Divine portal to the highest realm of the Akashic Records for (LEGAL NAME).

5) **Akashic Beings of Light,** guide me to the deepest Truth of my being, releasing any blocks & restrictions to my abundance & highest good.
6) **Great Creatress,** assist me to fully embody my Soul's Light, to fulfill my Soul's purposes, & to heal any accumulated karma.
7) **Surround me** with the enlightenment & wisdom of my Masters, Teachers, & Loved Ones.
8) **Clearly direct** my perspective & actions to those that manifest my Divine Plan.
   (Repeat lines 5, 6, 7, & 8 two more times, then say line 9)

9) **Free of all resistance, judgment, and fear,**
   I am now filled with Divine love & the Records are open.

33

In 1976, Annie's older sister, Carrie, introduced her to a psychic therapist named Mayla Riley. Having completed her senior year of high school a semester early, she was barely 18 years old, and felt swamped by conflicting feelings crashing through her. She was living on her own, struggling with a dicey live-in relationship with a recently sober guy 10 years older than herself, and questioning her own drinking. She was deeply in love with him even though he once said, "Annie, this is not the Alpha and Omega of relationships." Shocked and disappointed, Annie was undeterred. Secretly, she felt she was a failure at living life as a supposed "adult", as if, at the magic age of 18 the switch automatically flipped on and voila! She would know exactly what to do and how to live as an adult.

Annie had no idea what she was stepping into with her first appointment with Mayla. Her sister did not tell her how Mayla worked or what to expect. Carrie liked it and that was good enough for Annie, who desperately needed help. It didn't occur to Annie to ask for details.

After parking her second-hand 3-speed bike, she walked to what seemed like the front door. It was a rambling one-story house with a messy, overgrown yard. A handwritten note on the door directed her around the side of house to the back door. It was early spring in Northern California and the bright green grass was thigh-high and wet with dew. The path was completely covered with overgrowth and as she fumbled along, she worried that she had gone the wrong direction. Maybe she was supposed to walk around the other side of the house? It seemed like she was making her own path. When she opened the back door, she discovered what might normally be a laundry room, but instead of a washer and dryer, the room contained a very large, nearly enclosed, vertical plywood box. *

The enclosed box was much taller than Annie, about 3 1/2 feet wide on all sides, with a heavy, home-made, multi-layered curtain over a large opening in the front. An old grey, flexible metal hose snaked from inside the box into an aluminum pail half full of dirty water. Annie thought to herself "what's with the water?". Dust and a long hair floated on the surface.

Another note on the plywood box said, "get in, sit, and wait". Pulling the curtain aside, Annie stepped up onto the raised floor of the box and in the flash before the curtain closed, she located an old chair with two pillows with ruffles around the edges. Annie used one to fill in the pot-hole in the chair seat and the other pillow for her lower back. Her feet scuffed the loose gravel in the dark corners. She sat immersed in complete, velvet darkness. Automatically, Annie closed her eyes and waited, staring at the back side of her eyelids for what felt like a very long time.

Immediately, her inner screen was alive with lava lamp-style pulsating colors. The images flowed in and faded out. She began to cry. What was happening? She felt sad, deeply afraid, and dangerously confused. She wondered why her feelings were so intense. She felt helpless as she was swept into experiencing her uncontrollable feelings.

The colors on Annie's inner screen blossomed into full faces, then slowly shape-changed into a sidelong glance, then into a single eye staring back at her. The single eye reminded her of her boyfriend's eyes, like the eye of a whale. Aged, sad, knowing. The hot pink and orange colors felt safe and reassuring. But the faces were unnerving. They were stern observers, vaguely familiar, slightly judging. One face was red hot, devilish, with mean black eyes, slanted eyebrows, a spiked black beard, and devil-horns on its pointed head. The devil face formed and dissolved repeatedly increasing her fear, making her cry harder. The spectacle of images flowed on seamlessly. Annie watched, captivated, helpless as the fear continued to rise from deep within. She sobbed feeling dangerously lost and uncertain.

After a while, a woman that Annie assumed was Mayla Riley, pulled the curtain aside and looked quickly at her and said, "You're almost ready. A few more minutes."

Annie returned her focus to her feelings, watching the intense colors as they floated up from the bottom or drifted in from the sides of her inner screen. Oddly, it was satisfying to feel intensely everything she had tried to ignore. She had been trying to operate on top of the feelings she was now experiencing so intensely. The brilliant colors transformed into unidentifiable shapes and morphing into new hues. The devil face appeared repeatedly, only to disintegrate into blackness. Annie continued to cry.

Mayla finally came and got her, following her wobbly body down the hall to a small room on the left. The room had a messy twin bed pushed against the wall, covered with an antique patchwork quilt. Mayla directed her to lie down. Still crying, Mayla offered a handful of much needed Kleenex. Annie vaguely heard Mayla shaking some dry leaves and making sounds the likes of which Annie could not describe. Mayla rubbed her fingers and thumb together near Annie's ears, then snapped her fingers. She pulled at the air and flicked the invisible residue off. Annie cried harder in what she recognized as deep release.

Soon, it became clear that Annie was to verbalize her feelings. Eyes closed, out came the tentative words "I'm okay". To whom was she speaking? Her shaky tone wasn't quite right, so she tried again. Speaking aloud again, the words had more volume, but were slightly pleading, mixed with childish insistence, as if she was trying to convince her unconvinced parents. Annie tried again letting herself staunchly declare her feeling. "I'm okay!" On and on it went. She kept repeating the words with more intensity and they came out variously angry, argumentative, defensive, demanding. "I'm okay!". They sounded like a battle cry. As if they were the words she wanted to scream at birth. "I'm okay!" Her voice became hoarse from yelling "I'm Okay!" She was releasing the words that, in their simplicity, vocalized "stop criticizing!", "leave me alone", "stop worrying", "take me seriously", "I am free to be me!". The "I'm okay!" refrain eventually had the depth, authority, and command of what Annie now knows as the "I AM". A statement of fact. She felt acknowledged, validated, fully expressed, and finally, peaceful.

After a while the colors on Annie's inner screen settled into yellow-orange ripples that seemed to be vibrating in her lower belly. The gentle ripples moved continuously like sunshine reflected on the bottom of a swimming pool. Five months before this Annie had emergency major surgery. The surgeon removed her left ovary and fallopian tube containing a tubal pregnancy. The surgeon also removed scar tissue from a long-standing infection. Annie sensed the yellow-orange light as calming, healing, and re-regulating her reproductive organs.

Annie forced her swollen eyelids open and asked Mayla, "What is this light?" Mayla asked, "Do the words 'Christ Light' mean anything to you?"

Annie's family was not religious. She wasn't raised with a church or in a religion. Although she had been to a few churches and even tried being a Jehovah's Witness, God simply was not discussed much. Deeply influenced by San Francisco's summer of love, the Marin County Unitarian Universalist church had a weekend long "Be In" when Annie was 9 years old. It was wild and fun and disorganized. Outside, Annie and the other kids were running everywhere. They painted their legs with Day-Glo flowers. They sucked the helium out of balloons and talked funny, laughing so hard they nearly peed in their pants. They sewed leather wallets. Inside, in the main room, adults and children sang and danced the Hora. A white-haired man played familiar folk songs on the banjo, and everyone sang along. The kids slept in rumpled masses of sleeping bags on the bare floor. It was getting dark, and Annie was very hungry. She couldn't find either of her parents. She finally found a terse woman in the disorganized kitchen who seemed to be single-handedly making dinner for the whole group. Annie told her she was hungry. The woman responded gruffly, "You'll just have to wait. The spaghetti will be ready soon." That was church for Annie.

When Mayla said Annie was experiencing "Christ Light", she softly nodded. Annie thought, "Yes. Christ Light. Of course. It's Christ Light." Blissfully, that made absolute perfect sense.

Annie rode her bike back to her apartment. All the way home she voiced her new mantra. It gave her strength and clarity. Annie rode her bike hands free, arms wide, saying aloud "I'm Okay! I'm okay! I am okay!" She was free. She was inspired and unafraid. She was filled with colored Christ Light. All the broken uncertainty and cramping confusion had vanished. She felt restored to original purity.

To this day, it is Christ Light that holds Annie steady in the present moment and leads her forward on her spiritual path. To this day, she is not afraid to look within to find the unacceptable monster inside, the unlovable part of herself, or the scary devil that she had been absolutely certain was "in there". She can locate, identify, and feel her feelings. She's okay.

To this day, it is Christ Light that Annie is directed to see, to sense, to know, to follow as energy. It is The Light that works in and through her. It is The Light that is working in her students and clients. It is The Light that protects her. It is The Light that heals her. It is Christ Light that heals others. When all else fails, Annie knows to follow The Light, the infinitely wise, loving Light.

This is why the Akashic Beings of Light urge us to continually embody our Soul's Light as we Bring Forth Soul Consciousness.

*Footnote: Decades later, Annie discovered that the Orgone Box that Mayla had her sit inside was an unusual device invented by Wilhelm Reich that "helps a person accumulate energy for the purpose of accelerated healing".

Please write your responses to the interactive questions below.

~ Interactive Questions ~

Describe your introduction to "the Light", to Christ Light, or to perceptible beneficial energy?

What elements do you relate to in this chapter?

What does "the Light" or "Christ Light" feel like to you?

Who opened the doors to "the Light" for you?

Now close your Akashic Records by reciting the Closing Prayer below:

~ Closing Prayer ~

Thanking the Great Creatress & Her Holy Spirit for Love, protection
& healing received this day,
Thanking the Akashic Beings of Light for guidance,
Thanking the Masters, Teachers, & Loved Ones for wisdom &
direction.
The Divine Portal & the Akashic Records are now closed.
Amen. Amen. Amen.

CHAPTER 5

How I Learned to Channel

(Annie opened her Akashic Records to channel this segment. The Akashic Beings of Light are much better than Annie at telling Annie's story!)

Bringing Forth Soul Consciousness
Akashic Records Prayer

~ Opening Prayer ~

1) By the Power of Divine Light within me
2) Come Holy Spirit!   Spirit of Light!   Spirit of Truth!
3) For the highest good of all, throughout time, fill my heart with Divine Love as
4) I humbly ask permission to open the Divine portal to the highest realm of the Akashic Records for (LEGAL NAME).

5) **Akashic Beings of Light,** guide me to the deepest Truth of my being, releasing any blocks & restrictions to my abundance & highest good.
6) **Great Creatress,** assist me to fully embody my Soul's Light, to fulfill my Soul's purposes, & to heal any accumulated karma.
7) **Surround me** with the enlightenment & wisdom of my Masters, Teachers, & Loved Ones.
8) **Clearly direct** my perspective & actions to those that manifest my Divine Plan.

(Repeat lines 5, 6, 7, & 8 two more times, then say line 9)

9) **Free of all resistance, judgment, and fear,** I am now filled with Divine love & the Records are open.

In 1988, I received a letter inviting me to a new class offered by my spiritual teachers Sanaya Roman and Duane Packer called "Awakening Your Light Body". My entire body vibrated with excitement as I read the letter and I knew without a doubt that I was enrolling – even if I had to max out my credit card! I was only 30 years old when I learned to channel. My motive was simply to satisfy the prerequisite for this workshop, and I was absolutely determined to attend.

Sanaya Roman and her Guide Orin had done two life-changing readings for me that absolutely knocked my socks off. Along with answering numerous questions, her first reading for me visually demonstrated the power, complexity, beauty, and impact of my energy. My sense of myself was forever enlarged. The second reading contained information and processes that healed a grapefruit-sized ovarian cyst so that I didn't need surgery. At the time, I was recovering from two ectopic pregnancy surgeries only five months apart and was terrified at the prospect of a third surgery within seven months. I had attended a few one-day classes taught by Sanaya and Duane and read her book "Personal Power through Awareness". These fine teachers and their Guides were excellent examples of what conscious channeling was all about and how effectively this capability could serve others. I regularly used numerous spiritual growth and healing guided meditations channeled by Sanaya and Orin.

In preparation, I purchased Sanaya and Duane's book, "Opening to Channel", a Sony cassette recorder, and made my beginning. Loading a blank tape into the recorder I turned on the machine. I mean, what if right out of the gate, I brought through the next high guidance that freed humanity? I'd want the recording of that, now, wouldn't I? Well, that didn't happen, however . . .

I followed Sanaya's and Duane's suggestion to relax into a calm, receptive, meditative state. Per the book's instructions, with eyes closed, I opened the energy of the back of my head and neck which **Opening to Channel** said is the best location to receive my Guide. Automatically, my neck and head felt softer, as if the molecules had spread further apart, becoming more porous. As directed in the book, I silently asked for a high Guide whose purpose harmonized with my own higher purpose. Unquestioning, since I had absolutely no idea what my own higher purpose was, I waited for a response. After some time, I began to feel my body sensations quicken and a new energy began filling the core of my body. The energy in my head felt different, quiet, and open. Allowing this energy shift to continue for quite a few minutes, I let myself become accustomed to this flow, this guest consciousness inside of me. My thoughts and feelings were entirely peaceful. I sensed absolutely no danger, only peace. I watched a harmony of moving, undulating colors flowing across my inner screen. The brilliant paisley patterns that appeared and disappeared, reminding me of printed cotton bedspreads sold in Indian import stores and of the quality of my energy that I perceived the first time Sanaya channeled for me. After a while, I asked for this Guide's name. I received a complicated name that had Hindi tones to it. The name seemed to be 12 complex syllables strung together and was impossible for me to remember. The volume was also very soft and distant. Nevertheless, I sat with this imminently perceptible energy coursing through me and allowed this Guide and I to get to know each other in comfortable silence. About 30 or 40 minutes seemed to have passed and I felt ready to turn off the tape recorder and return to "ordinary consciousness" as Duane Packer is fond of saying.

A few days later, I was ready to sit down, slip into a meditative state, start the tape recorder again and invite my Guide to join me. I felt the energy shift as before and let things settle. This time I asked for a name I could both pronounce and remember. I waited for a response and I got 3 syllables. An. Nub. Iss. Anu Bis. Anubis. Okay fine. That works. Much better. I let our energies and consciousness blend. I wanted to get to know Anubis' energy so that I would feel and remember this Being's Light, consciousness and vibration. Without instruction, I created my own "memory file" that noted the vibration, feeling sense, volume, and peaceful harmony that signaled Anubis' presence. I wanted to be able to distinguish Anubis' consciousness and influence as distinct from my own. As the book instructed, I asked what Anubis' Higher Purpose was and I received the answer clearly, "Our purpose is to assist human beings to evolve personally and spiritually through re-unification with their Souls."

Mind you, I had no knowledge of my having either a Soul or a higher purpose. I had no idea that these topics would fuel my spiritual path for the rest of my life. I simply accepted, unquestioningly, this bold, clear and certain statement. I already had the belief and the experience that channeling brought forth Divine information and energy that healed emotions and bodies, expanded one's consciousness, and clarified one's perspective that resulted in a deeply effective shift.

So far, I had only heard Anubis speak in the very center of my inner mind and felt Anubis' energy. This Being came through clearly and firmly. So, I tried speaking the words I was receiving from Anubis. Surprisingly, Anubis spoke with a British/Indian lilt. For years this accent continued. I know now that as a novice, I needed the accent to quiet my self-doubt when it said, "This is just you and your overactive imagination." The difference was that what Anubis knew, I did not. I remembered Sanaya and Duane saying that my imagination was a safe, consciousness enhancing, spiritual doorway for me to access and use freely. These components confirmed my choice to be a "conscious channel" rather than a "trance channel". I wanted to hear and feel the calm wisdom and the confidence of Anubis' transmissions. I got to feel the immense love and respect that came through Anubis as I channeled. In the mid 1990's I stopped needing the accent. I trusted the feeling of Anubis' energy and the sensations, the tenor of Anubis' voice and the kinds of thoughts, the clarity of the concepts, the immense compassion, and the detailed visions that I received when channeling. I also had the feeling that we were kin.

Clearly, Anubis and I have grown individually and together. I can feel this Being has matured, deepened, gained in stature, and strengthened over the years. It feels as if Anubis has become more than just the junior voice of a group of Light Beings who "step down the energy" of their message so that I and other listeners can receive the whole elaborate package. Now, seems that Anubis is not only the voice of – but encompasses the entirety of this group of Light Beings and their messages.

In the beginning, the hardest part of channeling was developing trust in my ability to tap into my Guide and stay connected. Letting go of self-doubt is a process that takes practice and time. (Many of my clients and students have deep feelings of self-doubt, so the guides have developed and recorded a video class on "Healing Self-Doubt" that can be purchased on my website www.AnnieChannels.com and from my Etsy store https://soulsourcer.etsy.com)

Before I was led to the Akashic Records in 2014, I channeled with my eyes closed with my hands and arms moving the energy. Years after they had a reading with Anubis, clients would come up to me and tell me about how their reading changed their life. Even though back then, my readings took up to 2 hours, I wouldn't recognize their faces because my eyes had been closed the whole time!

Another challenging thing for me has been channeling future predictions. Psychics and channels are routinely asked to foretell the future. Those questions used to make me very nervous. To remedy this, I opened my Akashic Records and asked how to do future readings. The first thing my guides said was that I had to let go of my own fear of the future, and to stop going into agreement with clients about how threatened they feel about what may be coming down the road. Nowadays, I relax, trust, and verbalize what I am being shown, or simply say "I am not getting anything about that." The future is highly changeable and cannot be pinned down. The littlest thing can change the course of events such as a new decision about a morning routine, a left turn where the person normally turns right, a stop at a coffee shop that puts the person in contact with someone new, or a chance conversation with a stranger affects the course of events.

Even the purchase of a book can redirect your path!

I was shopping for Christmas presents in 2013, and even though it was 5pm and I was in a rush to get home to make dinner for my beloved Partner, I made a last-minute dash into a bookstore to find another gift or two for him. He is very generous and thoughtful with me, and I hoped to wrap a few more presents for him under the Christmas tree. I walked straight into the Spiritual section and, using my energy sensing abilities, I closed my eyes, held out my hand and used it to feel the energy in the form of heat, of possible books for him. In short order, I found three books for him. Later, I wrote loving notes on the inside covers with the date and wrapped them up. After Christmas, he was reading one and said "Hey Annie, I think you'd really like this one. It's right up your alley". A few days later, I started reading the book. It was **"How to Read the Akashic Records, Accessing the Archive of the Soul and Its Journey"** by Linda Howe. My Partner hasn't seen the book since then because I have underlined, indexed, and post-it-noted the heck out of it. This book taught me how to read the Akashic Records and I now do almost all my readings as Akashic Records readings. I've participated in nearly all of Dr. Howe's classes and been certified as an advanced practitioner and teacher of her classes.

Channeling and working in the Akashic Records turns out to be one of the demonstrations of my Soul purposes that helps people become reunified with their Soul.

We are always creating, responding to the outcome of our previous choices, and exercising our free will through choice. These seemingly insignificant elements can be game changers. **That is why little changes and seemingly insignificant choices lead to great transformations**. Small is good and, often, is easier for the personality to tolerate than gigantic changes that rock the boat and terrify everyone involved!

~ Interactive Questions ~

How do you feel about channeling?

Do you already have a "Spirit Guide" and what is your shared higher purpose?

What questions do you bring to your Guide?

Describe an experience where you felt you were spontaneously channeling?

What information came through?

How was it useful, applicable, and life enhancing?

Now, close your Records with the Closing Prayer.

~ Closing Prayer ~

Thanking the Great Creatress & Her Holy Spirit for Love, protection & healing received this day,
Thanking the Akashic Beings of Light for guidance,
Thanking the Masters, Teachers, & Loved Ones for wisdom & direction.
The Divine Portal & the Akashic Records are now closed.
Amen. Amen. Amen.

CHAPTER 6

How Healing Transpires
in the Akashic Records

Channeled by the Akashic Beings of Light

Bringing Forth Soul Consciousness
Akashic Records Prayer

~ Opening Prayer ~

1) By the Power of Divine Light within me
2) Come Holy Spirit!   Spirit of Light!   Spirit of Truth!
3) For the highest good of all, throughout time, fill my heart with Divine Love as
4) I humbly ask permission to open the Divine portal to the highest realm of the Akashic Records for (LEGAL NAME).

5) **Akashic Beings of Light,** guide me to the deepest Truth of my being, releasing any blocks & restrictions to my abundance & highest good.
6) **Great Creatress,** assist me to fully embody my Soul's Light, to fulfill my Soul's purposes, & to heal any accumulated karma.
7) **Surround me** with the enlightenment & wisdom of my Masters, Teachers, & Loved Ones.
8) **Clearly direct** my perspective & actions to those that manifest my Divine Plan.

    (Repeat lines 5, 6, 7, & 8 two more times, then say line 9)

9) **Free of all resistance, judgment, and fear,**
   I am now filled with Divine love & the Records are open.

The Akashic Records contain the entire record of your Soul, including everything that has ever happened to you as a Soul in all of your embodied lifetimes, and all of your in-between incarnations. The Akashic Records energetically connect you with your Soul. Healing begins as you access your Soul's Akashic Records with a sacred Prayer. The opening Prayer and the Closing Prayer create a sanctified container. This container allows you to safely explore challenging topics, and to obtain new perspectives of your Soul's purpose regarding key relationships, health issues, careers, money, and other significant events in your lives. Most importantly, your Akashic Records link you with your Soul's consciousness. Every time we activate the divine portal (the energetic elevator) to your Akashic Records, you receive healing by virtue of the conscious connection with your Soul. The Light of the Akasha amplifies the Light of your Soul, creating a deeper, more intimate connection between the human you and your Soul's expanded consciousness.

Further, your Soul is Divinely designed to be the connecting link between you and the Great Creatress, which adds grace to your life.

These connections enhance your spiritual growth and the assimilation of new wisdom. Being in the energy of your Soul through your Soul's Akashic Records enlightens your perspective, allowing you to make appropriate changes effectively and easily. Some of these changes happen without your conscious awareness of them. Your Akashic Records amplify the Light of your Soul
which does the healing as your Soul's Light is reflected inside your body through the spark of Soul Light within each cell.

The spark of Light in each one of your cells recognizes and responds to the Light of your Soul. Illumination reigns as the truth is revealed about the higher purpose of the problem or question you've presented.

In the Akashic Records, the spoken word, the written word, and thoughts all transmit energy, which are energetically impressed onto the very sensitive Akashic Records. The spoken word is the most powerful of these three, followed by the written word, and finally, thoughts. This is why we teach you to recite the Bringing Forth Soul Consciousness Akashic Records Prayer out loud and to write your responses to the interactive questions.

Transformation or healing can happen on three levels:
· At the level of the story you tell yourself,
· At the level of causes and conditions,
· At the level of your Soul's energetic blueprint.

All three levels increase your unconditional self-love, and the profound awareness of the fact of your own Soul's perfect presence.

"The Soul's journey is its evolution into awareness of its Divine origin and innate perfection. Many of you feel that you have been to the gates of hell and back, however, nothing you have experienced has the power to extinguish your Soul's Light."
Dr. Linda Howe

It is important to note that your perfect Soul cannot be dented, damaged, contaminated, lost, lent, stolen, divided, or destroyed. Your Soul is now, and always will be, perfect, even as it continuously evolves. The paradox of this spiritual journey is that despite harrowing, traumatizing events, and any beliefs you may have that you "need to be fixed", at the Soul level of consciousness, you are absolutely perfect. As you are realigned with your Soul, you are empowered in the moment, significantly diminishing the effects of past traumas. All of this contributes to healing.

Your Soul is yearning for intimacy with you, for deep connection with the human you, to assist you in solving problems. It longs to help you release unwanted influences from past lives and to dissolve restricting ancestral beliefs. Your Soul desires to heal your past traumas and injuries, so that you can fully enjoy the blessings bestowed upon you.

During Akashic Records readings and classes, you will know, see, and reflect these truths back to yourself – that you are perfect, whole, and complete. As you absorb the vibratory reflection of your Soul's perfection, you become healed.

By design, the Akashic Records illuminate how all illness, suffering, resentment, lack, frustration, and limitation are invitations to your healing and continuous spiritual growth. Every problem is an invitation, an occasion to grow in self-love, and Oneness with the Great Creatress.

Every distressing event in your life is your Soul calling you to come closer, and to connect with your Soul's wisdom, love, support, and healing Light. When this occurs, you can experience your Divine plan unfolding, rising from the ashes of the pain, chaos, and disorder of the past.

You feel fully present, whole, and empowered.

Healing also occurs when past lives are seen and recognized, and any negative carry-over energy is automatically neutralized. In the Light of your Soul's Consciousness, unwanted ancestral influences are lifted so both you, and your ancestors, are now free to evolve, unhindered.

Blocks to creativity and full self-expression are cleared with little or no processing, relieving you of suffering. Solutions to longstanding issues and judgments are lifted, liberating you to consciously travel your Soul's Path.

The Akashic perspective emancipates you from limitations that have hidden your Light, your intrinsic power, and your Oneness with the Great Creatress.

The Light of your Soul beckons you to a new era of peace, success, fulfilling relationships, and creative endeavors. Take the plunge, open your heart and receive the healing, stability, enduring love, of your Soul's Light and consciousness as it is freely offered to you.

Please write your responses to these interactive questions.

~ Interactive Questions ~

How do you feel with your Records open?

Please describe the Light of your Soul.

What do you detect as your Soul's consciousness?

How are you emotionally and physically affected by your Soul's Consciousness?

What are four Soul qualities you experience with your Akashic Records open?

Please describe your experience of your Soul's linking abilities to the Great Creatress.

~ Closing Prayer ~

Thanking the Great Creatress & Her Holy Spirit for Love, protection & healing received this day,
Thanking the Akashic Beings of Light for guidance,
Thanking the Masters, Teachers, & Loved Ones for wisdom & direction.
The Divine Portal & the Akashic Records are now closed.
Amen. Amen. Amen.

Please follow the exercise to Embody Your Soul's Light before reading the next chapter.

Exercise – How to Embody Your Soul's Light:

Close your eyes. Take 3 deep, cleansing breaths followed by complete exhalations to bring yourself fully into this moment.

1. Begin by becoming aware of a glowing sphere of radiant Light located 12 to 15 inches above your head. This is your 8th chakra (your Soul chakra). Let your sense of knowing tell you about the color, the shimmer, and the vibration in your Soul's Light. These qualities may change from time to time. Trust the changes. The Light is infinitely wise and knows what you need at every moment.

2. Observe as the Soul chakra pours its Light into the space between your Soul chakra and your crown chakra, creating a column of connecting Light.

3. Your crown chakra naturally opens to receive the Light of your Soul as it pours itself into your crown chakra.

4. Your Soul's Light fills your entire head, inside and out. Your Soul's Light fills your brain, scalp and hair, eyes, sinuses, jaw, and the atlas bone at the top of your spine. At any point in this process, you might feel a sense of your Soul's character.

5. Notice your Soul's Light as it fills your shoulders, arms, hands, and fingers.

6. Observe as your Soul's Light lovingly and affectionately touches all the organs and systems in the trunk of your body. Allow yourself to feel your Soul's love for this precious body It chose for you.

7. Observe your Soul's Light filling the entire trunk of your body, inside and out, including your skin. Your Soul's Light naturally pools in your pelvic cavity. It pauses in your hip sockets. Take a breath.

8. Follow your Soul's Light as it fills your thighs, knees, calves, ankles, and feet. Your Soul's Light fills the bones, muscles, tendons, and fascia tissues, as well as your blood system.

9. Take notice that very cell throughout your body contains a corresponding spark of Light reflecting your Soul's Light. Recognition in each of your cells of your Soul's Light generates a feeling of joyful reunion.

10. Remain focused on your Soul's Light and all your cells as they re-connect. Observe the interactions.

11. You might feel a click or a buzzing in your feet and legs as your body's connection with your Soul's Light is complete.

12. Ground your Soul's Light into the balance point of Mother Earth.

13. Now, send your consciousness up to the Great Creatress. Feel the sphere of Light that is the Great Creatress surrounding your Soul, you, and Mother Earth.

14. Spend as much time as you like here.

15. Create a memory file by placing the pointer finger of your right hand on the palm of your left hand so that you can fully embody your Soul's Light on command.

16. Easily and effortlessly, return to ordinary consciousness, wiggling your toes, rolling your shoulders, and enjoying a few relaxing breaths.

©Reverend Annie Bachelder 5-24-22

CHAPTER 7

How the Soul is Constructed

Channeled by the Akashic Beings of Light

Bringing Forth Soul Consciousness
Akashic Records Prayer

~ Opening Prayer ~

1) By the Power of Divine Light within me
2) Come Holy Spirit! Spirit of Light! Spirit of Truth!
3) For the highest good of all, throughout time, fill my heart with Divine Love as
4) I humbly ask permission to open the Divine portal to the highest realm of the Akashic Records for (LEGAL NAME).

5) **Akashic Beings of Light,** guide me to the deepest Truth of my being, releasing any blocks & restrictions to my abundance & highest good.
6) **Great Creatress,** assist me to fully embody my Soul's Light, to fulfill my Soul's purposes, & to heal any accumulated karma.
7) **Surround me** with the enlightenment & wisdom of my Masters, Teachers, & Loved Ones.
8) **Clearly direct** my perspective & actions to those that manifest my Divine Plan.
   (Repeat lines 5, 6, 7, & 8 two more times, then say line 9)

9) **Free of all resistance, judgment, and fear,**
   I am now filled with Divine love & the Records are open.

Welcome from the Akashic Beings of Light! We are delighted to communicate with you, imbuing you with our energy and Light, uplifting you, and providing information that assists you in **Bringing Forth Soul Consciousness**. We love helping you embody your Soul's Light, which helps you consciously unify with your Soul and the Great Creatress. This is our higher purpose, our Charter.

We had you do the exercise "Embodying your Soul's Light, as well as opening your Akashic Records before our greeting. This is so that your consciousness is fully illuminated and open to the imprinting of the esoteric information in this chapter.

The Akashic Records are the perfect platform to discuss **"Bringing Forth Soul Consciousness"** as the Records exist within the Soul Plane of Consciousness. The Soul Plane of Consciousness has greater perspective and is not limited by Earth's time or the world of form.

Today, we are discussing how the Soul is constructed **specifically** to be the amplifier of consciousness. The Soul structure is similar to computer software that runs the computer. The Soul is the software, and the physical human is the hardware that executes the Soul's software programming. The physical human experiences the drama, the pleasure, the pain, the growth, the development of wisdom, and the growing connection with the Great Creatress. The cumulative result is Soul Consciousness. Soul Consciousness functions as the funnel that condenses the energy that creates the manifested physical realm and the physical body. The Soul desires to experience the full array of feelings, physical states, mental thoughts, as well as states of creativity, love, inspiration, and imagination. The Soul has everything to do with earth life as it is experienced by humanity.

Taking a step back, it is important to know that Souls are created as individual sparks of the Great Creatress to experience Herself in infinitely greater and more detailed ways. These experiences are exponentially increased in diversified ways through the creation of free will and karma.

We are defining karma as "the vibrational accumulation of the Soul's choices, conclusions, and experiences on Its journey into oneness with the Great Creatress and all creation".

The incarnated Soul is temporarily housed in a Soul chosen body imbued with a personality that best expresses the Souls particular agenda for that incarnation. This brings in the element of **time**. Each incarnation reflects the historical time of that incarnation, the social development, the personal growth challenges, and the spiritual set points for that incarnation.

We suggest you use your spiritual imagination to visualize the following: Picture the vast expanse of the Great Creatress' entire creation. You understand this to be the dark silence of outer space, containing planets, stars, manifested, and un-manifested consciousness and energy. From this vastness, the Great Creatress focuses Her pure Divine Light, **with intention** to create a specific Soul. The Divine Light coalesces raw energy directing it toward the recipient energetic container to become the Soul. The Light intensifies, increasing in vibration, fusing with the Soul. This becomes the Permanent Atom of Light©, the unique energy signature of the Soul containing the Soul's blueprint and consciousness.

Your Permanent Atom of Light© combined with the sum total of your chakra light are what is invoked in the first line of the Bringing Forth Soul Consciousness Akashic Records Prayer: "By the power of Divine Light within me".

For human purposes, all energy is sourced within, and by, the Great Creatress. It then flows through the Soul creating a continuum.

*This is the primary mode and
basic format of all manifestation.*

Remaining connected to, and engaged with, the Great Creatress, the semi-autonomous Soul keenly and precisely feeds Its Light as life-force energy to the specifically chosen human physical body. The physical human develops multiple outer spheres of energy as gathering places for the Soul's Light and consciousness. These spheres of energy create the lustrous luminescence, known as the aura, that surrounds the human. These spheres also fuel eight major chakras, including the 8th chakra, the Soul chakra.

Soul infused life-force energy nurtures the physical human like the egg yolk feeds the embryo of a chick. Then, in a cooperative effort between Soul and the human body, the Soul fixates upon its chosen personality to the exclusion of all else. The personality is programmed with all the Soul's desired purposes, positive attributes, cracks, fissures, and developmental elements with which to experience fulfillment of Its Divine Plan. Thus, the fully formed human being begins functioning as an "experience module" with the Soul as the "modulator". (This is the same as the Soul being computer software and the physical human being the computer hardware.) The Soul continuously transmits to, and through, the chakras, and into various organs and faculties within the human system. In this way, the Soul demonstrates Its love, honoring, and familial possession of the human being.

A key developmental component of **Bringing Forth Soul Consciousness** is becoming aware of the Soul chakra, the 8th chakra, located 12 to 15 inches above the head, and the 7th chakra, known as the crown chakra. Notice, in particular, the dynamically active space between them.

> *When the human consciously fills in the space between the 7th and 8th chakras with Soul Light, the human begins to have a conscious experience of the Soul, Its love, Light, wisdom, and life-force energy.*

Embodying the Soul's Light throughout the whole body brings the physical human into direct connection with the Soul, Its Light, and consciousness. Through this Soul connection, the human has an informed "sense of knowing" about how the Soul is distinctly involved in all the activities and events the human being experiences. The human can then organize its perspective and actions toward the conscious creation of the Soul's purposes thereby fulfilling Its Divine plan. No longer is the human floundering in the dark, wandering alone.

Before actual physical incarnation, there is a convergence of consciousness, at which the Soul intends and aligns its purposes for this incarnation. In attendance are the Great Creatress, the Soul, the Soul's Akashic Masters, Teachers, and Loved Ones (a.k.a. your Akashic spiritual advisory team), and those other Souls whom the Soul is inviting to participate in Its experiential learning adventure. At this convergence, the Soul organizes the play, the players, the growth objectives, the Soul's purpose (or main theme for that lifetime), the time period chosen, and the environment most conducive to achieving the objectives for itself and for the other participants. This convergence of consciousness, and the "contracts" or agreements involved, becomes crystalized within the Soul. This crystallization formalizes the energies and intentions, signaling the energy has set up, and finalizes the Soul's Divine plan, much as **signing a** contract finalizes **the** contract.

The Soul transmits the crystalized essence energy to the human being. The contents are then shrouded, or "veiled" so that the human "forgets" its mission, the players, and agreements. With few exceptions, this ensures a blank experiential slate, a requirement for the human adventure.

The intrinsic connection between the Soul and the human is reinforced through conscious embodiment of the Soul's Light. This fills in the frequencies of Soul Light between Soul chakra and Crown chakra, and all the chakras below. This conscious activity purposefully brings forth the Soul's knowledge, revealed bit by bit, drawing forth the human on the specified path.

Trust is the major element to be developed at this stage. Trust in the Great Creatress and your Soul's intentions for you.

Conscious embodiment of the Soul's Light fills in the Soul frequencies in the physical human, so the Soul's consciousness can be experienced by the human. This activity draws the Soul's Light and consciousness into the significant space between the 7th and 8th chakras. Consciously embodying the Souls Light (and the consciousness the Soul's Light contains) amends and continuously builds the connection with the Great Creatress. Thus, the Soul becomes the connecting link between the human and the Great Creatress. As this link is consciously strengthened, the human finds it far easier to trust the Great Creatress, Her love for the human, and to trust that the Soul's Divine plan is unfolding. It also aligns the human self-will with the Great Creatress' will. This trust allows for easier evolution of the Soul on Its journey into oneness with the Great Creatress.

Allow us to return to the visual of deep space and raw un-manifested energy. Using your spiritual imagination, get a sense of yourself as a Soul-empowered human, with lines of Light connecting you to the pertinent experience points on your chosen timeline. Get a sense of the lines of Light connecting you to the other Souls who have agreed to participate in your current incarnation. Visualize yourself as a Soul-empowered human connected to all Souls in Creation, and to specific locations on earth that are meaningful for the execution of your Soul's purposes.

Just as other Souls have agreed to participate in your human drama, certain locations, conditions, and environments are the perfect match for a Soul to complete Its objectives. For example, a journey to Machu Pichu, or growing up in a war zone, or providing an impoverished village with physical or spiritual assistance or inhabiting a place of rare beauty and solitary silence, may be required by a Soul to achieve its objectives. The Soul may place an energy tag in the geographic location if the story is yet to be completed or if there is unfinished business from previous lives. Similar energy tags, or markers, are left within specific humans with whom the Soul has contracts or agreements. The tags have a resonance that make them magnetically attractive or magnetically repulsive. The energy tags contain a unique vibration, a tone that tells the story of the connection between the two humans. When examined in detail, within the magnetic connection is the story of past life connections, and the Soul purpose to be continued. If there is a purpose to fulfill, there will be a pull to connect, or a circumstantial context that forces the connection of the individuals or the group. Conversely, if there is no purposeful connection between these humans, the energy will be neutral, or simply unavailable to connection within the other Soul(s). There is a void.

For the purpose of **Bringing Forth Soul Consciousness,** knowing how the Soul is constructed results in:

- The ability to consciously inhabit the Soul, which is far wiser than the human personality or mind

- The development and execution of Soul purposes, imperatives, and growth opportunities

- Learning how to utilize and express your own wisdom because you are centered in your Soul's Light and consciousness, and connected to the Great Creatress

- Life moving faster, your choice points and bigger challenges arrive more quickly

- The conscious fulfillment of the purposeful connections with **all other life forms**, including the humans with whom the Soul has contractual agreements. This allows for completion of human relationships and a deeper love of Mother Earth

- The wherewithal to consciously execute the objectives the Soul has deemed important in the current incarnation, affecting the energy pathway for future incarnations

- Achieving more, producing the results planned during preparation for this lifetime

- Clearing more karma for yourself and your ancestors

- Making mature choices in alignment with your Soul purposes

- Consciously and effectively playing your part in other Souls' evolution (Sometimes you are a minor, but essential, player in others' dramas.)

- Developing loving detachment regarding others drama's

- The conscious fulfillment of the Great Creatress' overall Divine plan. This is the ultimate "call to service". You may even find you channel the Great Creatress or are in constant communication with Her. Embodiment of your Soul's Light allows you to do this easily and effectively, for yourself, and for others. Clarity will be your calling card.

In essence, there is a path of great beauty, stability, and expansion available to humans who **consciously embody their Soul's Light, consciousness, and Soul purposes**. Herein lie the directions for a joyful life, fulfillment, spiritual alignment, and harmoniously constructive relationships. You will find abundance comes easily and that you always have enough.

You trust that the Divine has already placed the resources you need at various points on your journey so that manifesting is not a distraction that requires extra effort.

This is the path of least resistance, despite the requirement for healthy self-determination and self-discipline.

The Importance of the Space Between the 7th and 8th Chakras

Filling in the Soul frequencies between the 7th and 8th chakras through embodiment of the Soul's Light, makes available key directives and information that assists the human to consciously accomplish their Souls purposes in this lifetime in a streamlined fashion. Information exists within these filled in frequencies at this location. Conversely, unpleasant memories, old cultural and ancestral programming can be removed. We provide you with an exercise that will give you the energetic experience that demonstrates our point.

Exercise: Interacting with the Space between the 7th and 8th Chakras

1. Close your eyes. Take three deep, cleansing breaths.

2. Inhale Light. Exhale grey energy.

3. Place your concerns in the lap of the Great Creatress while you focus on this exercise.

4. Become aware of your 8th chakra, the Soul chakra, about 12 or 15 inches above your head.

5. Embody your Soul's Light by witnessing your Soul chakra pouring Its exquisite Light into the space between your 7th and 8th chakras.

6. Notice that your Soul's Light forms a column of Light in this space, connecting the two chakras.

7. Allow your Soul's Light to entirely fill every part of your body until you vibrate in harmony with your Soul's Light.

8. When you are ready, return your attention to the space between the 7th and 8th chakras.

9. Zoom in on the column of Soul Light. Notice all you can about the quality of the Light. Notice the vibratory rate, colors, shapes, movement, or any vertical or horizontal frequency lines.

10. Energy is always changing. Simply observe the active energy inside the column of Soul Light.

11. Notice that there are no barriers to this column of Soul Light that

delineate the space. You can test this by running your hand through the space like moving your hand through a hologram.

12. Choose a Soul quality such as peace, unconditional love, or kindness, that you would like to experience.

13. Get a sense of this quality as a word held just outside the column of Soul's Light and insert the word into the column.

14. Give yourself a moment to feel and assimilate this Soul quality.

15. Follow the Soul quality as it moves into and around your physical interior.

16. Notice how this quality affects different body parts. Notice where it lands and integrates itself into your body.

17. Let that go for now and return your attention to the space between your 7th and 8th chakras and the column of Soul Light.

18. Now, get a sense of a symbol representing the fulfillment of a desired event.

19. Insert the symbol into the column of Soul Light.

20. Observe the energy as the symbol is absorbed into the column of Soul Light.

21. Observe as the symbol enters and moves around your interior.

22. Relax and observe. Don't force anything.

23. Notice if there are particular body locations where the symbol most easily settles or affects.

24. Make a memory file of this process and how it feels, looks, and how it changes your energy.

25. Return to the column of Soul Light between your 7th and 8th chakras.

26. Let an embarrassing situation, or a moment you regret, come into your awareness.

27. Notice where in your body you have stored this memory.

28. Observe as your Soul's Light gently brings it into the column of light.

29. Allow the Akashic Beings of Light to gently and firmly remove the memory and the sensations associated with this experience.

30. When the removal is complete, the Akashic Beings of Light kiss your forehead.

31. Gently and easily, bring your attention back to your Soul chakra. Thank your Soul. Come fully back into the room and open your eyes.

We resume. You can easily add DNA strands containing desired health, skills, other spiritual qualities, and selected Light frequencies, to this space between the 7th and 8th chakras. The human can use this process to manifest events, relationships, connections, and resources. We encourage you to open your Akashic Records and use this process to ask questions about the Soul, Its objectives, purposes, and methods of manifesting these elements.

As you explore this small, yet dynamic arena, a new world of options comes into play. Your alignment with Soul objectives becomes a natural directing force encouraging Soul-level interplay between you and others and your combined creativity.

Your expanded consciousness grooves the energetic routes for others to follow. Many, beyond measure, are benefited from this activity. The filled-in Soul frequencies and the embodiment of Soul's Light make available to all humanity additional evolutionary Light, energy, and healing.

The filled-in Soul frequencies dissolve the spiritual growth ceiling that many have felt as a superimposed limitation, like a glass ceiling pressing down. This activity opens fresh realms of possibility and new social constructs.

The benefit of Bringing Forth Soul Consciousness is this: the more deeply and consciously you are connected with your Soul, the easier and more fluid the journey.

Conscious connection with your Soul reduces resistance and density.

There are more choices from which to select. Due to the impact of Soul Consciousness, the menu of choices is more sophisticated, and refined. The selection is far wider than that for the human who is bumbling along, bogged down by attempts to control by human might, struggling to manage life without Divine assistance, in the absence of Divine Grace.

Grace has always been the province of the Soul. Grace is a Soul component. You receive Grace through your Soul alignment. The Soul is the intermediary between the human and Grace.

The crowning gift of **Bringing Forth Soul Consciousness** is that your **connection to the Great Creatress is conductive**, containing powerful frequencies of relationship, life-force energy, and communication. **Bringing Forth Soul Consciousness** allows for more precisely attuned alignment with Divine Will and the manifestation of your Soul's Divine plan.

That, we believe, is enough for today. We are grateful for your keen attention and willingness to engage with our messages for the greater good of all. We bid you adieu for now.

Please write your responses to the interactive questions below.

~ Interactive Questions ~

Utilizing the exercise "How to Embody Your Soul's Light", how do you feel when the column of Soul's Light between your 7th and 8th chakras is filled in with Soul Light and frequencies?

In the exercise, what changes for you when you interact with the column of Soul Light between your 7th and 8th chakra?

What Soul quality did you add to the column of Light? Why?

What desired event did you insert into the column of Soul Light?

Describe the embarrassing moment, or the regret, that the Akashic Beings of Light removed through your column of Soul Light. How do you feel now?

Knowing that you and your Soul are divinely designed to be intricately linked, what seems possible in your life now?

~ Closing Prayer ~

Thanking the Great Creatress & Her Holy Spirit for Love, protection & healing received this day,
Thanking the Akashic Beings of Light for guidance,
Thanking the Masters, Teachers, & Loved Ones for wisdom & direction.
The Divine Portal & the Akashic Records are now closed.
Amen. Amen. Amen.

CHAPTER 8

Following the Energy

Channeled by the Akashic Beings of Light

Bringing Forth Soul Consciousness
Akashic Records Prayer
©Rev. Annie Bachelder 1/22/2022

~ Opening Prayer ~

1) By the Power of Divine Light within me
2) Come Holy Spirit! Spirit of Light! Spirit of Truth!
3) For the highest good of all, throughout time, fill my heart with Divine Love as
4) I humbly ask permission to open the Divine portal to the highest realm of the Akashic Records for (LEGAL NAME).

5) **Akashic Beings of Light,** guide me to the deepest Truth of my being, releasing any blocks & restrictions to my abundance & highest good.
6) **Great Creatress,** assist me to fully embody my Soul's Light, to fulfill my Soul's purposes, & to heal any accumulated karma.
7) **Surround me** with the enlightenment & wisdom of my Masters, Teachers, & Loved Ones.
8) **Clearly direct** my perspective & actions to those that manifest my Divine Plan.

   (Repeat lines 5, 6, 7, & 8 two more times, then say line 9)

9) **Free of all resistance, judgment, and fear,**
   I am now filled with Divine love & the Records are open.

Greetings and welcome from the Akashic Beings of Light.

We welcome all who wish to make a beginning in **Bringing Forth Soul Consciousness.** We welcome you with Our open hearts. This experience will be different for each of you. If you reread some chapters, you will experience them differently each time. We begin with the individual you, where you are, as you are now.

Whatever preparation you may have done, or not done,
is not the issue.
You have arrived at this book.
Therefore, you have already been invited to partake
in these energies.

You are here with Us, and we wrap our Holy Hearts and supportive Love around you. All is well.

Bringing Forth Soul Consciousness is not as big or different as you might think. Many of you have already been here, some by accident, some by request, and some by instinct, and some by training. Simply center yourself in the moment as you read this. Center yourself in the lap of kindness and safety we offer you. We are gently transmitting energetically to you now. We suggest you open your Spiritual Heart (for further information see chapter 11 "Your Spiritual Heart") and tune your receiving to the energetic apparatus known as your Spiritual Heart. It is already within you. Feel your Spiritual Heart open, taking a shape that is suitable for you and for the moment. Allow it to form in its own way as it knows exactly what is most steady and most appropriate for you. Allow yourself to let go. Let yourself be enveloped by this energy.

Your Spiritual Heart contains the energy that you have craved
all your life.
The energy of Love, Light, healing, perfection, and momentary peace.

You have done well. We are aware of you. Now, as we transmit these words to you, let the images form, and the sensations move freely through you. In essence, you are coming into a calm channeling state. You, who are attracted to this information will recognize the flow coming through you. You will recognize the familiarity, the love, the respect, and the appreciation we have for you. You who are attracted to this information and energy will find solace, knowledge, and experiential energies that assist you, and open you up to the new. The information, the vibration, or the topic may be just what you need at this point in your life.

If your mind intrudes, simply relax and "expand to include" the intrusion. It is simply your mind making its presence known as it settles down for the duration of this transmission.

Throughout your reading of this missive, we suggest that you get centered, breathe in a relaxed, yet free and full fashion. Opening your Akashic Records at the beginning of each chapter assists greatly with centering and calming. Become aware of your chakras, let them settle into the rhythm that this transmission stabilizes for you. Now become aware of the 8th chakra, about 12 to 18 inches above the head. (Please see the final chapter titled "Prayers, Invocations, and Exercises" for the exercise called "How to Embody Your Soul's Light") Let yourself become familiar with this chakra. Observe Its Light, texture, and intensity. Observe how the lower chakras easily accept this additional chakra in the vertical line-up. Observe the 8th chakra as it gently pours its limitless sparkling Light into the space between it and the crown chakra. Note the color. Allow that to shift and change, as it will do so periodically. Feel the Soul Light filling your skull. Feel its precision and spatial arrangement. You may have noticed the crown chakra automatically receives this Light, offering no resistance. This is the light of your ever-present Soul, that brought you into existence as the physical human with a personality, to fulfill Its higher purposes. (For further information see chapter 7 "How the Soul is Constructed")

Continue to receive the Light of your Soul as it pours into your whole body. Follow the Light as it fills your head, your shoulders, neck, arms, and hands. Open to receive this Light as it fills your upper body, then fills the lower body. Notice how easily it flows into the pelvic floor and the hip sockets, down the legs and into the feet. Pause for a moment to observe. Notice the Light of your Soul connecting with each and every cell in your body.

Feel the recognition and the love being exchanged
between your cells and your Soul's Light.
It is a festive, heartwarming occasion!

Take as much time as you need to acknowledge the connection and the recognition of your Soul's Light within each cell, each organ, each system in your body. Recognize the teamwork in the precise functioning of your body.

Your physical body is an important participant in the execution of your Soul's purposes.

If you choose, you may ground the Light of your Soul into the center of the Earth, the balance point of the Earth. Some of you may be naturally drawn to "grounding up" to the Great Creatress. You may find yourself being weightless and very buoyant. If so, allow your Soul's Light to go all the way up to Source and rest there for a breath or two. Keep your options open, trying both methods at different times. You won't need to force either method.

Ground in the way you are most easily drawn to do as you follow the energy.

This is a marvelous beginning, or a marvelous continuation of a theme. Some of you will use the process above to bring peace and calm into your experience. Some of you will use this process to channel your Soul, and some will use this process to center yourself and prepare to channel your Guide's energy.

Return your awareness to your Spiritual Heart. Filled with Soul Light, notice how far out your Spiritual Heart extends. Notice that your Spiritual Heart has taken on the shape of a star and that you are able to reach out with the arms of the star to touch upon planets or distant forms of consciousness that reside at this set of coordinates, or who have come to meet you. Notice that you can use your Spiritual Heart to reach out and touch Souls in need. Or simply without touching their energy, surround them with your Spiritual Heart's energy field. You can use this for healing, soothing, and refreshing yourself or others in need, as long as those in need are sending out prayers requesting assistance. Offer only what you have in abundance. Offer only what is "costless" to you. If there is a drop in your energy or a reduction in your focus, please return your awareness to your Spiritual Heart and embodying your Soul's Light.

Following the Energy

We have brought in the concept of "Following The Energy". This will take on more and more significance as you continue **Bringing Forth Soul Consciousness**.

Soul Consciousness is re-acquiring, and re-engaging, certain abilities forgotten upon entering your body in this incarnation.

Feel and sense the words as we assure you that you already have the ability to sense the energies present.

Begin distinguishing your own energy from another life form or person's energy. This could be understood as learning to use your discernment. Discernment is another ability already in existence within you. At a very basic level it is where, as a child, you begin to have likes and dislikes. These progress into preferences, hardening into opinions. As a Soul in a body, you have energy sensing capabilities that function largely beneath your conscious awareness and which, unfortunately, your culture teaches you to ignore, fear, question, or suppress. Our goal is to bring your energy-sensing capabilities to the forefront and to support you in trusting the data acquired. Except in extreme situations such as a near death experience or sudden enlightenment, this is not an overnight experience. That is very good news as it means that you can be trained, and you can train yourself through practice, to acknowledge and further develop this skill.

As you continue to read, you may find yourself resonating with, or rejecting, some of our proposals. This is as it should be.

We will always support you, lovingly, as you use your discernment and innate energy sensing abilities. We encourage you to remain open rather than in a defensive posture about the information in this book. Rather than defensively rejecting any information, as if it would harm you, simply allow what disagrees with you to glide past you. Allow it to flow past you and it will dissipate on its own. This will require little or no resistant physical energy and occupy your experience only for a brief period, leaving no trace.

The attitude of resistance is what is harmful to you.

Detachment and discernment are far easier on your physical and psychic energy.

So, we arrive at the understanding that Following the Energy combined with discernment, or choice, is a self-empowering stance. If you choose to follow and observe the energy we are presenting, we honor that, as well.

Following the energy requires you to be fully present in the moment, experiencing your experience, observing from a neutral posture.

As you read and listen to this book, we suggest a stance of neutral curiosity, allowing yourself to be led from chapter to chapter by your discernment of the energy and information within it. Write your responses to the interactive questions at your own pace and in the order you are drawn to explore them. You may find it valuable to return to certain chapters for further study or to sharpen your skills, or to simply to open your Akashic Records and engage with the Akashic Beings of Light and your Masters, Teachers, and Loved Ones. As we have stated, we are aware of you individually and are transmitting to you specifically with your permission. You are at choice here!

At this juncture Annie is being shown a memory.

During the early 1990's we had a female dog, an Akita, named Callie. Akitas are large, heavy coated creatures, bred in Japan as property defense animals. This Akita, while being of somewhat imposing size was a very gentle, well trained, and calm dog. Late one night as my former husband and I were walking Callie in the well-lit neighborhood, Callie began following a skunk. She was clearly following in an attitude – not of aggression or even play – but of distinctly neutral curiosity. What was alarming to us was that she was following this skunk with her nose literally six inches from the skunk's rear end. Callie steadily maintained her six-inch distance precisely in tune with the skunk's zig-zagging pace. This went on for nearly three minutes. We watched, stunned, not wanting to raise an alarm that would cause the skunk to release its stink. After a while, the skunk slipped under a fence where Callie could not follow, and we three resumed our walk unharmed. The Akashic Beings of Light are using this memory to illustrate several key concepts:

Simply follow it.

1) the value of remaining in a state of neutral curiosity,
2) observing without judgment,
3) free of resistance or interference
4) steadily following the energy.

The objective is to stay as close to the energy and follow where it goes, allowing yourself to be led where the energy is taking you. Observe the energy, your thoughts, and sense of knowing about the energy, and trust that all is for your higher good. You don't need to force an agenda or try to influence the energy. Simply follow it.

Please write your responses to these interactive questions and explore them with your Records.

~ Interactive Questions ~

Describe a time when you felt drawn to follow the energy or felt led by the energy.

Describe there times and methods you used to ground yourself.

How do you feel about the messages from the Akashic Beings of Light?

Describe your experience of your Spiritual Heart.

~ Closing Prayer ~

Thanking the Great Creatress & Her Holy Spirit for Love, protection & healing received this day,
Thanking the Akashic Beings of Light for guidance,
Thanking the Masters, Teachers, & Loved Ones for wisdom & direction.
The Divine Portal & the Akashic Records are now closed.
Amen. Amen. Amen.

Great Creatress Invocation

Oh, Great Creatress!

I invite your Divine and Holy Presence to flow through me now.

Opening my Spiritual Heart, I receive the fullness of your gifts.

Perpetually aligned in Divine partnership with you, I offer my mind, body, and spirit in unity with Your Power and Purpose.

Surrendering all obstacles, Your pure Light flows gracefully through me.

Receiving your Divine instructions for this day, all thoughts, words, and deeds that most serve You arrive pre-formatted with Your Impeccable timing, love, and strength of purpose.

Inspire me to proceed in the direction and manner that You prescribe.

Born of Your Divine Light, and filled with gratitude, your steady Presence gives me the energy, clarity and empowerment needed to fulfill Your Divine Plan.

Gratefully, I say **And so it is, Dear Goddess! Amen!**

CHAPTER 9

The Development of Soul Consciousness

Channeled by the Akashic Beings of Light

Bringing Forth Soul Consciousness
Akashic Records Prayer
©Rev. Annie Bachelder 1/22/2022

~ Opening Prayer ~

1) By the Power of Divine Light within me
2) Come Holy Spirit!   Spirit of Light!   Spirit of Truth!
3) For the highest good of all, throughout time, fill my heart with Divine Love as
4) I humbly ask permission to open the Divine portal to the highest realm of the Akashic Records for (LEGAL NAME).

5) **Akashic Beings of Light,** guide me to the deepest Truth of my being, releasing any blocks & restrictions to my abundance & highest good.
6) **Great Creatress,** assist me to fully embody my Soul's Light, to fulfill my Soul's purposes, & to heal any accumulated karma.
7) **Surround me** with the enlightenment & wisdom of my Masters, Teachers, & Loved Ones.
8) **Clearly direct** my perspective & actions to those that manifest my Divine Plan.
(Repeat lines 5, 6, 7, & 8 two more times, then say line 9)

9) **Free of all resistance, judgment, and fear,**
I am now filled with Divine love & the Records are open.

Greetings and welcome from the Akashic Beings of Light. We request that you practice the "Exercise: How to Embody Your Soul's Light" before beginning today's discussion.

Exercise – How to Embody Your Soul's Light:

Close your eyes. Take 3 deep, cleansing breaths followed by complete exhalations to bring yourself fully into this moment.

1. Begin by becoming aware of a glowing sphere of radiant Light located 12 to 15 inches above your head. This is your 8th chakra (your Soul chakra). Let your sense of knowing tell you about the color, the shimmer, and the vibration in your Soul's Light. These qualities may change from time to time. Trust the changes. The Light is infinitely wise and knows what you need at every moment.

2. Observe as the Soul chakra pours its Light into the space between your Soul chakra and your crown chakra, creating a column of connecting Light.

3. Your crown chakra naturally opens to receive the Light of your Soul as it pours itself into your crown chakra.

4. Your Soul's Light fills your entire head, inside and out. Your Soul's Light fills your brain, scalp and hair, eyes, sinuses, jaw, and the atlas bone at the top of your spine. At any point in this process, you might feel a sense of your Soul's character.

5. Notice your Soul's Light as it fills your shoulders, arms, hands, and fingers.

6. Observe as your Soul's Light lovingly and affectionately touches all the organs and systems in the trunk of your body. Allow yourself to feel your Soul's love for this precious body It chose for you.

7. Observe your Soul's Light filling the entire trunk of your body, inside and out, including your skin. Your Soul's Light naturally pools in your pelvic cavity. It pauses in your hip sockets. Take a breath.

8. Follow your Soul's Light as it fills your thighs, knees, calves, ankles, and feet. Your Soul's Light fills the bones, muscles, tendons, and fascia tissues, as well as your blood system.

9. Take notice that very cell throughout your body contains a corresponding spark of Light reflecting your Soul's Light. Recognition

in each of your cells of your Soul's Light generates a feeling of joyful reunion.

10. Remain focused on your Soul's Light and all your cells as they re-connect. Observe the interactions.

11. You might feel a click or a buzzing in your feet and legs as your body's connection with your Soul's Light is complete.

12. Ground your Soul's Light into the balance point of Mother Earth.

13. Now, send your consciousness up to the Great Creatress. Feel the sphere of Light that is the Great Creatress surrounding your Soul, you, and Mother Earth.

14. Spend as much time as you like here.

15. Create a memory file by placing the pointer finger of your right hand on the palm of your left hand so that you can fully embody your Soul's Light on command.

16. Easily and effortlessly, return to ordinary consciousness, wiggling your toes, rolling your shoulders, and enjoying a few relaxing breaths.

©Reverend Annie Bachelder 5-24-22

Excellent. Well done. Now, let us delve more deeply into the Development of Soul Consciousness, how you can merge with your Soul, and what this involves. The Soul chakra, located 12" to 15" above the head, is the energetic repository of the Soul's Light. Your Soul's Light contains the method of Soul formation, Soul structure, Soul purpose, and coding, as you might call it. The Soul chakra contains the imprinting as it pertains to the human personality and physical body for this particular lifetime. The Soul chakra also contains the energy patterns most conducive to achieving the Soul's purposes for this lifetime.

It is important at this juncture to state that although the Soul is in an eternal state of evolution and expansion, the Soul is always perfect, even in Its process of evolution.

> **Your Soul cannot be contaminated, corrupted, co-opted, torn, chipped, broken, damaged, stolen, or lost.**

How could the Great Creatress create an imperfect creation? How could the Great Creatress lose something It created? How could the Divine create a mistake? All things are made of energy and no energy is ever lost or wasted in this universe; hence, nothing can be lost. Humanity's sense of separation is often mislabeled as the Soul being lost, damaged, or disconnected.

Feeling disconnected is simply the way the human is called to rejoin Its Soul for nourishment, fulfillment, connection, comfort, direction, and conscious reunification with the Great Creatress.

The apparent lack of connection leads to feeling lost, alone, and unloved. This apparent lack of connection emphasizes your belief that you, your body, and your Soul are three separate, unrelated, elements. This is a great example of your human mind's ability to compartmentalize. We are using the terms "the body" and "the human" interchangeably. Purposefully, the Soul uses your emotional longing for connection to fuel your interest in spiritual growth and your desire for Oneness with the Great Creatress.

As we have noted before, the space between the Soul chakra and the crown chakra is of interest. When you pour your Soul's Light into this space and into your body, this space contains the energetic link between Soul Consciousness and human consciousness, including consciousness of the body. Within this space is a complex set of energy lines that functions as a multicolored bar code. These are continually updated as the Soul evolves and Its communication with the you and your body is strengthened through expanded Soul Consciousness. Your Soul communicates with you and with your body. Often, your Soul communicates through your body the messages which you are prone to ignore. These tend to be in the "physical self-care" category, such as "slow down", "rest", "relax", "consult with a doctor" or "take a nap, please". The human and the body respond by sending information on current receptivity and assimilation settings which influence the rate of flow from the Soul to human. The multicolored bar code lines increase or decrease, changing vibration as needed depending on the circumstances and the need being addressed. The multicolored bar code lines reflect the state of communication between Soul and human. A snapshot, as it were. Significant energy exchanges between body and Soul are reduced if the body is in a state of overwhelm, agitation, disorder, pain, panic, extreme fatigue, or significantly ill, essentially whenever the microcapillaries are too compressed. This is because there is little receptivity. Conversely, when the body is calm, peaceful, open, and divinely organized, the multicolored bar code lines are stable, abundant, and flowing, and so are the microcapillaries.

[For further elucidation, Annie is being advised to clairvoyantly "look" at the vibration rate, colors, and overall state of the space between 7th and 8th chakras of channeling and Divine Energy Healing clients. Annie is also advised is to clairvoyantly "look" at the beginning, middle and the end of the reading and to take note of the qualities expressed. The Akashic Beings of Light are recommending that she understand that this is simply a sounding, a registration of energy, and is not a judgment of the reading or healing as to whether the reading is good or bad. Nor is it an assessment of the value and quality of the reading. It is simply a registration of the energy state of the space that connects the physical human with its Soul. This state will be in constant flux and reflects the consciousness of the client – not the consciousness or abilities of the channel.]

When the embodied human is consciously connected to her Soul, energetic communication occurs, and harmony ensues. Healing occurs in this environment. Vibrational coherence and unity of body, Soul, and human is essential to peace of mind and sound health.

When the body, human consciousness, and the Soul are in resonance all is well and a new benchmark of vibratory harmony is set.

Each time a human being consciously communes with the Soul, fully embodying the Soul's Light, an enhanced vibratory resonance is established. A real sense of Soul presence comes to the forefront of human consciousness. Perhaps subtle at first. Repetition is key here, and mastery through repetition of this method of embodying your Soul's Light, of communication and connection, is of tremendous import to continued spiritual growth and harmony.

[Annie feels the statement about repetition as a physical weight, a heaviness upon her crown and shoulders, and a slight dimming and dizziness, as a way of the Akashic Beings of Light emphasizing their point.]

Filling in the gap between the 8th and 7th chakras via embodying your Soul's Light causes the connection between Soul and human to deepen and strengthen. Filling your entire body with your Soul's Light perpetuates healing. From what you may feel is a tenuous beginning, a strong bond is consciously formed that cannot be broken or withered. Each time new benchmarks are set they become fact. They become the new starting point. Many wonderful, life enhancing experiences become available as a working part of the human consciousness. Your "law of attraction vibration" has been raised, therefore what comes to you is of a higher caliber.

As the saying goes "You can't un-ring the bell." Hence you need not be concerned with backsliding.

The increased Soul connection, or Soul Consciousness, allows old energies and obsolete beliefs to loosen their grip so they can be replaced with newer, higher vibrational perspectives, thought forms, and experiences.

We suggest that whenever you have a moment, standing in line at the grocery store, or particularly when you are struggling, that you practice embodying your Soul's Light and bringing it into the whole body. The sensation of unity and uniformity brings peace and balance to the nervous system. Over time the sense of love and being "Soul Directed" occurs. From there, a sense of Oneness with the Great Creatress replaces any sense of separation.

Experience the downward flow of embodying your Soul's Light as a form of grounding, even while the practice results in a rise in consciousness.

Harmony is a wonderful state of being, in any case. As the intentional state of embodied Soul Consciousness becomes the new norm, many stubborn problems resolve, dissipate, or disappear. This occurs with far less effort than before. These may be problems experienced within yourself, outside of yourself, in the family, or at work. These problems may have been societal and cultural.

The Light of the Soul has great potency for restoration, recalibration, and reorientation.

Experiences of this nature are cumulative within the human and thus changes outside of the human are a natural consequence. As Soul Consciousness grows, and as the sense of Oneness with the Divine grows, many new paths, solutions, and inquiries into consciousness arise. Divisions between humans are reduced or simply become unnecessary.

We bid you adieu for now.

Please write your responses to these interactive questions.

~ Interactive Questions ~

What do you notice about the state of your consciousness as your Soul pours Its Light from the 8th chakra into the space between it and your 7th chakra?

Describe your sensations as you completely embody your Soul's Light.

Describe your state of consciousness while embodying your Soul's Light.

In what ways has your longing for your Soul's Light and connection moved you forward on your spiritual path?

Describe your sense of the complex set of lines (bar code) in the space between your Soul Chakra and the 7th chakra?

What qualities and colors are present in the bar code?

How does it change under different circumstances?

~ Closing Prayer ~

Thanking the Great Creatress & Her Holy Spirit for Love, protection & healing received this day,
Thanking the Akashic Beings of Light for guidance,
Thanking the Masters, Teachers, & Loved Ones for wisdom & direction.
The Divine Portal & the Akashic Records are now closed.
Amen. Amen. Amen.

CHAPTER 10

Embracing Soul Qualities and the Great Creatress

Channeled by the Great Creatress

Bringing Forth Soul Consciousness
Akashic Records Prayer
©Rev. Annie Bachelder 1/22/2022

~ Opening Prayer ~

1) By the Power of Divine Light within me
2) Come Holy Spirit! Spirit of Light!   Spirit of Truth!
3) For the highest good of all, throughout time, fill my heart with Divine Love as
4) I humbly ask permission to open the Divine portal to the highest realm of the Akashic Records for (LEGAL NAME).

5) **Akashic Beings of Light,** guide me to the deepest Truth of my being, releasing any blocks & restrictions to my abundance & highest good.
6) **Great Creatress,** assist me to fully embody my Soul's Light, to fulfill my Soul's purposes, & to heal any accumulated karma.
7) **Surround me** with the enlightenment & wisdom of my Masters, Teachers, & Loved Ones.
8) **Clearly direct** my perspective & actions to those that manifest my Divine Plan.

    (Repeat lines 5, 6, 7, & 8 two more times, then say line 9)

9) **Free of all resistance, judgment, and fear,**
   I am now filled with Divine love & the Records are open.

Greetings. I am the Great Creatress.

Greetings Blessed Souls. Greetings to your essence. Greetings to all you are creating, and greetings to all the elements with which you are created.

I want to speak to you today, as an advocate of connecting with your Soul. Your Soul, and by design, your personality or human self, are my beloved and blessed creations. While you are gallivanting though your life you may be unaware of My Presence. But I am ALWAYS aware of yours. I hold you in My creative awareness with great esteem, love, respect, and care. I am fully generating all you are wanting to experience and create, at all moments throughout time. No, My Beloved Beings. I have never forgotten or forsaken you. The constant flow of My life-force energy is always in you, with you, around you, even as you are transitioning from bodily form to pure consciousness and energy.

It is My Will that you know your own Soul. Through Me, your Soul is the primary animating force for your human embodiment. As the Akashic Beings of Light have discussed in previous channelings, your Soul is the primary link to my Holiness. As you learn to embrace your Soul, you are learning to embrace Me, and to access ever-increasing aliveness, help, purpose, healing, consciousness, and direction.

> *Qualities of the Soul are so like Mine as to be one and the same.*
> *This is by design. This is what is meant by "made in the image and*
> *likeness of Me".*

Hence, every time you consciously choose to embody your Soul, to merge with your Souls Light and consciousness, you are in essence joining your consciousness with Mine. Do not make too much of this connection ritual. Big or small, fast or slow, elaborate or simple, the same or different, all attempts are acknowledged, and We respond to you by extending our Enlightenment to you.

> *For every step toward the Light you take,*
> *the Light takes 100 steps toward you.*

This is a function of My design, and hence, your consciousness. From time immemorial, humans have reached for, engaged with, been fascinated by, and deeply desired connection with Me. The temporal rules of engagement may have appeared to change over time, but humanity's desire for connection, (for envelopment, really), has remained strong and consistent throughout time.

Prayer before and after are always good ways to begin and end your formal engagements with Me. These tokens of ritual help your human mind settle and the prayer draws to you the energy connection you crave. Prayer grooves the energy pathway to Soul connection and connection with Me. Prayer sets the energy parameters for reabsorption into My Allness. Utilizing your Soul as the linking mechanism with Me is the perfect way to merge with Me. Embodying your Soul's Light and consciousness is a simple way to accomplish what seems to you to be a challenging feat.

Notice and release any misunderstandings you have about Being Your Soul. Let your Soul's Light fill in the space that the misunderstanding used to occupy.

Some of you have no idea what constitutes your Soul. Notice and release that. Let your Soul's Light fill in the space that the misunderstanding used to occupy. Your Soul is the energetic animating consciousness of your body and personality.

Some of you have rejected your Soul or have been convinced that your Soul has rejected you. Notice and release that. Let your Soul's Light fill in the space that this misunderstanding used to occupy. Now, draw your Soul's Light even closer to you. Like Me, your Soul is always extending love, connection, and support to you.

Some of you think I have rejected you, your Soul, and the entire planet. Sweet Ones, this is not true. Notice and release that misconception. Let your Soul's Light fill in the space that the misconception used to occupy. Feel my life-force energy all around you, your body, your Soul, and Mother Earth. In truth, Mother Earth and I, the Great Creatress, are having a love affair, are having a life affair. It is expressed as unification, merging, embodiment, embracing, engagement, inclusion, fusing, joining, bonding, coalescing, creation, and partnership. You are invited to partake of this.

As you embrace your Soul, and as you thusly embrace Me, you will feel my love, care, and quiet but certain, inclusion.

Some of you have felt disconnected from your very own Soul and are now consciously rejoining It.

As you reclaim your Soul, you will feel My unmistakable, ever-present life-force flow through you. My life-force energy runs through everything your eyes can see, and all that your eyes cannot see. My Presence is even in those early hints, thoughts, and formulations of what you wish to feel, and create.

The more innovative your ownership of yourself and your Soul as one, the more My creativity can enliven your human self and Soul purposes.

The more you serve as My example the more I can work miracles through you. Notice and release the fears that somehow My working miracles through you will result in harm, judgment, or death, for you or others. Trust Me. That time has passed.

During this time in human history, as Great Creatress, my creations give life.

I have reselected my creative powers to creating life with love. Your safety, health, freedom, and the fullest experience of Love are my keenest objectives. Having heard many empty promises from leaders, your skepticism is warranted. Notice and release that. As you release the old spiritual paradigms and their elaborate supporting beliefs, you open to Me. You open to my Divine assistance, to the restoration of My Divine order within you and within your consciousness. You shift into the moment, here now, fully relaxed and alert. Clearly, many readers of this book have noticed that the paradigm shift is fully underway. Preparation time has passed.

The focus now, is on graceful navigation via adaptations to your perspective, and to receiving My Divine guidance.

I am ever alert to your requests and turn none away. Fulfillment of these requests may be modified, or perfected, due to your limited viewpoint and creation skills. These modifications create elegant solutions to your problems and allow you to substantially rise in consciousness. They suit My Divine plan to provide greater life, love, and healing to this Beloved Planet, and all her inhabitants.

"This you shall do and more." All of you reading this book are healers in one form or another. Your physical body is designed to heal, to support life, to serve Life. As you embody your Soul's Light and consciousness, you automatically increase your healing at many levels. The higher vibration brought about by embodying your Soul increases your basic vibrational setting. Embracing your Soul and embracing Me, allows you to hold and utilize a greater variety of Light frequencies. As you do so, and as you consistently represent the Light in thought, deed, and word, you heal even further. The integrity of your Divine Design is restored.

Your own healing, or what We intend as restoration, radiates outward which heals others. By Divine Design, your healing and restoration opens a conscious pathway that others can choose to follow. It is adaptable to individual needs. That is why I made the Light Infinitely wise. That is why I made the Infinite Light your first consciousness of My Greatness. The Light is always pure, innocent, blameless, genderless, myth-less, and it can travel anywhere! Even underwater to the deepest depths of the sea. No crack is too tiny for the Light to enter, to shine through. It touches the most minute fragment. No trauma or infection is too grave for My Light to restore. *(See chapter 4, My Introduction to the Light.)*

Embrace your Soul and embrace Me. Absorb My genuine love and honor of you in the form of Light. I created you to be thusly and I have not deserted you. I have not turned my back on your vigorous attempts at healing, following Divine Guidance, or helping others. My eyes and ears, and even more relevant, My Heart embraces yours. Perpetually aligned in Divine Partnership with you, hand in hand we step into Light for the Highest good of all.

I give you this prayer to support your connection with your Soul and to me. You may be receiving this prayer as words, as Light, or as frequency. All are perfect paths to your embracing your Soul, gaining from Its Light, wisdom, and connecting with me, the Great Creatress. Your Source.

~ Integrating Soul Prayer ~

For the highest good of all, Great Creatress,
please, open my Spiritual Heart to full vibrancy.
Awaken me to your Divine Design.
By the power of your Spirit within me, I presence my Soul.
I embody Its Light and consciousness.
Oversee my Soul and physical experience as we become One.
Safe in Your embrace, my Soul's Light fills me to the brim.
Recognizing my Soul's Divinity and alliance with You,
I open to receive Its beneficial influence.
Embodying my Soul's Light, I am strengthened.
I am awakened to Its consciousness.
Like you, Great Creatress, my Soul embraces me kindly,
Guides me wisely,
Fills my heart with Its love,
Sweetens my thoughts, words, and deeds with compassion.
My Soul naturally forms my link with Thee, Great Creatress.
May all consciousness be of the Light.
And so, it is.

Amen

Let the Light of your Soul flow into your crown chakra. Notice the natural ease of the Light flowing into the space between your Soul chakra and your crown chakra. Let the Light of your Soul penetrate you thoroughly. If you find yourself efforting at this, please relax. Breathe. **Let the Light do the work.** We started many of you on your spiritual path using the Light as the focal point. Let the Light of your Soul fill the rest of your body all the way down to your toes. Take as much (or as little) time as you need. There is no race to get anywhere.

Filled with the Light of your Soul, extend your awareness beyond your body. You will find me here, enveloping you, and your Soul. We three belong together. We three are inextricably linked and the inexhaustible connection is Love. Sweet, gentle Love. Embodying your Soul's Light as the link lets you fully feel my Presence. You may be feeling my "Always-ness". That is because you are recognizing the familiar sensation of My embrace. Everything you do, all the thoughts you think, all the activities you do, are within My Presence. My Presence is Love. I am Peace. I radiate Light. You are welcome to take in as much of My Presence and the qualities I radiate as you like. There is, of course, an infinite supply, and there is even more after that.

Light, one of My chief qualities is one of your chief Soul qualities, remains the default connection. Your Soul's Light opens your beautiful, enigmatic Spiritual Heart.

We think it bears repeating that the Light is Infinitely Wise. It functions as My medium of healing, connection, and vivification.

Light slips in when you are not protecting, separating, defending, or dividing yourself into compartments. The Light is your friend. Its effective communication is beyond words, language, cultures, and races. The Light speaks volumes. Light creates pictures which are worth thousands of words. The Light contains sensations as a part of my connection with you, all of which are my Blessed Gifts to you to use as you like. You cannot perform My miracles without it. You cannot misuse the Infinitely wise Light.

The beneficial qualities you ascribe to Me are endless, bountiful, good, kind. They are free and in abundant supply. Therefore, I can and do help you with anything and everything. My fingerprint is always evident in your creations, for you are creating with Me, through Me, because of Me. This is why you will always benefit from your willingness to partner with Me in every way. I am in the very fabric of life, no matter what, so you might as well invite Me to dinner.

~ Interactive Questions ~

How do you feel when you read and/or hear the Great Creatress's message?

What questions arise after taking in this chapter?

What creations are you working on where you can feel Her Divine Presence?

Describe a time when the Light slipped in surreptitiously and you were healed or comforted?

~ Closing Prayer ~

Thanking the Great Creatress & Her Holy Spirit for Love, protection & healing received this day,
Thanking the Akashic Beings of Light for guidance,
Thanking the Masters, Teachers, & Loved Ones for wisdom & direction.
The Divine Portal & the Akashic Records are now closed.
Amen. Amen. Amen.

CHAPTER 11

Your Spiritual Heart

Channeled by Anubis

Bringing Forth Soul Consciousness
Akashic Records Prayer
©Rev. Annie Bachelder 1/22/2022

~ Opening Prayer ~

1) By the Power of Divine Light within me
2) Come Holy Spirit!   Spirit of Light!   Spirit of Truth!
3) For the highest good of all, throughout time, fill my heart with Divine Love as
4) I humbly ask permission to open the Divine portal to the highest realm of the Akashic Records for (LEGAL NAME).

5) **Akashic Beings of Light,** guide me to the deepest Truth of my being, releasing any blocks & restrictions to my abundance & highest good.
6) **Great Creatress,** assist me to fully embody my Soul's Light, to fulfill my Soul's purposes, & to heal any accumulated karma.
7) **Surround me** with the enlightenment & wisdom of my Masters, Teachers, & Loved Ones.
8) **Clearly direct** my perspective & actions to those that manifest my Divine Plan.

(Repeat lines 5, 6, 7, & 8 two more times, then say line 9)

9) **Free of all resistance, judgment, and fear,**
I am now filled with Divine love & the Records are open.

Greetings and Welcome from Anubis.

As your escort into and through this information, I am holding the overall connecting vibrations of this information. Whether you are the author or the reader, we are aware of you throughout time and are holding you lovingly in the Light. We are with you whenever you read and whenever you think of the Akashic Beings of Light or of Anubis. We are providing guiding steps, new vibrations, and energy that assists you on your unique spiritual pathway.

For many months now, we have been adding the element of "Your Spiritual Heart" to Annie's guided meditations, Akashic Readings, and Akashic energy processes. As we explore the topic of Your Spiritual Heart, we are also drawn into key details about how your Spiritual Heart is involved with channeling.

Let us explain: First, there exists your physical and emotional heart. This is the muscle that pumps blood and oxygen throughout your body. It is about the size of your fist. The physical heart is also the organ and location where humans feel and sense love, loss, heartbreak, disappointment, attraction, challenge, insecurity, inspiration, upliftment, and informs the brain as to action and response. This heart is sourced at the physical level.

The Heart chakra exists at the energetic level closest to the body and is most closely connected to the body and its various functions. The Heart chakra, or 4th chakra, at rest, can extend its energy about 10 to 20 feet out from your body. It opens or restricts the flow of love and connection with other objects of affection, depending upon the physical and emotional experiences of the human, its family programming, and cultural beliefs. The Heart chakra is a gathering place for the lower three chakra energies to coalesce and clarify before moving the energy up into the 5th, 6th and 7th chakras. The Heart chakra, when clear and balanced, adds clarity and love to the 1st, 2nd, and 3rd chakras below, and fuels the open receptive energy and activities of the 5th, 6th, and 7th chakras above the Heart chakra.

Also, in the region of the chest and upper torso, is your Spiritual Heart. The Spiritual Heart significantly encompasses and surpasses in size and volume of energy the Heart chakra and the physical heart. Your Spiritual Heart purifies and intensifies the Heart chakra and physical heart energies. Every time we guide Annie to become aware of, or to activate her Spiritual Heart, she experiences an immense expansion and a corresponding visual.

(Trust what you receive if your visual or "sense of knowing" is different.) Annie's visual shows an unlimited energetic range with a deep red center, and an outer layer that becomes a diffuse red. This bullseye begins horizontally and extends outward in all directions. When fully open your Spiritual Heart forms a sphere around the body. The intensity of your Spiritual Heart may fluctuate from day to day, but it is always larger, more substantial than the radiations extending from the physical heart and the heart chakra.

Your Spiritual Heart is always more magnetic in its attraction and manifestation capabilities and is more powerful in its reception and transmission of Universal Spiritual Love. The Spiritual Heart, while compact for its ability to project, is made of a dense, higher, and finer, substance, and vibration. It is very steady and extremely stable in its radiation.

As a point of functionality, activating your Spiritual Heart immediately releases you from attachment to your personal agenda, grants you the objectivity needed in the moment to navigate potentially treacherous emotional waters, and lifts your spirits. Steeped in acceptance, it causes you to be in the flow. You naturally move into a state of harmony each time you activate your Spiritual Heart.

The Spiritual Heart forms the center of your energy sensing capabilities. Love is the first energy a developing embryo senses, then learns to transmit, even as a single cell becoming multi-celled. Love is the fundamental ray of Light a human being senses when it becomes conscious of "The Light". Love is the fundamental vibration a human being senses when becoming spiritually aware. Love is the carrier wave upon which a complex transmission is sent so that it bypasses the traps in the ordinary human mind. Love enters the Spiritual Heart, and is unerringly transposed into words, symbols, concepts, and motivations, which the heart chakra and the physical heart can receive.

The Spiritual Heart contains a skill set instilled in every human, in every sentient earth creature, and in all transcendent Beings of Light. Allowing reception of communication at the level prior to language, the

Spiritual Heart contains the potential to be developed into a highly complex and erudite receiver, transponder, and communication device. The Spiritual Heart transposes energetic information into language, visions, and sensations, fulfilling the requirements for channeling. That is the technical explanation of what happens when you channel. Messages of any worth always contain the core carrier frequency of love. This is the benchmark of quality, of universality, and the value of messages that reach beyond the world of form, the limits of time. The message stands the test of time – generations of time – is carried upon or woven into the core frequency of love. Love is the center frequency of this missive. Activating your Spiritual Heart is a Soul-level activity, which amplifies the messages you receive, whether as intuition, channeling, or from your Akashic Records.

The Spiritual Heart mixes with your Soul's Light and consciousness, connecting you with the Divine. Whereas the Heart Chakra is centered in the body, preparing you for connection with your Soul, and connection with the Great Creatress. Activating your Spiritual Heart makes it safe for the personality (your human self) to receive and transmit channeled information and energy. Built into the experience of the Spiritual Heart is the establishment of **trust**. Trust in the human receiver's capability, trust in the Entity transmitting the message, trust in the accuracy, quality, and usefulness of the information being transmitted.

Annie has noticed that the issue of trust is a common theme in learning to channel, in learning to receive information and energy from the Akashic Records, and for any person walking a spiritual path. As a channel, she has learned that she is a **transmitter** of information and energy. "Transmitter" is defined in your dictionaries as "A set of equipment that generates, modulates, and transmits electromagnetic waves carrying messages, signals &/or frequencies, and conveys it to the antenna."

Annie, or any channel for that matter, functions as an antenna receiving energy and information which she transmits as signals, frequencies, and messages specifically designed for the intended receiver.

As the message is transmitted, the receiver (the channel) physically incorporates the vibration of the message within their body and consciousness, matching the vibration. The vibration is increased as the message begins, crescendos, and wanes as the transmission comes to completion. The receiver (the channel) assimilates the vibration, the information, and becomes the living carrier of the message. Literally, the message exists within her. It cannot be removed, only modulated, up down, left right, zoomed in, or zoomed out, amplified, or reduced, or enlarged. It cannot be removed as it has now become part of her.

The Spiritual Heart functions within the human as the receiver and the transmitter for the Soul, the Soul's Light, and the Soul's guidance.

The Soul transmits Its love for the human through the Spiritual Heart on a carrier frequency of love. Meanwhile, the Soul serves as the connector to the Great Creatress' Light and Love.

All are One and One are All. Simplified, the Spiritual Heart is where the Great Creatress dwells. This is the "indwelling Divine". The Spiritual Heart and the Permanent Atom of Light© are the consciousness that precede the physical, which naturally indicates the connection with the Great Creatress predates all else.

The human is encased within the Soul. The Soul is completely, totally in exact contact with all of the human, inside and out: the physical cells, the micro-components of the body, and the entire consciousness of the human. Surrounding the Soul, in complete contact with and pervading all energy identified as the Soul, is the Great Creatress. There is no place in which the Great Creatress is not. The Great Creatress is in and around everything, everywhere, all the time, including you. The Great Creatress occupies the spaces within, and in between, all minute and large particles, as well as the particles themselves. The Great Creatress is the context within which the entire infinite, ever expanding universe exists, except there is no edge, no beyond, in which the Great Creatress is not. Hence, the Great Creatress Is. She continually births all, enlivens all, with her generous breath of life-force. Your Spiritual Heart makes possible, the consciousness of all these parts. Your Spiritual Heart makes love and trust of the Great Creatress possible.

The Soul's consciousness is permeated by that of the Great Creatress. Separation is impossible. The Soul permeates all that is the human, hence, separation between human, Soul, and Great Creatress is impossible.
Take a moment to experience this marvel of grandeur.

Take a moment to appreciate that your personality, your physical body, and your consciousness, are totally in contact with the Light and energy of your Soul. All the time. Feel the size of your Spiritual Heart. Now, sense the Great Creatress permeating your Spiritual Heart, your Soul, and all that you hold as you. Here is a substance and a state of being that herald's peace, quiet, unity. There is no conflict. No chatter, no questions, no argument. Just peace.

The Spiritual Heart is always available and will always bring you into this realm, the realm of the Great Creatress, of your Soul, of unity, drenched in peace. This multi-dimensional inseparable connection soothes all upsets, eases all tensions, and calms the racing mind. This connection cues the next vital action that is in accordance with the unfolding of your Divine Plan and your Soul's purpose(s). This is the Source of Creation. Revelling in this ever-present multi-dimensional connection will add life-force energy to you, your creative endeavors, and will illuminate the next action steps on your path. The Spiritual Heart makes it possible for you to experience great good, to have thoughts and motivations that empower your actions for the good of all. The Spiritual Heart makes it possible for you to be tapped in, to receive, and to operate beyond the ordinary limitations of time, space, matter, money, education, apparent resources, etc.

You may need to pause here. Take a few deep breaths to help you incorporate this information. Refresh your brain with oxygen. Move your body for a moment or two.

The expansion that results from repeated engagements with the Spiritual Heart is multi-faceted. The human is expanded, the Soul is expanded, and the Spiritual Heart expands into deeper and deeper realms of consciousness. Consequently, the Great Creatress expands, and with that her acknowledgment of you, for your engagement with Her creations, pours forth in a limitless, timeless manner. The sensation is a great inhalation culminating in a great exhalation.

Through the Spiritual Heart you have a doorway into levels of creativity, knowledge, and experience. Through the Spiritual Heart you have connections with all that has been created and all that is ready to be created. That is how you find your own creativity enlarging and functioning in the seamless way it is meant to function.

The Spiritual Heart feels good, very natural to you.
It is an ingenious way to entice you to use this access point to gain
inspiration and to know your next action steps.

That is more than enough for now. It might be useful for you to reread esoteric chapters such as this. You may be surprised at how much more you can assimilate.

[Here are Annie's personal examples of the Spiritual Heart in action:

One evening, I was on overnight duty, attending to my 91-year-old father and his 93-year-old wife who had dementia. My Dad had had some small strokes, but it was the chronic urinary tract infections which compromised his usually clear thinking, and radically affected his rationality. A retired math teacher and builder of our childhood homes, my dad preferred logic and mathematics, and lived by his personal code of "Selfish Altruism". His "reason for being" was family, plain and simple. His natural setting was geared to making life better for us kids, his wife, relatives, friends, even for their apartment tenants. When he had a urinary tract infection, he became paranoid, referring to the flocks of birds flying over the San Francisco Bay as being "mechanical. They're watching us." He became distrustful, wild-eyed with fear, and reclusive. Thankfully, the previous night he voluntarily took the antibiotics that clear up the urinary tract infection. This day was only day two on the antibiotics, which meant his thinking and emotions were still altered. I felt vulnerable to his criticism but when I remembered to open my Spiritual Heart, I was immediately rewarded with a sense of open-hearted love, kindness, humor, patience, and deep wisdom. I was completely relieved of all self-centered fear, fatigue, and the sense of being "put upon".

Another morning, I was in 90% meltdown, feeling used up, impatient, and irritated by everything. In addition to caring for my elderly parents, I had also been caring for my Sweetheart, who had knee replacement surgery 3 weeks prior, and was using crutches to ambulate around the house. He needed help with most things, such as getting fresh ice packs many times per day, carrying a cup of coffee or water for taking pills, and bringing him meals. To top it off, my mother had carpal tunnel surgery the week before and her needs were on my mind, as well. Somehow, I remembered to activate my Spiritual Heart, and was lifted into a heavenly awareness and energy that made gravity and my personal life less dense, and sig-nificant. Instantly, access to greater realms and different dimensions of consciousness became my playground, inspiring my cadence and problem solving. Frustration and fatigue melted away.

Channeling for over 34 years, I can attest to the tentative and gradual development of trust in myself and Anubis. I had been channeling for many years and had intense training and practice in sensing energy and consciousness through "Awakening the Light Body" seminars when I was drawn to the Akashic Records. I learned to sense and trust the Akashic Beings of Light, and my Masters, Teachers, and Loved Ones, and the Akashic Records themselves. Channeling has been a process of surrender, trust, and personal investment of time, attention, and consciousness.

When channeling, I do several things consciously: I turn down the volume of my personality, open the back of my head and neck, and hollow out a space in the center of my body for the energy of the Guides. I place myself on "receive". My personality becomes one of the thin layers surrounding the hollow space, pressed to the side within my inner being, for the period of time that I am channeling.

- **I have learned to listen to the specifically chosen words and phrases the Guides use.**
- **I have learned to pay attention to the precise visuals and memories that are cues for me to describe.**
- **I have learned to feel the emotions rising and receding that are part of the message I am to verbalize.**
- **I have learned to sense and describe the physical sensations and the qualities of energy in my body that contribute to the channeling.**
- **I have learned to describe the colors, intensity, vibration, and density of the frequencies of Light the Guides use to heal, to shift, and to prepare or adapt me (or the client) for growth that is coming.**

These elements (and so many more!) are all part of the transmission I am receiving. These very elements are what make the transmission heart-felt, rich, compact, and complete. I know for certain that absolutely everything in my awareness, my consciousness, my memory, and my experience are all available to, and utilized by, these benevolent Entities and Guides as communication devices. Also, everything that my consciousness can reach out to and comprehend is available as information and energy I am to channel. The more subtle threads are the most powerful and the most challenging to follow but yield the highest and most precise transmissions for me to channel. I have had to learn to trust these images, perceptions, and concepts that aid me in doing an accurate reading.

My "investment" has paid off generously. I gained a multi-dimensional spiritual guidance team that always treats me with unconditional love, understanding, respect, patience, humor, trust, intimacy, confidence, and objectivity. I gained a heavenly career that allows me to be a transmitter of these same qualities. Anubis, loyal as ever, stands by me still. Patient and encouraging, Anubis supported me as I was learning how to channel; as I became ill with multiple sclerosis; as I was missing in action in drug and alcohol addiction; as I got sober and had to concede that I didn't know what or who my Higher Power would be as a sober person; and as I recovered from disability due to multiple sclerosis. Never have I been chastised or negatively critiqued for my poor performance, lack of faith, or for my human fallibility. The Guides have always been encouraging, validating and supportive. Meanwhile, my trust of the Entities grows, my skills increase, and I am given access to information, energy, and healing that stands the test of time. I can look back and be affirmed in my choice to continue this path. Mind you, this 34-year process continues to this day as I learn to relax and trust, again and again, what comes through me that blows my mind! I am honored, humbled, and inspired.]

Please write your responses to the interactive questions below.

~ Interactive Questions ~

Please describe your experience of your Spiritual Heart.

Please describe your experience of your Soul surrounded by your Spiritual Heart.

Being specific, what do you notice about the availability of the Great Creatress when you are connected to your Soul and your Spiritual Heart?

What core carrier frequencies do you detect in this chapter?

How do you feel when you read and/or hear the Great Creatress's message?

What questions arise after taking in this chapter?

What creations are you working on where you can feel Her Divine Presence?

Describe a time when the Light slipped in surreptitiously and you were healed or comforted?

~ Closing Prayer ~

Thanking the Great Creatress & Her Holy Spirit for Love, protection, & healing received this day,
Thanking the Akashic Beings of Light for guidance,
Thanking the Masters, Teachers, & Loved Ones for wisdom & direction.
The Divine Portal & the Akashic Records are now closed.
Amen. Amen. Amen.

CHAPTER 12

Masterful Manifesting

Channeled by the Akashic Beings of Light

Bringing Forth Soul Consciousness
Akashic Records Prayer
©Rev. Annie Bachelder 1/22/2022

~ Opening Prayer ~

1) By the Power of Divine Light within me
2) Come Holy Spirit! Spirit of Light! Spirit of Truth!
3) For the highest good of all, throughout time, fill my heart with Divine Love as
4) I humbly ask permission to open the Divine portal to the highest realm of the Akashic Records for (LEGAL NAME).

5) **Akashic Beings of Light,** guide me to the deepest Truth of my being, releasing any blocks & restrictions to my abundance & highest good.
6) **Great Creatress,** assist me to fully embody my Soul's Light, to fulfill my Soul's purposes, & to heal any accumulated karma.
7) **Surround me** with the enlightenment & wisdom of my Masters, Teachers, & Loved Ones.
8) **Clearly direct** my perspective & actions to those that manifest my Divine Plan.

(Repeat lines 5, 6, 7, & 8 two more times, then say line 9)

9) **Free of all resistance, judgment, and fear,**
I am now filled with Divine love & the Records are open.

Greetings from the Akashic Beings of Light.

Welcome to today's conversation. We are discussing how you can energetically prepare yourself by connecting to your intended audience, customers or clientele, and how you bring your information and services forward as a public communication.

In preparation, as your read this, embody your Soul's Light, filling your entire body with Its constancy and brilliance. (See Exercise "How to Embody Your Souls Light" in the final chapter "Prayers, Invocations, and Exercises") Stand tall in the Light of your amazing, Divinely created Soul. Then begin to speak to your audience or connect remotely with them. You will be heard. Perhaps not by all, but you will be heard by those that can receive, make the most use of, and benefit the most from, your message.

Often, your notion of "being heard" includes being heard by absolutely everyone and not the defined group that resonates with your message at this time. Of course, we always urge you to do the energy work first, before taking physical action.

The energy work prior to action is always the preparation.

What follows are directions on how to prepare yourself energetically. Be sure to open your Akashic Records and invite your Masters, Teachers, and Loved Ones to assist you. You are invoking their presence through the **Bringing Forth Soul Consciousness** Akashic Records Prayer. To further empower your work, ask the Great Creatress for assistance with this process, and for successful completion of your work or projects.

When you think of your audience, listeners, or readers, activate your Spiritual Heart. *(See chapter 11 "Your Spiritual Heart")* Feel your love and allegiance to these Souls. Notice that there are brilliant lines of Light going out from your Spiritual Heart to their Spiritual Hearts. You might sense that they are gathered in a circle around you. Connect with them. Trust that your Soul, your Masters, Teachers, and Loved Ones know what, and how, to do this in the highest and best way for all involved. Connect Soul to Soul with this group. The Souls you are connecting with are the ones you already love or are the people you are most able to love without effort. These are the Souls with whom you are meant to share your deepest truths. This is the intimate group, the first and most primary group.

The ease of energy connection is the indicator of their receptivity.

If you find yourself forcing the connection, simply focus on the Souls that are open and receptive. The brilliant lines of Light that emanate from your Spiritual Heart locate them automatically. Rather than using your self-will to make the connections, simply observe as the Spiritual Heart makes the connections. Your job, throughout this entire process, is to stay focused on experiencing your "sense of knowing", the energy, or feeling, or seeing the energy as it does the work for you.

The Light, including your Soul's Light, is infinitely wise and knows what is best for all, including for you.

With your Akashic Records open, you are functioning from your Soul's Light, your Spiritual Heart, and within the rarified Akashic atmosphere, free of judgment, resistance, and fear.

Now, reach further out with your Soul's consciousness to the next layer of your audience. Observe the lines of Light extending from your Spiritual Heart to their Spiritual Hearts. Use your Spiritual Heart and its unique core frequency of love to connect with this group of Souls. This may feel like a less solid or intense Love. Temper your expectant vibration with judgment-free acceptance. This is a larger group than the first. Be aware of the first layer's connections with some of the Souls in the second layer of your audience. This represents information being spread via personal recommendations and word-of-mouth referrals. Hold the energy focus for a few more moments. You can trust your Soul and your Masters, Teachers, and Loved Ones to know when that is complete.

Now reach even further outward to the third layer of your audience. The third group is akin to the general public, the broadest and most diverse group. Dare yourself to know this group as the entire population of the Earth. Using your Spiritual Heart as the medium of connection, let the flood of Universal Love flowing through your Soul and your physical self flow out to all people. Feel those whose eagerness and hunger for your message matches your commitment to express it. Feel, or sense, their hunger for the pure carrier frequency of love that your Spiritual Heart radiates. Feel their desire for the spiritual support, validation, and encouragement that your message contains. Hold the images and sensations you are receiving in a loose but stable focus. This group, being so large, takes a lot of focus. You may need to repeat this sequence once or twice more.

Now, open to receive.
You have sent energy from your Soul and your Spiritual Heart to many recipients and now you receive love and Light from them, much as a gift is reciprocated.

Energy, and the Spiritual Heart in particular, are two way streets. Remember to balance the out-go of love, Light, and acceptance with the in-flow of love, gratitude, and appreciation.

Give AND receive, preferably in equal measure.

There will be an exact moment when the transmission is complete and without warning the connection will cease.

You need not know exactly who is receiving these transmissions of Love and Light in any of the three groups. You might recognize some Souls. You are working at an energy level beyond the personality. You are working at Soul level, loving, and connecting with them at Soul level. You can trust the Great Creatress, the Divinity of your own Soul, and the pure Universal Love that is flowing through you and your Spiritual Heart.

You are functioning as a channel, in the energy realms, and it is not necessary that you know all the personalities connected to these Souls.

Know that younger, less experienced Souls may not be able to receive and absorb as much as more seasoned Souls can receive and absorb. That is fine. Also, some Souls will receive faster and some more slowly. That is also fine. It is essential to do this process repeatedly, at different times in the creation of the project. Trust what happens and place your expectations of certain results in the lap of the Great Creatress. She is most pleased with your passion to do good, in service of others. Passion is the root of commitment to success. As always, She is observing your energy as you function in this way.

We bring this energy preparation process to your attention because it makes you and your work magnetic to the many readers and listeners who are tuning in. It may take a while for the material presented in this book, or in your own work, to take hold, get traction, and thus become known as a stand-alone entity, as a masterful resource in and of itself. This process teaches you how to manifest energetically, in a general and loving way, calling to you those whom you can most serve. This process can be adapted to any cause or project you are bringing forth, at any stage of inception or completion. We recommend repeated transmissions so that many catch on and respond to your message. And we suggest that this is a wonderful way to share Love and Light with others, with groups of people, other earth life forms, and with the planet as a whole.

Having done your preparatory energy work, you can now create and send flyers, public messages, and Soul purposes out into the world. You have built the lines of connective Light, born on the essential carrier frequency of love.
You have called your "Public" to you.

Remember, every message sent on the frequencies of Love, appreciation, and willingness to serve others, begets the best results. Do not be too surprised if you must **enlarge your receiving** to accommodate those who are drawn to your work.

This approach is subtle, quiet, and gentle.
It is easier on the sender and the receiver.

When you feel you are competing with others, perhaps those whom you have deemed are louder or "better" than you, or more experienced marketers than you, or with whom you feel are absconding with **your** customers, listeners, or readers' attention, you are minimizing the "grass roots movement" effect. You have slipped into the illusion of competition and shortage consciousness. You are the only one who can effectively serve those who respond to your work. You must also appreciate the Great Creatress' plan to test the effects of infinite paths to illumination, healing, and evolution. It is the Great Creatress' goal to have many tiny sparks come together to make a flame that grows into a fire of inspiration and acceptance.

Remember: When it comes to making changes, many small changes are easiest to enact.

Small is flexible, adjustable, and can grow in many ways and directions. The smallest root fibers of Redwood trees feed, protect, and reproduce these ancient monoliths. New trees grow up in a circle inside or around the grandmother trees. Some of them are born from a stump, and some grow from the roots of other trees who are part of the circle. Small connected to small counts! Small bursts of Light can be very effective, much like exercising with intense bursts of maximum output for short periods then returning to a more measured pace, then another burst of maximum output. Small, consistent energy work produces the desired results. Don't give up. Make this a regular practice of sending and receiving energy.

You are doing very well. For now, we bid you adieu.

Please write your answers to these interactive questions. We assure you that writing your answers will deepen, intensify, and strengthen the process.

~ Interactive Questions ~

Please describe your experience of the first layer of recipients of the connective lines of Light.

How do you feel as you project Light from your Spiritual Heart Center?

What did you experience when projecting lines of Light from your Spiritual Heart to the second layer of recipients?

Describe your experience with the third layer.

Was the Light different at different send points?

Please describe your experience as you received Light coming back to you from your intended recipients.

How did you feel when you balanced sending Light from your Spiritual Heart center with receiving Light from your intended recipients?

~ Closing Prayer ~

Thanking the Great Creatress & Her Holy Spirit for Love, protection & healing received this day,
Thanking the Akashic Beings of Light for guidance,
Thanking the Masters, Teachers, & Loved Ones for wisdom & direction.
The Divine Portal & the Akashic Records are now closed.
Amen. Amen. Amen.

CHAPTER 13

Feeling Your Soul's Light in Your Body

Channeled by the Akashic Beings of Light and by Anubis

Bringing Forth Soul Consciousness
Akashic Records Prayer
©*Rev. Annie Bachelder 1/22/2022*

~ Opening Prayer ~

1) By the Power of Divine Light within me
2) Come Holy Spirit! Spirit of Light! Spirit of Truth!
3) For the highest good of all, throughout time, fill my heart with Divine Love as
4) I humbly ask permission to open the Divine portal to the highest realm of the Akashic Records for (LEGAL NAME).

5) **Akashic Beings of Light,** guide me to the deepest Truth of my being, releasing any blocks & restrictions to my abundance & highest good.
6) **Great Creatress,** assist me to fully embody my Soul's Light, to fulfill my Soul's purposes, & to heal any accumulated karma.
7) **Surround me** with the enlightenment & wisdom of my Masters, Teachers, & Loved Ones.
8) **Clearly direct** my perspective & actions to those that manifest my Divine Plan.
(Repeat lines 5, 6, 7, & 8 two more times, then say line 9)

9) **Free of all resistance, judgment, and fear,**
I am now filled with Divine love & the Records are open.

Greetings from the Akashic Beings of Light and from Anubis.

We welcome you again you to the rarified air of your Soul's Consciousness. Let yourself be comforted by taking a moment to embody your Soul's Light. Let your Soul's Light fill the frame of your body and illuminate the fundamental thinking abilities of your mind. Now, let the Light of your Soul fill the creative center within you. Notice that by embodying your Soul's Light you are easily able to engage your Spiritual Heart.

There is a tendency in humans to push, to control, to charge forth, armed to the teeth with self-will, only to run into the proverbial brick wall.

This is very painful for you to experience and similarly painful for us to observe. You are getting the vision of Us wincing as we watch you do this. Settle in and allow the sense of simply being to overtake you. Your being is enough for the moment. This moment is big enough to hold you, your good intentions, and all your grand plans to accomplish in one day.

If you are getting the sense that we are reigning you in, that assumption is partially correct. What we are doing is calling you back from your tendency to speed toward the next moment whilst wearing yourselves out with effort and struggle. We are simply calling you back into the moment such that all of you is collected firmly and stably in the one moment before moving forward.

This is actually a very nice moment.
This singular moment, here, now.

To help you embrace this moment we offer this exercise.

Exercise: Feeling Your Soul's Light in your Body

1. Close your eyes. Allow yourself to fully arrive in this moment. Yes, simply this moment.
2. Scan your body inside and out. Take it all in.
3. Feel the quality of this moment.
4. Ask your mind to stop rushing you.

5. Ask your mind to help you to focus on this moment as your total experience.

6. Now, take a few very deep, relaxing, and calming breaths to aid your centering.

7. Take a moment to notice your inner screen on the inside of your eyelids.

8. You may be seeing, sensing, or "knowing" your Soul as beautiful Light that is illuminating your body.

9. Observe the color, or colors, of your Soul's Light.

10. Does your Souls Light have a misty outline? Or a crisp demarcation, a clear and defined boundary?

11. Observe your Soul's Light deep inside your body.

12. How does your Soul's Light adjust to best harmonize with different organs?

13. Notice the wisdom of these adjustments, measured by the vibrance of the life-force energy these organs now exhibit.

14. Notice that your Soul delights in these excursions as you invite it to participate in unity with your blessed body and your consciousness.

15. Flowing between your physical body and your Soul's Light, is a mutual respect and adoration of your blessed body.

16. There is an intimacy between each individual cell and your Soul's Light as it flows gracefully through your blessed body.

17. In chapter 7, "How Your Soul is Constructed", we discussed how your Soul specifically chose your body and your personality, lovingly, as the perfect choice to be your Soul's expression on Earth.

18. Your Soul created you as Its experience module. This was done with respect and care. This is the bond between Soul, personality, and body. This is the agreement between your Soul and your physical self.

19. Your Soul's Light is wise and knows exactly what you need at this moment.

20. Let your body absorb all the Light it needs. Revel in the peace and fulfillment of this moment.

21. Place your pointer finger in the center of your palm as a physical reminder of this experience.

22. You have the wisdom of the ages within. You know there is no other self that you need to be, to see, to feel, to know. The deeper you flow into your Soul, the more rarified and clarified are your perceptions and the more connected to you are with the Great Creatress. And when you call out to your Soul, saying, "Come Soul, come Holy Light," you are calling all the forces of Light to you. You are ultimately calling the Divine to you. You are asking to be unified with your blessed body, your Soul, and the Great Creatress.

23. Well, then you have everything you need, for the moment, for the day, and for continually improving life, don't you?

24. When you feel calm and ready, return to reading the rest of the chapter.

From this aligned place of attention, you are ready to experience the Light of your Soul as it ebbs and flows, pulses and radiates, in and around you.

Indeed, we are pointing out the fact that you and your Soul are an unbeatable team! The physical self, when filled with your Soul's Light, has all the qualities that you desire. Infinite energy, quiet patience, an endless well of love, Divine perspective, and all the wisdom needed to fulfill the objectives your Soul set forth for this lifetime. Together, you and your Soul are the "dream team", perfectly aligned in the fulfillment of your Soul's Purposes. Perfectly aligned in harmony with the Divine Herself! The Akashic Perspective is that "Every Soul has everything it needs and nothing it does not need".

As you experience your Soul's Light in your body, please open your Spiritual Heart. Open to the love that your Soul has for you. Feel that in your body. It wants no other. Feel that in your body. Your Soul never leaves you. It faithfully receives you. It desires to fulfill your needs. Feel that in your body. It loves you beyond reason.

It accepts you wholly and totally. It wants you whether or not you want yourself. It neither judges nor condemns you. Feel that in your body.

How could your Soul reject you?
You are the pinnacle of Its creative endeavors.

You are the apple of Its eye and the glow in Its heart. Feel that in your body. Your Soul loves you with the tenderness of a mother toward her precious newborn.

Your Soul claims you as Its own!

Now, allow yourself to sense, to see, and use your knowingness to claim your Soul as your own. Yes. Claim your Soul as your own. Say out loud, "I claim my Soul as my Own!" Say it again. "I claim my Soul as my Own!" Again. "I claim my Soul as my Own!" Celebrate your unity with your unique and Divinely inspired Soul. You have dispelled the sense of separation often felt strongest through body sensations.

You have done well. For now, we bid you adieu.

Write your responses to these interactive questions.

~ Interactive Questions ~

Activate your spiritual heart. Claim your Soul. Now, describe how you feel.

How do you feel when claiming your Soul in your Spiritual Heart?

You and your Soul belong together. Describe your experience of belonging.

You can see through the eyes of your Soul. What do you see?

You can love through the Spiritual Heart, the Heart of your Soul. How does that feel in your body?
You are supported by your Soul. As you take in this Divine knowing, what softens?

You are inspired by your Soul. What becomes possible? What options open up for you? Do you detect new solutions coming into your awareness?

~ Closing Prayer ~

Thanking the Great Creatress & Her Holy Spirit for Love, protection & healing received this day,
Thanking the Akashic Beings of Light for guidance,
Thanking the Masters, Teachers, & Loved Ones for wisdom & direction.
The Divine Portal & the Akashic Records are now closed.
Amen. Amen. Amen.

CHAPTER 14

Embodiment of Your Soul's Light and Consciousness

Channeled by the Akashic Beings of Light

Bringing Forth Soul Consciousness Akashic Records Prayer

©Rev. Annie Bachelder 1/22/2022

~ Opening Prayer ~

1) By the Power of Divine Light within me
2) Come Holy Spirit!   Spirit of Light!   Spirit of Truth!
3) For the highest good of all, throughout time, fill my heart with Divine Love as
4) I humbly ask permission to open the Divine portal to the highest realm of the Akashic Records for (LEGAL NAME).

5) **Akashic Beings of Light,** guide me to the deepest Truth of my being, releasing any blocks & restrictions to my abundance & highest good.
6) **Great Creatress,** assist me to fully embody my Soul's Light, to fulfill my Soul's purposes, & to heal any accumulated karma.
7) **Surround me** with the enlightenment & wisdom of my Masters, Teachers, & Loved Ones.
8) **Clearly direct** my perspective & actions to those that manifest my Divine Plan.

   (Repeat lines 5, 6, 7, & 8 two more times, then say line 9)

9) **Free of all resistance, judgment, and fear,** I am now filled with Divine love & the Records are open.

Welcome! We Akashic Beings of Light are here with you today.

Dear readers, you are already feeling the deep strength and love of your own sweet Soul flowing through you. There can be a tenderness to your connection with your Soul. Kind, loving, light as a feather – but strong in the way that many varied experiences can strengthen a being of consciousness. Your Soul has experienced many embodied lives; some easy and simple, some difficult, treacherous even. Some embodiments were traumatic, and some have been filled with great Light and healing. For now, we simply ask you to gather up and embrace the sum of these lives, the wisdom gained, the love shared, and multitudes of realizations of spiritual truth threaded throughout all your embodiments.

> ***At this time in humanity's history, the embodiment of your Soul's Light and Consciousness is paramount. You are seasoned enough to know that being anything other than your Soul is to live an inauthentic life.***

It is the authenticity of your spiritual connection with your Soul and the Divine that enthuses you, inspires your actions, provides the challenges that cause great hunger within you to proceed!

Before we continue, we urge you to practice the step-by-step exercise "How to Embody Your Soul's Light", found here and at the back of this book in Prayers, Invocations, and Exercises.

Exercise – How to Embody Your Soul's Light:

Close your eyes. Take 3 deep, cleansing breaths followed by complete exhalations to bring yourself fully into this moment.

1. Begin by becoming aware of a glowing sphere of radiant Light located 12 to 15 inches above your head. This is your 8th chakra (your Soul chakra). Let your sense of knowing tell you about the color, the shimmer, and the vibration in your Soul's Light. These qualities may change from time to time. Trust the changes. The Light is infinitely wise and knows what you need at every moment.

2. Observe as the Soul chakra pours its Light into the space between your Soul chakra and your crown chakra, creating a column of connecting Light.

3. Your crown chakra naturally opens to receive the Light of your Soul as it pours itself into your crown chakra.

4. Your Soul's Light fills your entire head, inside and out. Your Soul's Light fills your brain, scalp and hair, eyes, sinuses, jaw, and the atlas bone at the top of your spine. At any point in this process, you might feel a sense of your Soul's character.

5. Notice your Soul's Light as it fills your shoulders, arms, hands, and fingers.

6. Observe as your Soul's Light lovingly and affectionately touches all the organs and systems in the trunk of your body. Allow yourself to feel your Soul's love for this precious body It chose for you.

7. Observe your Soul's Light filling the entire trunk of your body, inside and out, including your skin. Your Soul's Light naturally pools in your pelvic cavity. It pauses in your hip sockets. Take a breath.

8. Follow your Soul's Light as it fills your thighs, knees, calves, ankles, and feet. Your Soul's Light fills the bones, muscles, tendons, and fascia tissues, as well as your blood system.

9. Take notice that very cell throughout your body contains a corresponding spark of Light reflecting your Soul's Light. Recognition in each of your cells of your Soul's Light generates a feeling of joyful reunion.

10. Remain focused on your Soul's Light and all your cells as they re-connect. Observe the interactions.

11. You might feel a click or a buzzing in your feet and legs as your body's connection with your Soul's Light is complete.

12. Ground your Soul's Light into the balance point of Mother Earth.

13. Now, send your consciousness up to the Great Creatress. Feel the sphere of Light that is the Great Creatress surrounding your Soul, you, and Mother Earth.

14. Spend as much time as you like here.

15. Create a memory file by placing the pointer finger of your right hand on the palm of your left hand so that you can fully embody your Soul's Light on command.

16. Easily and effortlessly, return to ordinary consciousness, wiggling your toes, rolling your shoulders, and enjoying a few relaxing breaths.

We resume. As you embody your Soul's Light, you deepen your connection with your Soul, and acquire its consciousness. Automatically, feelings of calm and centeredness follow. Even feelings of wisdom and preparedness. Automatically, you are encircled by the Great Creatress. Automatically, you experience the inner peace you are seeking, and which is essential for having a smoothly productive day.

> *There is no shame in you becoming "dependent" upon this Soul Consciousness. It is now required for you to feel your best.*

Practice embodying your Soul's Light and Consciousness is essential to your further growth, for "ascension" or enlightenment, as your wise ones would say. It is essential for rising or expanding outward into new vistas of consciousness. It is essential for you in order to grasp potential possibilities and probabilities of new social structures, education, and familial arrangements.

You are already growing into these probabilities so you might as well stretch all the way out into them. Stretch as if you were spreading your angel wings wide and the farthest tips of the feathers gently touch these social possibilities.

> *Just touching these possibilities brings them into mortal focus, adding the needed physical energy to bring them into physical existence.*

Touching these possibilities with the tips of your angel wings is like the white feathers dipping ever so slightly into colored paint pots. The feathers begin absorbing the color which flows into neighboring feathers, turning your Angelic wingspan into a virtual rainbow of color, of Light, of ecstatic expression. Eventually, this rainbow of color reaches your Spiritual Heart *(see chapter 11 "Your Spiritual Heart"),* and your consciousness is changed by the very witnessing of such a creative act!

Symbolically speaking, we are talking about altering the combinations of energetic factors (represented by the colored paint pots), combined with awareness of spiritual law (represented by the feathered Angel wings), such that social ideas and constructs automatically shift and change (represented by your Spiritual Heart).

*Do you feel the premise of equality for all humanity at the foundation
of these social changes?*
Do you feel how freedom of choice is enhanced?
Do you feel the higher vibrational Light held within these options?

The bondage of old heart breaks and old fears dissolve, returning to the
Divine for revision and renewal. Your Spiritual Heart is free to love in the
way it is designed to love. Your consciousness is free to express itself as
new concepts, new ideas, new thoughts, and experimental paradigms.
There is a great opening outward.

*You may even have to take off the "social hat", or the identity you
have assumed in this life in order to delve deeply into this.*

You can do this on a temporary basis if it makes you feel safer. If you get
lost or lose the consciousness thread, simply return to embodying your
Soul's Light.

We ask you these questions:
*What if your identity is not a compilation of the current
arrangement of ideas, values, cultural history, and social standing
that you are in this lifetime?*
Who, then, are you free to be?

What if you are not limited by the ponderous history of all the lifetimes
you as a Soul have had as you entered the physical realm? Who and how
are you free to be? Are you now able to arrange anew the very molecules
of the things you desire and the body you inhabit? Are you now able to
generate the necessary energy, resources, and money required for your
further expansion and fulfillment of your Soul's purposes?

From this consciousness, creation is so easy. You can easily affect the
physical realm to further your Soul's purpose and plan for you, and
therefore fulfill the Great Creatress' Divine Design of love and unity
with all life.

*Set your sights high. Work repeatedly with your Masters, Teachers,
and Loved Ones requesting a clear, well-developed vision,
and feeling sense of how to manifest your vision and
how to perfect your purpose as it unfolds.*

Be sure to witness in advance the benefit to humanity and society in the unfolding of your vision and Soul's purposes in action. Feel the benefit to others as a relaxing of defenses, of peaceful hearts and minds, as proof of your manifesting abilities.

Exercise: Manifesting as Your Soul

You will want to take notes during or after this exercise. Make sure you have your pen and paper or laptop close by.

1. Take 7 deep, cleansing breaths. Exhale each one fully and completely. Take your time. You are oxygenating your brain and increasing your heartbeat.

2. Embody your Soul's Light. Sense the closeness of your Soul. Feel your Soul's love for you. Feel your heart area opening like a flower.

3. Get a sense of the Great Creatress' presence. Get a sense of Her love for you.

4. Focus on a heart's desire, something you need to experience during this lifetime. You may need to ask your Masters, Teachers, and Loved Ones to bring a heart's desire to your attention. Accept what they offer even if it different than what you planned.

5. Set your heart's desire on a table in front of you.

6. Silently, tell yourself the story of this heart's desire. What is it? What does it look like? How does this heart's desire make you feel? What does it do for you? What does it do for others? Why is this heart's desire so important to you? How does it fulfill a Soul purpose? Who else is involved?

7. Feel intensely the importance of this heart's desire. Pause here, if you need more time to really, really, really feel everything about this heart's desire.

8. Using your spiritual imagination, breathe life-force energy into your heart's desire. Do that again. And again.

9. Ask your Soul to help you. Observe what your Soul does to manifest your heart's desire.

10. Is your Soul bringing any energy out of your body and using it?

11. Or is your Soul removing something inside you that restricted the fulfillment of this heart's desire?

12. Ask your Masters, Teachers, and Loved Ones to assist in this process. Observe them closely.

13. Embodying, again, your Souls Light, and sense the Great Creatress' presence.

14. Ask Her to demonstrate the next step in manifesting this heart's desire? Feel Her intention. Feel Her focus. Feel her single-minded attention.

15. Ask Her why she installed this heart's desire in you?

16. Ask Her how it serves Her Divine Plan for you?

17. Ask Her how it serves Her overall Divine Plan?

18. The Great Creatress now allows you to witness the benefit to humanity.

19. The Great Creatress now allows you to witness how this heart's desire plays out in your life, and in others' lives.

20. When this feels complete, thank the Great Creatress, thank your Masters, Teachers, and Loved Ones. Thank your Soul. Feel the rearrangement inside of you.

When your identity is Soul's Light and Consciousness, manifesting is not about creating money or shiny objects, although some of that will materialize. This is about healing of entire villages, counties, provinces, states, countries, and continents. This is phenomenal spiritual enhancement at "Earth as a planet" level. Simply reading or hearing this you are participating in the unfoldment of a higher vision, and a finer future. Through the experience and restoration of harmony within, through Soul reunification, and Oneness with the Great Creatress, manifestation of your healing ripples out to the rest of the world. The more peace you experience within, the more beneficial you are to society.

To prepare yourself to receive the results of Manifesting as Your Soul exercise, consider these interactive questions and write out your responses:

~ Interactive Questions ~

How do you envision yourself exercising these potent freedoms?

What effects ripple out from your actions and decisions?

What new ideas arise in those wily, unpredictable human minds and spirits?
How creative and adventurous do you envision being in your co-creations with the Divine Designer?

How outlandish can your requests for help and inspiration be when you pray to the Great Creatress for assistance?

Describe your willingness regarding redirecting?

Will you ask that the Great Creatress take over and provide a new opportunity to expand, to gingerly place your consciousness in a new framework, so that many are led to experience the uncharted territory ahead?

How much more adaptable are you when embodying your Souls Light?

Describe your vision and your increased creativity while embodying your Soul's Light?

What creative endeavors seem possible with the aid of your Masters, Teachers, and Loved Ones?

With the aid of the Great Creatress?

What bursts into possibility when your Angel wings dip into the color pots?

~ Closing Prayer ~

Thanking the Great Creatress & Her Holy Spirit for Love, protection & healing received this day,
Thanking the Akashic Beings of Light for guidance,
Thanking the Masters, Teachers, & Loved Ones for wisdom & direction.
The Divine Portal & the Akashic Records are now closed.
Amen. Amen. Amen.

CHAPTER 15

Living as Your Soul

Channeled by the Akashic Beings of Light
under the Auspices of the Great Creatress

Bringing Forth Soul Consciousness
Akashic Records Prayer

©Rev. Annie Bachelder 1/22/2022

~ Opening Prayer ~

1) By the Power of Divine Light within me
2) Come Holy Spirit! Spirit of Light! Spirit of Truth!
3) For the highest good of all, throughout time, fill my heart with Divine Love as
4) I humbly ask permission to open the Divine portal to the highest realm of the Akashic Records for (LEGAL NAME).

5) **Akashic Beings of Light,** guide me to the deepest Truth of my being, releasing any blocks & restrictions to my abundance & highest good.
6) **Great Creatress,** assist me to fully embody my Soul's Light, to fulfill my Soul's purposes, & to heal any accumulated karma.
7) **Surround me** with the enlightenment & wisdom of my Masters, Teachers, & Loved Ones.
8) **Clearly direct** my perspective & actions to those that manifest my Divine Plan.
   (Repeat lines 5, 6, 7, & 8 two more times, then say line 9)

9) **Free of all resistance, judgment, and fear,**
   I am now filled with Divine love & the Records are open.

Please be open to a very different chapter format.

Integrating Soul Prayer

For the highest good of all, Great Creatress,
Please, open my Spiritual Heart to full vibrancy.
Awaken me to your Divine Design.
By the power of your Spirit within me, I presence my Soul.
I embody Its Light and consciousness.
Oversee my Soul and physical experience as we become One.
Safe in Your embrace, my Soul's Light fills me to the brim.
Recognizing my Soul's Divine alliance with You,
I open to receive Its beneficial influence.
Embodying my Soul's Light, I am strengthened.
I am awakened to Its consciousness.
Like you, Great Creatress, my Soul embraces me kindly,
Guides me wisely,
Fills my heart with Its love,
Sweetens my thoughts, words, and deeds with compassion.
My Soul naturally forms my link with Thee, Great Creatress.
May all consciousness be of the Light.
And so, it is.

Amen

A samurai knows when to act and when not to act.
Living as my Soul, my Soul knows when to act and when not to act.

Greetings and Welcome from the Akashic Beings of Light!

Rather than have them at the end of the chapter, We have created this chapter as in-depth, exploratory questions that orient you to living your daily life as your Soul. It is imperative that you open your Akashic Records each time you write responses to these questions. Plan to have a few hours of uninterrupted time, over several days, to write about and incorporate your experiences of Living as Your Soul. Take your time. Please have your notebook and pen (or the equivalent) at hand so that you can write your responses to the questions. We have asked Annie to write her responses in italics and are providing them as reference information to these interactive questions about Living as Your Soul. This writing exercise helped Annie to further develop, and to demonstrate to herself, the link she has already forged with her Soul. You may need to break up this chapter into several writing sessions with your Akashic Records open. Please remember to close your Akashic Records after every writing session.

Living as your Soul is the priority now.

Support your process of living as your Soul by praying the "Integrating Soul Prayer" every day for 30 days. Use the prayer to integrate your Divine assignment within the Great Creatress' plan. Everything is energy and consciousness expressed as Light. Continue to embody your Soul's Light. Anchor your Soul's Light in your physical body. Practice seeing how many Soul Qualities (see list below) you can incorporate into your daily life. Tally how many times in a day you expressed Soul qualities. This is a practice, and nowhere in this practice is there judgment, resistance, fear, criticism, or condemnation. You cannot fail. Your Soul qualities outshine such obstacles.

Remind yourself everyday of the Great Creatress' profound, enduring, love for you.

Everything begins as energy. You are now receiving, from your Future Self, these Soul Qualities in action, in profusion. Receive from your Future Self these emanations as they deeply penetrate your consciousness and your behavior patterns. You are integrating these qualities and upgrades very quickly. Assume this to be true, permanent, and a sound foundation upon which you build your life. You are actively stepping into these qualities as you are living as your Soul. *(See Exercise: Receiving Light from Your Future Self in the last chapter.)*

Integrate the Light of Being that is your Soul.

The gift of Living as Your Soul is that the presence of the Divine automatically surrounds you within and without. Softly at first, like a cloud of delicate Light. Soon you will find that Her gentle embrace is constant, sturdy, and reliable. Her Divine embrace places you squarely in the center of your being, whole, grounded, perfectly on course. Restfully active. Charged. Aligned like an arrow pulled taught and released from the Divine's bow into the heart of the Great Creatress' Divine plan.

Begin absorbing, integrating, and expressing these qualities of your Soul:

Love
Light
Compassion
Wisdom
Peace
Trust
Acceptance
Joy
Being
Stillness
Kindness
Freedom
Inclusivity
Oneness
Discernment
Surrender
Vision

Ask yourself what Soul quality are you focusing on today?

We are speaking into your spiritual imagination, speaking to you as your Soul in a body. Explore Living as Your Soul through these interactive questions. Look for your Soul's perspective, the Akashic perspective, and write your responses.

1. **With the Soul Qualities above in mind, consider how your Soul responds to self-judgment?**
   My experience of living as my Soul, keeping the above Soul qualities brightly in my consciousness, the volume and intensity of self-judgment is greatly reduced, even on the "hot topics" like aging, my diminishing beauty, my higher body weight, or evaluating how a client's reading went.

2. How does your Soul respond to habitual judgment of others?

I am finding it easier to step out of habitually judgmental thoughts of others such as sizing people up at the grocery store, comparing myself to other women, my automatic classification of race and gender, and my automatic body responses to these classifications.

3. How do you, living as your Soul, respond to comparison?

Living as my Soul allows me to be more accepting of myself, my age, beauty, my weight, far more generously. The critical nature of these comparisons is often outweighed by my sheer joy at seeing other people. I must stay relatively focused on completing the task at hand, while grocery shopping or running errands, which is the bulk of my out-of-the-house experience. Living as my Soul, comparison is a non-topic, a non-issue, irrelevant. As my Soul, I am aware of my Light, my gifts, talents, and abilities, and the genuine satisfaction I feel at being able to spend much of my time expressing them. Living as my Soul, I am often focused on the ongoing conversation with the Akashic Beings of Light as they prepare me for more writing topics. This conversation is active almost all the time, at various degrees of volume and consciousness. The conversation is becoming the backdrop of my life. Where is there room for comparison? My brain-mind is occupied with detecting the specific words the Akashic Beings of Light are using to elaborate on certain topics. My personality, which used to be subject to emotional derailment via critical comparison, is calm and quiet with these more interesting topics to think about. I really wasn't aware of this until I began writing about my personal experience with Living as My Soul.

4. Living as your Soul, what is your experience of worry?

My Soul does not have the capability of worrying! That's news. Worrying is the experience of the untrained mind that thinks it is preparing for an uncertain and fear-filled future. Thankfully, my Soul exists in the present moment and experiences life anchored in the Spiritual Heart. My Soul experiences "things must be the way the great Creatress wants them to be". My Soul trusts in the goodness of the moment, that all is well, and automatically trusts the route that the Great Creatress is taking.

5. How do you, living as your Soul, respond to worry?

My Soul naturally calms my personality when I worry and forget to trust the Great Creatress. My Soul soothes my personality until I can regroup and follow It's lead. My Soul is enveloped in the Great Creatress and moves as One with her. My Soul breathes me, reminding me to relax, unwind, calming my inner "hypervigilant Chihuahua".

6. How would you, living as your Soul, exhibit Oneness?

Living as my Soul, staying present in the moment is an act of conscious Oneness. Living as my Soul there is no separation, no concern that my attention is wandering, and getting off track. Living as my Soul, I feel the generous embrace of the Great Creatress and Oneness constantly. This translates easily and effortlessly into a peaceful and confident personality.

7. How does your Soul experience Oneness?

My Soul experiences Oneness as a constant, steady stream of inclusion, and absolute acceptance of everything as it is. My Soul experiences everything without complaint or editing, judging, rearranging, or efforts to control. My Soul automatically knows Its eternal place is One with the Great Creatress. This is fact, not a goal, or a vague hope. My Soul breathes the Great Creatress, just as my body naturally and automatically breathes Earth's air. My Soul fully expects to be enveloped in this bliss of belonging to continue uninterrupted. My Soul exhibits Oneness the way a tree exhibits leaves. There is no other option. It just is. My Soul does not make an effort. It remains in alignment with the Great Creatress in a state of Oneness and beyond.

8. How would you, living as your Soul, exhibit Oneness?

I imagine unity with the Great Creatress like being in a happy cartoon, one piglet in an enormous group of piglets happily and constantly fed and provided for by the Great Creatress, running around in nature with no disagreement or conflict with other creatures, plants, weather, or geography. I feel my place is assured, no fear of the future, and lots of room to run about, playfully, childlike.

9. How does your Soul demonstrate unity with the Great Creatress?

My Soul demonstrates unity with the Great Creatress through being part of Her flow, by joining wholeheartedly with Her projects for me. My Soul is unified with the Great Creatress through awareness of Her directives, and realizing Her Divine objectives, through expanding and melding my Soul's energy and consciousness with Her Allness. My Soul rests in Her compassionate embrace when there is nothing to do. My Soul demonstrates unity with the Great Creatress and her creations as absolute acceptance of Her Divine Order. Acceptance keeps appearing in this conversation. My Soul has no obstacles to overcome, nothing to fight, and no resistance. My Soul is powered by the Divine so carrying out Her wishes is like effortlessly floating downstream. My Soul receives Divine direction as perfect order and being so aligned, feels joy in carrying out Her plans. It is as if I and my Soul keep saying, "Okay, that's a great idea."

10. How would you, living as your Soul, create and manifest?

Living as my Soul, I create and manifest as I am directed by the Divine or through the advice of the Akashic Beings of Light, and my Masters, Teachers, and Loved Ones. When the energy is ripe (as Anubis puts it) and the full push to act arrives, it is a clear imperative. If the time to act has not yet arrived I feel blocked, un-surrendered, uncertain about taking action, or unclear which action to take. When the energy for action is "ripe", I feel quite certain, even compelled to act, and to act on specific projects in a specific way. For example, there will be words to write on the class flyer, there will be class outlines and objectives, there will be a call to serve. The time needed to take these actions seems to appear in my schedule as well.

The Akashic Beings of Light are telling me that I, the human, need to embody my Soul's Light, hold the project in my Spiritual Heart, harmonize my body with my Soul, my Spiritual Heart, and the project. Then expand my consciousness outward all the way to the Great Creatress. Linking in this way allows the project to adhere to me as the agent of manifestation with no distortion.

11. How does your Soul create and manifest?

My Soul creates and manifests through matching Its energy with that of the Great Creatress. Holding continued focus on the objective, surrendering into the project, my Soul literally falls into the conceptual energy of the project, devoting Its whole self to the creation. My Soul invests Itself fully in the actions needed to manifest. No distractions. No dilution. My Soul becomes One with the objective. My Soul opens to receive the energy from the Great Creatress that carries it forward into the material world.

12. How does your Soul prioritize activities?
How does your Soul prioritize states of Being?

Living as my Soul is a state of being. It is drastically different than living as my human self, with all the complications and slipperiness of my personality. Living as my Soul, I am uniquely qualified to fulfill my Soul's purposes and fulfill my Soul's part in the Divine plan. As seen from the Akashic perspective, living as my Soul creates the state of being that is most harmonious and capable of functioning as an agent of the Divine. Not only do the people with whom I have relationships perform their parts in fulfilling my Divine plan, I fulfill my part in their Divine plans. Living as my Soul allows the necessary energetic shifts with little or no resistance, and the subsequent lessons in mastery are acquired and assimilated. Living as my Soul prioritizes meditation, calming the personality, before action. As Sanaya Roman said in one of her channelings for me, "A samurai knows when to act and when not to act." My Soul knows when to act. Living as my Soul guides me to "expand to include" the higher purpose of the urges to act, to inhabit them, quietly letting the energy of the action percolate into my experience. This allows me to know how putting an idea into action may affect others, and to see who of my clients, students, family and friends, known and unknown, are able to receive the benefits of the action, experience, or the information.

We encourage you to continue this process by writing your responses to these questions:

13. Living as your Soul, what do you envision your life to be like?

14. Living as your Soul, how would your mind operate?

15. Living as you Soul, what ideas pervade your mind and imaginings?

16. Living as your Soul, how would you greet challenges?

17. Living as your Soul, how would you handle problems?

18. Living as your Soul, how would you make decisions?

19. Living as your Soul, how would you address attachments?

20. Living as your Soul, how would you address "control" concerns?

21. Consider how you would feel if your entire being was animated by your Soul's peace, joy, and acceptance?

22. Living as your Soul, how does your Soul contribute to others?

Living as your Soul is the priority now.

~ Closing Prayer ~

Thanking the Great Creatress & Her Holy Spirit for Love, protection & healing received this day,
Thanking the Akashic Beings of Light for guidance,
Thanking the Masters, Teachers, & Loved Ones for wisdom & direction.
The Divine Portal & the Akashic Records are now closed.
Amen. Amen. Amen.

For your convenience and further investigation we are providing the list of all the questions below.

1. With the Soul Qualities above in mind, consider how your Soul responds to self-judgment?

2. How does your Soul respond to judgment of others?

3. How do you, living as your Soul, respond to comparison?

4. Living as your Soul, what is your experience of worry?

5. How do you, living as your Soul, respond to worry?

6. How would you, living as your Soul, exhibit Oneness?

7. How does your Soul experience Oneness?

8. How would you, living as your Soul, exhibit Oneness?

9. How does your Soul demonstrate unity with the Great Creatress?

10. How would you, living as your Soul, create and manifest?

11. How does your Soul create and manifest?

12. How does your Soul prioritize activities?

13. How does your Soul prioritize states of veing?

14. Living as your Soul, what do you envision your life to be like?

15. Living as your Soul, how would your mind operate?

16. Living as you Soul, what ideas would pervade your mind and imaginings?

17. Living as your Soul, how would you greet challenges?

18. Living as your Soul, how would you handle problems?

19. Living as your Soul, how would you make decisions?

20. Living as your Soul, how would you address attachments?

21. Living as your Soul, how would you address "control" concerns?

22. Consider how would you feel if your entire being was animated by your Soul's peace, joy, and acceptance?

23. Living as your Soul, how does your Soul contribute to others?

CHAPTER 16

Soul Consciousness – Next Steps

Channeled by The Akashic Beings of Light

Bringing Forth Soul Consciousness
Akashic Records Prayer
©*Rev. Annie Bachelder 1/22/2022*

~ Opening Prayer ~

1) By the Power of Divine Light within me
2) Come Holy Spirit!   Spirit of Light!   Spirit of Truth!
3) For the highest good of all, throughout time, fill my heart with Divine Love as
4) I humbly ask permission to open the Divine portal to the highest realm of the Akashic Records for (LEGAL NAME).

5) **Akashic Beings of Light,** guide me to the deepest Truth of my being, releasing any blocks & restrictions to my abundance & highest good.
6) **Great Creatress,** assist me to fully embody my Soul's Light, to fulfill my Soul's purposes, & to heal any accumulated karma.
7) **Surround me** with the enlightenment & wisdom of my Masters, Teachers, & Loved Ones.
8) **Clearly direct** my perspective & actions to those that manifest my Divine Plan.

(Repeat lines 5, 6, 7, & 8 two more times, then say line 9)

9) **Free of all resistance, judgment, and fear,**
I am now filled with Divine love & the Records are open.

Greetings and welcome from the Akashic Beings of Light.

Being bound by time, you will want to consider the next steps. To this we say practice, practice, practice. We also suggest you use the previous chapters energy instructions and exercises to explore, explore, explore. Forget about getting it perfectly correct and let go of standing out. You are accessing your Soul's Light and consciousness. It is time for you to get to know one another. This familiar connection is the first thing forgotten upon entering a body on earth.

The gravitational field pulls the familiar connection with your Soul out of your physical body leaving only traces, hints, and faint shadows.

This is because Mother Earth has been given the task of storing the energetic memory and experience of your Soul and Its consciousness.

Therefore, grounding yourself with the balance point of Mother Earth is so helpful in Bringing Forth Soul Consciousness.

This is also why so many of you feel reconnected and whole while in nature. Mother Earth releases some of the information and energy of your Soul each time you engage with Her Earthly realm from a place of devotion. At the same time your Soul remains interactively connected to its Soul Group and the Great Creatress in the upper realms. That is also why you feel steadied and fulfilled when you both ground down into Mother Earth and at the same time connect upward to the Great Creatress. Your next steps may include regular walking, or hiking in the hills, at the beach, or anywhere you feel calmed and connected to nature.

While practicing **Bringing Forth Soul Consciousness**, you will find yourself being guided by your Soul as it lights up the next steps on your path. It is true that many of you do not have a specific vision, or a "sense of knowing", about your current life purpose. Keep opening your Akashic Records and more will be revealed. We notice that when you are shown the long view that you either run away, as if threatened by being all that you already are, or laughingly deny all involvement with such impactful purposes.

To accommodate your personality, your Soul reveals only the next small steps in furtherance of Its goals and the ultimate goals of the Great Creatress.

Again, we emphasize that you increasingly trust in the wisdom of the Great Creatress, your Soul, the Akashic Beings of Light, and your Masters, Teachers, and Loved Ones. All of Us help you along the way. This book lays the groundwork for you to acquire many more skills and Light-filled attributes that fuel your Souls Purpose.

Giving you small indications of what is next on your path bypasses the distractions of the ego's snatch-and-grab for recognition.

We see you becoming willing to develop humility, serenity, and sovereignty in the process of becoming conscious of your next steps.

In moments of desperation, seek to align yourself with Divine Will. (See the Exercise: How to Align Your Self-Will with Divine Will at the back of the book.) Surrender to your Soul, the Great Creatress, and her Divine plan for you. Align yourself with being of service to those in your sphere of influence. Embody your Soul's Light and all argument and resistance become unnecessary. Other than exercising free will, accept that you are not in control of outcomes. You become willing to play your part in the personal dramas that your Soul has arranged for your growth and for the completion of karmic scenarios.

Resistance causes friction, irritability, and slows your progress. Resistance lowers your vibration.

Please remember that your happiness is at the center of these dramas. As the result of your connection and alignment with your Soul and the Great Creatress, you will feel your inner well of happiness steadily filling. Through practice embodying your Soul's Light and harmonizing with Divine Will, the weight of the past lightens, and you'll feel happier, fulfilled.

The more you
- **embody your Soul's Light,**
- **align your self-will with Divine Will, (see last chapter for Exercise: Align Your Self-will with Divine Will)**
- **accept yourself as you are,**
- **and allow the Light to lead and change you,**
- **follow what increases your energy and enthusiasm, the easier your path, the clearer your Soul purposes, and it will be easier to carry out your next steps.**

You are essentially consciousness. You were consciously created. The more you **opt into** expanding your consciousness, the easier your path unfolds.

> *Next Steps include much preparation on the inner planes. You are*
> *aided in preparation for your next steps by opening your Akashic*
> *Records and following the suggestions you receive from your Masters,*
> *Teachers, and Loved Ones. Preparing by doing the energy work first*
> *makes manifestation of your next steps much clearer and easier.*

(See Exercise: Masterful Manifesting at the back of the book.) Refine your energy sensing skills *(See Exercise: Interacting with the Space Between the 7th and 8th Chakras.)* Continual practice aligning with Divine Will grants you exceptional creative freedom and awareness of next steps.

Many humans are fond of the "Rewards Game", so here is your reward. Create with your spiritual imagination. Create your dreams. Create new frontiers. Create with vision. Most of all, create from your beautiful Spiritual Heart in concert with your Soul and the Great Creatress.

> *When beginning your day, invoke the Great Creatress.*
> *When beginning work on your project, invoke the Great Creatress.*
> *Learn from the Great Creatress, the Highest Mistress*
> *of Manifestation.*
> *Ask, how would the Great Creatress go about creating this project?*

Some of your preparation for next steps has already been accomplished by making sense of the past. Annie is reminded that in having to give the adopted baby back to his birth family, she played her part perfectly. In that experience she learned that she has a strong tendency to avoid conflict that blinds her to the obvious. Avoiding conflict makes her deaf to advisors, especially if they conflict with what she wants and is pre-emptively (even obsessively) focused upon. To know her next steps, Annie learned that she needs to face facts. She must consciously register the warnings she is receiving, and proceed with heightened caution. She learned not to assume that others have her best interests at heart. Others have **their** best interests at heart and may not be able to see beyond their personal gains or losses. Just like Annie, they may be unable to see how their actions affect others. It is her responsibility to be aware of possible breakdowns, inklings of doubts, fears, and limitations. Most pointedly, she learned that no amount of disappointment could deflate her natural tendency to reach for, and to raise her consciousness.

> *It may take some time to be revealed, however,*
> *increased consciousness always clarifies next steps.*

Preparation for next steps has occurred through what you call "day-dreaming" where you let your mind roam. This allows creative ideas, discoveries, and revelations to present themselves. Preparation for next steps happens through conscientious application of spiritual principles, begetting specific results, whether silently unknown, or resulting in elegant solutions that far exceed what the person might have conjured. This gives the person a glimpse into the magnanimous nature of the Great Creatress and the possibilities available through alignment with Her Divine Will. Preparation has occurred through experiencing relationships in different permutations with Soul-designated people. This broadens your perspective and enhances compassion, reducing the ego's grasping attempts to control.

> *Preparation has occurred over many lifetimes,*
> *solving increasingly complex problems,*
> *with the deeper wisdom acquired.*

Next steps unfold as you respond to each moment's temptations, urgings, indications, and intuition. Next steps are revealed in the projects you return to again and again, with renewed energy and attention to detail. Next steps reveal themselves in your daily activities, in your idle questions such as "I wonder what would happen if I . . . ? Next steps are revealed as deeply sourced actions, when you feel called to act with certainty, when you rise out of your chair with resolve and move in the direction of achieving your desires. Next steps are revealed when you ask for and receive spiritual guidance to act that seems natural to you, that seems all a part of the plan, even effortless.

Pease write your responses to the interactive questions below.

~ Interactive Questions ~

You have practiced opening your Akashic Records over a dozen times while studying *Bringing Forth Soul Consciousness*. Describe 3 beneficial things about your "practice" utilizing the Akashic Records?

Describe an experience of receiving valuable information relating to your next steps while being out in nature?

Describe how your path has gotten easier through Soul Consciousness and connecting with the Divine?

What spiritual principles have you applied that have amplified and encouraged your spiritual growth?

What Soul Qualities are helping you the most now?

~ Closing Prayer ~

Thanking the Great Creatress & Her Holy Spirit for Love, protection, & healing received this day,
Thanking the Akashic Beings of Light for guidance,
Thanking the Masters, Teachers, & Loved Ones for wisdom & direction.
The Divine Portal & the Akashic Records are now closed.
Amen. Amen. Amen.

CHAPTER 17

Loving Your Fear

Channeled by the Angelic Healing Conclave

Bringing Forth Soul Consciousness
Akashic Records Prayer
©Rev. Annie Bachelder 1/22/2022

~ Opening Prayer ~

1) By the Power of Divine Light within me
2) Come Holy Spirit! Spirit of Light! Spirit of Truth!
3) For the highest good of all, throughout time, fill my heart with Divine Love as
4) I humbly ask permission to open the Divine portal to the highest realm of the Akashic Records for (LEGAL NAME).

5) **Akashic Beings of Light,** guide me to the deepest Truth of my being, releasing any blocks & restrictions to my abundance & highest good.
6) **Great Creatress,** assist me to fully embody my Soul's Light, to fulfill my Soul's purposes, & to heal any accumulated karma.
7) **Surround me** with the enlightenment & wisdom of my Masters, Teachers, & Loved Ones.
8) **Clearly direct** my perspective & actions to those that manifest my Divine Plan.

   (Repeat lines 5, 6, 7, & 8 two more times, then say line 9)

9) **Free of all resistance, judgment, and fear,**
   I am now filled with Divine love & the Records are open.

Welcome. We are the Angelic Healing Conclave.

When you make a strong statement such as, **"By the power of Divine Light within me, come Holy Spirit, Spirit of Light, Spirit of Truth!"**, among others, we are often requested to respond to your summons. We are a specific Angelic healing faction working with the Akashic Beings of Light, providing our healing presence and services for this missive. We work wholly at the energetic level. We work with your Soul energy, resulting in physical effects. Just like the author, we serve and answer to the Great Creatress. Much of our assistance is clearing detritus of the past so that you can better function as your Soul's agent on Earth. We work with 100% pure Divine Light to heal what ails you most, and that is fear.

This period of time and consciousness is a direct face off with Fear.

Fear is being used to corral you, to limit your freedoms, to trap you in a moment in history in which you were told what to do, when to do it, and for how long. In this phase, you'll be developing new attitudes regarding fear. New attitudes to outside influences. You will be making choices about your behavior, actions, thoughts, beliefs, and the consequences of your choices for others. You need to be willing to choose, and choose strongly, what you want to think and feel in each moment. Are you going to hop on the mindless bandwagon of danger, fear, potential consequences, right vs. wrong, and one side or the other's mass media agenda? We support your critical thinking skills and personal way of determining the truth for yourself, while you experience the consequences of your choices. We support your ability to see and think beyond the limits of dualistic thinking, to a third, fourth, or fifth option. Yes, there is danger, but there is heightened experience of aliveness, as well.

You know very clearly how to care for yourself in these unusual times.

What the Angelic Healing Conclave wants you to know is that We are here to sanctify your thoughts, actions, and beliefs. Are you willing to release mass thought and choose to live in a higher way of being, to choose a third, fourth or fifth option, that relaxes your grip on defending yourself, as if against death?

You have always been as you are, at this very moment, reaching the pinnacle of choice. However, you have always been choosing, choosing to feel or deny the fear, choosing to work with it or to resist it, choosing to opt in or opt out of mass fear consciousness. You have always been asked to make life and death choices. Your brain is designed around this basis. Sometimes the fear scale is minor, but the result was the same. For example, "Are you going to eat the cake, or are you going to eat the apple?" This example is not about immediate life or death, but over time, due to the cumulative nature of the consequences of your choices, it will become a choice about life or death. This is true if repeatedly choosing to eat the cake negatively effects your health and your peace of mind. Over time this choice compromises your ability to independently care for yourself, makes you a burden on society, causes you to be unable to work to support yourself, makes you dependent upon your family or paid caregivers, and makes you dependent upon medications to compensate for your choices. From the Angelic Healing Conclave's perspective, in this example, you must embrace the fear and feel it fully before taking action. You must feel your fear of failure, fear of denying the physical cravings, the fear that that is the last piece of cake on earth, and you had better eat it before someone else does.

You must feel the fear, love it, accept it unconditionally. By experiencing and accepting the fear, the natural consequence is that the fear dissolves. Loving fear until it dissolves creates space, frees you from resistance, allowing new choices to be energized and arise.

In another example, feeling fully, accepting, and loving fear allows a choice to change your behavior that assists many life forms, for the greater good. In a past life 400 years ago in North Africa, Annie was the Headman of a village during a deadly drought and was tasked with making the choice for the entire village to stay and wait or the rains or to uproot everyone to look for water and food. The Headman chose to stay, experiencing and accepting the fear that his choice would be the death of the entire village including himself. Regardless of his fear, he hoped the rains would arrive very soon and he reasoned that fewer tribe members would suffer – and die – if they were not under the additional strain of travel.

Through many long sleepless nights, the Headman prayed fervently, asking for Divine guidance, asking the Divine to speak louder than his fears and more vividly than his terrifying visions. Over and over, he placed his fears in the hands of the Divine. Over and over the Divine bade him wait while showing him love and understanding of his uncertainty. Unfortunately, the rains were some time in coming and some villagers died while the Headman survived. A few villagers left on their own to search for food and water. As Headman, he took the deaths and the departures very hard, feeling his failure to keep his villagers safe and his fear of a future that repeated this harsh experience.

However, from then on, he tracked on a stick the rainy years, the drought years, and he began to see a pattern. He and the villagers dug multiple wells and created several ponds for water collection for the villagers, for agricultural, and for livestock use. He realized that plans had to be made, and effort taken, to secure the future well-being of as many people as possible. Many of the choices the Headman made in that past life were difficult and required significant contribution of work from the villagers to build the ponds and dig the wells. It was fear and guilt for the lives lost in the drought that motivated him to look for new choices. He had to choose repeatedly over the years to continually advance the work on water storage, and to educate the villagers how the past taught him that this additional work saved human lives, livestock, and allowed the village to grow enough crops to store for the lean years.

No matter the times, you have had to choose. Sometimes your choices ended in disaster, and sometimes your choices ended in delight. Sometimes it felt as if your choices made no difference in the outcome. Regardless, no God has ever come to feed you to the lions for what you deemed your error.

You are always welcomed back for another try at the experience called human life on Earth. This is the inherent Grace in reincarnation.

You must offer up to the Divine your fear of choosing "wrongly". Place your fears in the lap of the Great Creatress while we, the Angelic Healing Conclave stream 100% pure Divine Light and Love from the Great Creatress into you.

Get quiet within. Know that you are Love and you are loved. Know that We, the Angelic Healing Conclave, are assisting in your healing, in your progression, in your evolution, and subsequent elevation. We heal everyone regardless of crimes, fears, insults, violence toward themselves, or toward others. We heal all, whether they are in a body or

in between bodies. All humans are deserving of the rightful restoration of their own dignity and divinity.

In Our realm, there are no hierarchies of power, wealth, or influence. These stratifying judgments cause fear, division, and resentment. In our realm of consciousness, We have loved them into harmlessness. We experience only the constant desire and objective to be one with the Great Creatress and with All That Is.

Oneness with the Great Creatress unifies all consciousness in this one moment, untainted by the so-called past, with its past misdeeds, and limited understanding.

In most cultures on Earth, in order to realign with their Soul and the Divine, it's completely acceptable to choose death by disease. This is offered as an honorable exit strategy, if chosen. Becoming ill and dying is absolutely acceptable in your culture. That's why you have cancer at such alarming rates. There are no other socially acceptable ways to opt out. Taking an overdose may accomplish the task but will be looked upon as suicide, the result of depression and not fitting in. It will be seen as tragically sad, and an opportunity for others to "wish they had seen it coming and done more".

You can spend your life fearing the unexpected, dreading the unknowable, hyper-vigilant to warning signs of danger.

Fear does not bring you closer to the Great Creatress.

Conversely, fearlessly seeing Her in everything, at every location, sensing Her in every Soul that you have the good fortune to meet, brings you into oneness with the Great Creatress.

Constant awareness of the infinite creations, the infinite experiences, the gradations of aliveness – this is the Divine living in and through you.

This is a state of honoring the Great Creatress. Absolutely thrilling.

Your choice is to love every second of life, or to fear discomfort and death. Your choice is to see through the gauze of fear to the satisfaction, and fulfillment of a life well lived. Fully accepted, your complicity in its creation is through your appreciation. Your life may only be so many years, or, it may be many endless moments of experience, many endless opportunities to shine vibrant with life. You may be lifted up by life, carried on the infinite stream of life-force energy until you choose to change playgrounds. We say to you that it's important that you know that you are choosing at every moment, with every thought, with every daydream.

The Great Creatress, and We, the Angelic Healing Conclave, care for the least of you, at your worst, at your lowest, at your least powerful, and your most vulnerable. We care for you and are here, awaiting your slightest call, your faintest motion of surrender, of acceptance of help. Then, We and you, make a team that is infinitely more able, powerful, and effective.

> *It is in loving yourself, including the sense of fear,*
> *that loosens fear's grip upon you.*

It is through welcoming your whole experience, fear included, that you are free to experience without control, without hypervigilant monitoring for danger.

> *Resisting fear is what emboldens it. Resisting fear leads to the*
> *mind searching for evidence supporting the fear. Imagining the*
> *feared outcome ensures that the most feared thing is manifested.*
> *Remember, what you think about most is most easily manifested.*

The mind is certain to find abundant evidence. It takes great faith to trust that there is no death to be avoided, dodged, or fought off. These forms of resistance beget more fear and resistance. However, if fear is welcomed as one component of your experience, then you are free to acknowledge all the other bits and pieces that make up the whole of your experience. Therefore, fear can simply be ONE of the many ingredients in your experiential soup. It is non-resistance and loving fear that allows fear to slip into rightful inclusion, rather than dominance, in your experience.

Regardless, this moment becomes the next which brings with it the pleasure of a new menu of choices to fill your awareness! As you say, "this too shall pass". People and other life forms will pass, as well. Let this go. The more you can accept what is happening in your experience at this moment, the more you can have this moment of precious aliveness, love for self and others, and the pure promise that life always contains!

It has been our pleasure love you into healing and to spend this time with you.

Please write your responses to these interactive questions:

~ Interactive Questions ~

Ask your Masters, Teachers, and Loved Ones to show you a past life that involved great fear and leadership.

What helped you face important choices that prompted fear in you?

What gifts have you received from your Soul or the Divine in times of fear?

[If you would like to have a Divine Energy Healing utilizing the Angelic Healing Conclave please visit www.AnnieChannels.com to schedule.]

~ Closing Prayer ~

Thanking the Great Creatress & Her Holy Spirit for Love, protection, & healing received this day,
Thanking the Akashic Beings of Light for guidance,
Thanking the Masters, Teachers, & Loved Ones for wisdom & direction.
The Divine Portal & the Akashic Records are now closed.
Amen. Amen. Amen.

Integrating Soul Prayer

For the highest good of all, Great Creatress,

please, open my Spiritual Heart to full vibrancy.

Awaken me to your Divine Design.

By the power of your Spirit within me, I presence my Soul.

I presence Its Light and consciousness.

Oversee my Soul and physical experience as we become One.

Safe in Your embrace, my Soul's Light fills me to the brim.

Recognizing my Soul's Divinity and partnership with You,

I open to receive Its beneficial influence.

Embodying my Soul's Light, I am strengthened.

I am awakened to Its consciousness.

My Soul neither dominates nor condemns me.

Rather, my Soul embraces me kindly,

Guides me wisely,

Fills my heart with Its love,

Sweetens my thoughts, words, and deeds with compassion.

My Soul naturally forms my link with Thee, Great Creatress.

May all consciousness be of the Light.

And so, it is.

Amen

CHAPTER 18

Healing the Separation

Channeled by Anubis

Bringing Forth Soul Consciousness
Akashic Records Prayer
©Rev. Annie Bachelder 1/22/2022

~ Opening Prayer ~

1) By the Power of Divine Light within me
2) Come Holy Spirit!   Spirit of Light!   Spirit of Truth!
3) For the highest good of all, throughout time, fill my heart with Divine Love as
4) I humbly ask permission to open the Divine portal to the highest realm of the Akashic Records for (LEGAL NAME).

5) **Akashic Beings of Light,** guide me to the deepest Truth of my being, releasing any blocks & restrictions to my abundance & highest good.
6) **Great Creatress,** assist me to fully embody my Soul's Light, to fulfill my Soul's purposes, & to heal any accumulated karma.
7) **Surround me** with the enlightenment & wisdom of my Masters, Teachers, & Loved Ones.
8) **Clearly direct** my perspective & actions to those that manifest my Divine Plan.
   (Repeat lines 5, 6, 7, & 8 two more times, then say line 9)

9) **Free of all resistance, judgment, and fear,**
   I am now filled with Divine love & the Records are open.

Greetings and Welcome from Anubis. We welcome you here for the purpose of Healing the Separation you have inherited in the human design, with its weakened link to the Divine and your own Soul. Each chakra functions specifically. The Spiritual Heart is one of the healing components. The separation is most evident when the Soul chakra, the 8th chakra, is **not** included in the conscious use of your energy system.

Over time, through historical misunderstandings, and simple, forgivable ignorance, humanity has felt increasingly isolated. Humans feel the loss of belonging. The loss of connection to a greater intelligent source, has caused the experience of disassociation from your Soul, lack of abundance in all areas, and disconnection from the Great Creatress' dependable, infinite supply of love and resources.

As a result of this disconnection, humanity suffers from disconnection from Mother Earth, poor problem solving, poor nutrition, impossibly low income, and crude decision making. It is as if in choosing relationships they are drawn to the lowest quality partners, disrespectful friends, or to continuing in a job that doesn't feed them and their family. Their gifts, talents, and abilities are not seen, utilized, or respected. All of this is overcompensated with obsessive pride and resistance to asking for help, either Divine or human, and fear of, and resistance to being dominated.

We are working to remedy these very things. It has always been our higher purpose to unify humans with their Soul, and to heal the separation. Even if you had no idea that your Soul is a part of you and your journey, we are making available to you the energy needed and activities for re-connection with this cohesive whole.

Humans have been plunged into male dominated social and religious hierarchical structures from time immemorial. Until the last 100 years, little had been said or done to advance the idea that separation from your Soul and the Great Creatress (the Divine Feminine) is a grievous misunderstanding. The idea of separation between Soul and human has been used against you to support the "top-down power schemes" of political and religious leadership. This imposes "outside-in" belief systems, which aid hierarchical social and religious powers and their financial gains.

The misunderstanding is the belief that your human body and personality are not connected to Soul from within because Soul is separate spirit energy, outside of the human body, imperceivable, and inaccessible.

Further, we categorically state that the Soul is intrinsically allied with the Great Creatress.

This alliance encourages autonomy, social and environmental awareness, and independent thinking. We are here to reinstate your original, essential, intimate connection between you and your Soul. We are here to encourage the re-establishment of this connection, encourage a reorientation toward, and cooperation with, your Soul. Reconnection and reunification with your Soul heals the separation. No longer will you feel lost, or ousted from, the Great Creatress' inner circle. By Divine design and by purpose, the more you reintegrate your connection with Soul, the more you will feel the loving connection, direction, and life-force energy flowing through you from your Soul. One of the chief functions of the Soul is providing and maintaining the link between you and the Great Creatress. This naturally means that you will feel that you deservedly belong with Her.

Astoundingly, many of you have felt that you neither owned, nor belonged to, your own Soul.

Mysteriously, your Soul became your responsibility. You were threatened with ensuring your Soul would either burn in hell or be cut off forever from the approval of a violent, unforgiving God. Despite your ignorance, lack of awareness of your erroneous actions, undisciplined thoughts, and honest mistakes, you were given no information, much less any authority, about how or why this ghostly appendage became your responsibility. This concept seems to have taken root in the murky swamplands of confusion and guilt. We suggest you release these antiquated beliefs from your innermost being and begin anew. Begin as if you had a fresh, spotlessly clean whiteboard.

To heal the sense of separation and recondition your thinking, please recite out loud these affirmations every day for 30 days:

"I and My Soul Are One" Affirmations

I and my Soul are One.

I and my Soul are inseparable.

I and my Soul belong together.

I and my Soul walk hand in hand on the path of enlightenment together.

I trust my inseparable Soul to love me no matter what transpires.

I trust my inseparable Soul to stand by me.

My Soul has never, and will never, reject me.

Consciously linked, my Soul and I are clearly directed to the highest and best outcomes for our mutual benefit.

My Soul and I safely grow, expand, and explore together.

My Soul is my best friend and the keeper of my innermost gifts, talents, and abilities.

My Soul assists me with solutions, insights, and inspiration.

My Soul never abandons me in times of trouble.

My Soul aids in my healing, maturation, and supplies the courage needed to progress on my path.

My Soul actively draws me toward uplifting opportunities and abundance.

The more I merge with my Soul the more healed and whole I am.

The more my Soul merges with me, the more we can accomplish together.

The more I identify as my Soul, the capabilities for achieving my aspirations increase.

The more I identify as my Soul, the fewer limitations, distractions, and obstacles I experience.

The more my Soul becomes my human identity, the more peace, inclusivity, and harmony I experience.

I now see through the loving eyes of my Soul.

I now experience through the expanded awareness of my Soul.

I now love with my Spiritual Heart, the heart of my Soul.

I now clearly hear and follow the wisdom and direction of my Soul.

I and my Soul are indivisible.

My Soul and I are One, we are One with the Great Creatress (the Divine).

Thank you, Soul. Thank you, Great Creatress.

As you assimilate unification with your ever-loving, ever-loyal Soul, and as you identify as your Soul, many wonders become available. In fact, the state of wonder becomes your common experience.

The mysterious and often mentioned "flow" becomes your norm. The anxiety and fear caused by separation dissolves. The return to peace is instantaneous. Unified with your Soul, you easily trust that you are being Divinely guided and this holds you steady. The more you incorporate your Soul connection, the easier it is to follow your spiritual path because your connection with Soul and the Divine are constant. The present moment is the only moment of interest. You sense that this is a friendly Universe in which you intrinsically belong.

Trust that your Soul is precisely placing each footfall.

You are created by, and aligned with, all that is Holy, and you are fully on purpose.

In the moments when you feel disconnected from your Soul, please remember this: **"Enlightenment is not how long you can stay in the flow as much as how quickly you can return to it."** *quote from DaBen, Duane Packer's Spiritual Guide*

Please write your responses to the interactive questions below.

~ Interactive Questions ~

Rereading the "Integrating Soul Prayer" how does your body feel?

Reciting the "I and My Soul Are One" affirmations, how does your body feel?

What do you notice today about your connection with your Soul?

What is different about embodying your Soul's Light compared to when you first began the practice?

How do your thoughts and feelings change when you utilize your Soul as your link with the Divine?

What does "being in a state of wonder" mean to you?

What is your Soul inspiring you to do?

~ Closing Prayer ~

Thanking the Great Creatress & Her Holy Spirit for Love, protection, & healing received this day,
Thanking the Akashic Beings of Light for guidance,
Thanking the Masters, Teachers, & Loved Ones for wisdom & direction.
The Divine Portal & the Akashic Records are now closed.
Amen. Amen. Amen.

CHAPTER 19

The Etheric Planes of Light, Claiming Your Soul

Channeled by the Akashic Beings of Light

Bringing Forth Soul Consciousness
Akashic Records Prayer
©Rev. Annie Bachelder 1/22/2022

~ Opening Prayer ~

1) By the Power of Divine Light within me
2) Come Holy Spirit!   Spirit of Light!   Spirit of Truth!
3) For the highest good of all, throughout time, fill my heart with Divine Love as
4) I humbly ask permission to open the Divine portal to the highest realm of the Akashic Records for (LEGAL NAME).

5) **Akashic Beings of Light,** guide me to the deepest Truth of my being, releasing any blocks & restrictions to my abundance & highest good.
6) **Great Creatress,** assist me to fully embody my Soul's Light, to fulfill my Soul's purposes, & to heal any accumulated karma.
7) **Surround me** with the enlightenment & wisdom of my Masters, Teachers, & Loved Ones.
8) **Clearly direct** my perspective & actions to those that manifest my Divine Plan.
   (Repeat lines 5, 6, 7, & 8 two more times, then say line 9)

9) **Free of all resistance, judgment, and fear,**
   I am now filled with Divine love & the Records are open.

Greetings, Dear Reader, from the Akashic Beings of Light. As you read this, We are transmitting from the Etheric Planes of Light, placing ourselves at your service as you assimilate our messages, and explore these realms. These are consciousness planes of prismatically colorful, geometric shapes of Light and energy, gracefully in motion. They are available to you now, via the Akashic Records combined with embodiment of your Soul's Light and the consciousness therein. We have brought you to the Etheric Planes of Light, your soul's dwelling places, as an introduction to claiming your Soul.

The Etheric Planes of Light are different than the Akashic Plane of consciousness, they are the territory of the Soul. This is the Soul's Resting Place, the Soul's rejuvenation energy field, and the Soul's reformulation region. For those who embody their Soul's Light and consciousness, the energy here is uniquely palatable, and easily absorbed. Our purpose in bringing you here to explore, is to remind you experientially, that everything begins as energy. In keeping with this universal principle, embodying your Soul begins as energy, the energy of your essential consciousness and formatting.

You are simply, eternally, and consciously embodying your Soul in present time.

This is not a "do over".
This is a multi-layered process of rejuvenation and evolution.

Every time you as a human makes a significant leap in physical, emotional, mental healing, and spiritual growth, your Soul is similarly rejuvenated, and evolved. Every time your Soul makes a significant upgrade, you the attendant human is similarly upgraded. The evolutionary layers are similar in essence to the layers of a pearl. Each layer adds chatoyancy, the aurora borealis-like light and depth, to its emanation.

The Soul's ability to radiate Light is expanded and your Soul's influential reach is greater than it was prior to the most recent rejuvenation.

Embodying your Soul is a strong peaceful priestess/priest stance of acquisition, of ownership, of illuminated being. It is an authoritative act of summoning the Soul to your human self. It is a command, a demand that you and your Soul join in conscious partnership. Be willing to take on this advancement, to add this level of connection to the

Great Creatress, as your rightful place. All else will develop over time. Embodying your Soul is, at this point, the first step.

Annie began connecting with her Soul, unbeknownst to her, in her teenage years. Embracing her Soul, followed by embodying her Soul, has been an ongoing process with plateau years, and years of extreme growth brought on by great physical and emotional upheaval. Some of her deepest wisdom was engendered by her decade of solitude when she was disabled with multiple sclerosis. Nothing has been wasted, no time has been lost. All is in accordance with her Divine plan, her Soul's path, and her human experience as her Soul's experience Module. [See chapter 7 "How the Soul is Constructed"] We wish to encourage those who may feel they have lost valuable time, missed important opportunities, or outright failed at your spiritual expansion. Not so.

Know with all certainty, that any so-called delays, detours, distractions, and procrastination, are stages of Soul infusion and inclusion within the human. Yes, the path is winding and fraught with obstacles, each of which has tested your mettle and you have not been found recalcitrant or wanting. All has been used to good purpose. Enough. Onward.

Embodying Your Soul is a process that began with your first physical incarnation however short, uneventful, or elementary. For example:

Annie did an Akashic Records reading for a woman who wanted to know why she was deeply afraid of death. The woman's Akashic Masters, Teachers and Loved Ones revealed an ancient past life as an early amphibious, salamander-like creature, defenselessly small in size and structure, taking its first exploratory journey out of the water at the edge of a deeply shaded pond. Not two steps out of the water, the amphibious creature was gobbled up by a dinosaur-sized animal which, of course, ended her life. The astonishing brevity of that life, and the experience of being eaten on a maiden voyage (read: brave new experience), was so shocking it stayed with her for hundreds of lifetimes as a pronounced fear of death. So too, was the experience of being defenseless and small in stature. These two elements alone were enough to set the stage for many lifetimes of feeling helpless, powerless, and chronically afraid of dying. Having reviewed this very early past life, this woman was able to readdress her choices. She could now face life from an empowered and free state of consciousness, far more in tune with her current life as a middle-class, well-educated person living in the USA.

Embodying Your Soul has exhibited your stealth and your skills as you navigated the Path of Congruence. This path is your ever-unfolding Soul Path. It is punctuated by phases, sometimes lasting lifetimes. These periods are characterized by lost faith, distrust in the Universe, lack of connection with the Great Creatress, distrust of your inner wisdom's voice, and overwhelming existential angst. This path is about rediscovery of faith and connection to the Great Creatress. Your elevated guidance systems are in full force as you live your life, regularly enveloped in gratitude, your Soul's Light, and trust in the friendliness of the Universe. You live in a state of safety, infused with your Soul's Light. This links you with the Great Creatress. She underscores the Divinely inspired events in your life which generate happiness, joy, and fulfillment. This is the Path of Congruence.

You are at this place, brought here by your hunger for connection, for inclusion, for belonging. You have always wanted to BE your Soul and now you are, with our gentle assistance, learning to live as your Soul.

This is the crossroads upon which you stand. Breathe with relief, grant yourself a moment of acknowledgement, celebration even, as you recognize the long, often scary path that you have taken to get here, to arrive at this juncture, this preordained moment of truth, securely centered in your essence.

Acknowledge the effort, the dedication, the willingness, and the massive amount of blind faith required to arrive here.

As We stated before, the time for preparation is over, you are here now, fully engaged and equipped to embody your Soul, to inhabit your Soul.

The Great Creatress does not err. Her works are perfect. You, as human, and you as Soul, are perfect. The Great Creatress invented "Process" as a way of expanding the states of learning, and of absorbing the stages.
"Process" allows for integration and assimilation.

Exercise: Claiming Your Soul

1. Begin by embodying your Soul's Light, energy, and consciousness.

2. Become aware of your Soul chakra, the 8th chakra, about 12 to 15 inches above your head.

3. Sense the Light and energy in it.

4. Open your crown chakra and allow the Light of your Soul to enter your other chakras and your physical body.

5. Sense your Soul's Light as it fills every part of your body, even your toes.

6. Include your Soul's Light, energy, and consciousness in your physical experience.

7. Sense your Soul's Light as infusing with your body.

8. Wear your Soul as invisible clothing, as internal reckoning.

9. Orient your vision so that you are gazing through your Soul's eyes.

10. Listen with your Soul's hearing.

11. Feel your Soul's Light in your palms and fingers. Activate your Soul's sense of touch.

12. Activate your Spiritual Heart, your Soul's Heart.

13. From the deepest, tenderest part of the human you, send an invitation to Your Soul asking it to show you how it claims you.

14. Open your receiving as wide as you can and receive your Soul's connection, your Soul's claim of you.

15. Notice where it connects, and how. Notice Its gentle demeanor.

16. Perhaps there is an embrace. A deeper infusion of love.

17. Offer your Soul the best part of you, the part that is willing to grow, to play, to change.

18. Feel the acceptance, the partnership, the cooperation between you.

19. Silently claim your Soul.

20. Communicate with your Soul your willingness to see, hear, and know all that your Soul see's, hears, and knows.

21. Feel how secure you feel now.

22. Embody your partnership with your Soul often, while navigating even the simplest of moments. Do this regularly, and you will discover that this feels natural, and you can hardly remember a time when you did not feel the loving infusion and partnership of your Soul.

23. When this ends, bring your attention back into the room, and into ordinary reality.

Begin by embodying your Soul's Light and consciousness during simple, everyday activities, for example, washing the dishes or watering the plants. Include your Soul during any meditation. Engage with your Soul upon arising, while driving, walking, and before going to sleep. Ask your Soul to be with you as you sleep, deepening your rest, and bringing forth what it may, in your dreams. Embody your Soul while daydreaming, problem solving, or asking for insights.

Always be respectful toward your Soul, allowing it free reign in your Spiritual Heart. Let It guide you step by step. Employ your faith in these moments, invest your trust in your Soul, for it has guided you to the tops of mountains and through the valley of the shadows, and it has done so lovingly!

Please write your responses to these interactive questions.

~ Interactive Questions ~

Describe your sense of knowing, your vision of, or the feeling you have when reading about the Etheric Planes of Light.

At this point in your study of this book, how does your Soul's Light and energy feel to you? How has it changed since you began reading this book?

Describe and acknowledge 3 examples of the effort, the dedication, the willingness, and the massive amount of blind faith required to arrive here in this moment.

Describe a past life or a fear that is relevant for you or has caught your attention while reading this chapter.

~ Closing Prayer ~

Thanking the Great Creatress & Her Holy Spirit for Love, protection, & healing received this day,
Thanking the Akashic Beings of Light for guidance,
Thanking the Masters, Teachers, & Loved Ones for wisdom & direction.
The Divine Portal & the Akashic Records are now closed.
Amen. Amen. Amen.

CHAPTER 20

Alternatives to Worry

Channeled by the Akashic Beings of Light

Bringing Forth Soul Consciousness
Akashic Records Prayer
©*Rev. Annie Bachelder 1/22/2022*

~ Opening Prayer ~

1) By the Power of Divine Light within me
2) Come Holy Spirit! Spirit of Light! Spirit of Truth!
3) For the highest good of all, throughout time, fill my heart with Divine Love as
4) I humbly ask permission to open the Divine portal to the highest realm of the Akashic Records for (LEGAL NAME).

5) **Akashic Beings of Light,** guide me to the deepest Truth of my being, releasing any blocks & restrictions to my abundance & highest good.
6) **Great Creatress,** assist me to fully embody my Soul's Light, to fulfill my Soul's purposes, & to heal any accumulated karma.
7) **Surround me** with the enlightenment & wisdom of my Masters, Teachers, & Loved Ones.
8) **Clearly direct** my perspective & actions to those that manifest my Divine Plan.

(Repeat lines 5, 6, 7, & 8 two more times, then say line 9)

9) **Free of all resistance, judgment, and fear,**
I am now filled with Divine love & the Records are open.

Greetings and Welcome from the Akashic Beings of Light!

We are in receipt of Annie's request for calm, detachment, peace, and successful completion of all the tasks that are hers to perform. After her father and stepmother died, Annie has been working hard on paying her deceased parent's bills. The big obstacle has been switching bank accounts from her parent's bank account over to the new Trust account. Also, she is managing two small apartment buildings in the estate as well as researching the best way to sell some of these assets. All of these tasks have more details within the details, and she is experiencing a steep and stressful learning curve. She is thoroughly engrossed in worry. Hence, today's topic.

If you are experiencing similar circumstances, we encourage you today to listen to Annie's YouTube recording of "Overwhelming Peace". (See the chapter in this book under the same name. The YouTube recording of this chapter can be accessed via this link: https://youtu.be/cQh7KbchRyI.) You may wish to play it softly in the background while you are doing other activities. Please bookmark it on your phone for use on the go, and at night while falling asleep.

When in distress, the fastest way to accommodate your sanity is to stop. Face the distress. Feel your beautiful body-servant as it is experiencing the effects of the distress. Greet the distress.

Ask the distress:
  · What do you need to know about this distress?
  · Which inner child of your human self is most engaged with the distress?

**All angst is born of self-will. There are usually 3 topics:
fear, frustration, and anger.**

Like Sisyphus, you are probably trying to push the rock up hill with your incredible self-will and self-determination. This leaves no room for the Divine to assist you.

We suggest you process your feelings using the **Akashic Transformation Process Master Questions©** below.

What is my resistance regarding _____?

How have I judged myself regarding _____?

How have I compared myself unfairly regarding _____?

What are the hidden obstacles to the resolution of _____?

What action can I take today regarding _____?

To this list of queries, we add:

Embodying Soul's Light and Consciousness, how can you trust the process that is already under way?

How do you feel when you choose faith in the orderliness of the universe, knowing that the solution to your problem is also already on its way?

It is the human mind that obsesses about the problem, generating fear. In this circumstance we encourage you to exercise. Even a short walk blows off stress energy, quiets your mind, and relieves your body of tension. The physical movement helps shift the energy and open you to new options and solutions.

Worry is obsessive repetitive thought and prayer is the simplest and best way to heal this thought pattern. Early intervention with prayer is highly useful as it breaks they cycle of addictive chemicals released by the brain with each repetition of the obsessive thought. Prayer is spiritual intervention, embodying your Soul's Light, and calling upon and the all powerful Great Creatress for help and healing. Repeating a favorite line or two of the Akashic Records Prayer is enough to reroute your thoughts to a higher energetic plane. This avoids the resulting poor outcome of manifesting the worry and creates an ecosystem capable of manifesting increased inner peace.

Worry is unexpressed fear, a desire to fix the unfixable, to change what is not yours to change, such as other people, time, or the external causes that worry perceives as the problem. Through self-will, it is the desire to force an outcome that conflicts with opening to the revelation of alternatives and possibilities that are better than what your worries had imagined. Here again, we suggest you stop for a moment. Let your shoulders drop. Let your lungs be open, breathing slowly and deeply. Feel your beautiful body-servant. (We are calling your body "your beautiful body-servant" as an aid to transforming any habitual criticism and self-consciousness about your body shape or function.) Your beautiful body-servant is trying to help you master this so-called "problem" in the physical world. Your beautiful body-servant is required equipment for **Bringing Forth Soul Consciousness**. Hence, we add another query to your repertoire:

Embodying fully my Soul's Light and consciousness, what is the Soul's perspective, or the Akashic perspective of the issue causing my worry and distress?

It's always useful to engage fully with your Soul's Light, and Consciousness, and call upon our blessed Great Creatress for Divine Help.

Asking the Great Creatress for help is a masterful act.

It automatically softens your stance, opens your heart to Divine Love, and opens your mind to different options and resolutions to the stuck point.

Asking the Great Creatress to help you while fully embodying with your Soul's Light allows the energy to shift toward fulfillment of your Divine Plan. You are calling upon the most creative source, the most intelligent being, the divine designer, of all that is. Drawing your Soul's Light into your whole being, you are automatically aligning with your Soul, its higher purposes and the ability to navigate these purposeful and potent choice points.

Choice Points are the big turning points in your life.

Will you move forward in the old worrying way, or will you take the risk of making a new choice? Are you going with habit, or "going along to get along"? Or are you standing in the Truth of your Soul and Its divine connection, wide open to divine guidance, moment by moment? Are you going to fret about the future or maximize the power and peace of the moment to manifest a higher result?

Worry is being certain that you are not going to get what you want, in the form that you have envisioned, and that you will end up feeling disappointed. Worry is always about the future.

Worry perpetuates the anxious state from which no better future can be created. Worry and its attendant visions and assumptions are never about the present moment. Clearly, the fears and worries you obsess about are not empowering a higher, better future or a future representing your highest vision. You are merely inserting more worry into your future.

> ***Your Future Self is absolutely certain that you are successful in resolving the issue and experiencing happiness and fulfillment.***

We recommend that you get quiet and receive Light from your Future Self. When you receive Light from your Future Self, she/he is always showing you that you have not suffered and died, as your personality believes will happen. Your Future Self shows you that you successfully mastered the current set of obstacles.

Exercise: Receiving Light from Your Future Self

1. Begin by taking seven slow, deep inhalations followed by strong, complete exhalations.

2. With every inhalation you are bringing in your Soul's Light and Consciousness. 3) With every exhalation you are releasing density and complexity.

3. Inhale and feel your Soul's Light as it fills your whole beautiful body-servant.

4. Exhale, forcing all the old energy completely out of your lungs.

5. Inhale Soul Light. Exhale density.

6. Inhale Light and exhale overwhelm. Relax.

7. Inhale Soul Light. Exhale and relax.

8. Your Future Self stands in front of you. This is your Future Self of 2 months, 2 years, 20 years, even 2 lifetimes in the future.

9. Your Future Self looks kindly upon you. It is clear, calm, and composed.

10. Your Future Self emanates brilliant multicolored Light.

11. Your Future Self begins to direct its brilliance toward you.

12. This Light feels like a secure force for good.

13. Your Future Self is letting you know that everything is all right. Everything has worked out for your highest and best good.

14. Your Future Self makes clear that you have become stronger and clearer in the process. You become more your Soul Self in the process you are currently undergoing.

15. Your Future Self may have an important detail or message to share with you.

16. Your Future Self may simply be saying, "Relax. Everything is okay. The problem got solved. The dilemma got resolved for every ones highest good. You may now make peace with all your frustrations and all that has been bothering you."

17. Drink in your Future Self's Light. Soak up its presence. Fill yourself with your Future Self's peace. Soak up your Future Self's wisdom. You easily trust your Future Self and know it is on your side, on your team, working for your highest good.

18. Now ask to be in the Light radiating from your Future Self of 2 lifetimes from now.

19. What is different about this Light? How have you grown?

20. What do you have to adjust in your present self to receive Light from this Future Self?

21. How does this Future Self deal with problems and dilemmas?

22. Ask if there is another message from this Future Self?

23. Thank your Future Selves, reserving a future opportunity to share your Future Self's bountiful Light and wisdom.

24. Bring to mind a problem that causes you fear and anxiety. Write out your responses as you apply the Akashic Transformation Process Master Questions©.

What is my resistance regarding _____?

How have I judged myself regarding _____?

How have I compared myself unfairly regarding _____?

What are the hidden obstacles to the resolution of _____?

What action can I take today regarding _____?

What information did you receive from your Future Selves regarding a problem that has caused you to worry?

[Here is Annie's example exploring her worry and distress using the Akashic Transformation Process Master Questions:

What is my resistance regarding the change-over of my deceased parent's Bank accounts? I felt out of control, inept, and frightened of disastrous consequences to all the heirs of the estate. In my attempts to manage the apartments and tenant problems, I felt "put upon", out of my depth, dangerously inexperienced.

How have I judged myself regarding the bank accounts and apartment management? I judged myself a faker, a fraud, acting as if I knew what to do and how to handle these situations. Situations I egotistically thought I had in hand. I didn't want my siblings to know how ignorant I really was. I didn't know how to ask for help in managing the apartments. The only solution I had in mind was to sell the apartments and get the heck out of the Landlord business.

How have I compared myself unfairly? I compared myself unfairly to my father who had been a landlord for 46 years. He had many years of experience in solving tenant problems, fixing things, and dealing with the personalities of the tenants, and with the Housing Authority. Although I compared myself to an imagined, experienced Trustee who had been through all these mysterious processes, while in truth, I had almost no previous experience whatsoever.

What are the hidden obstacles to the resolution of these issues? Looking back, I would say patience is essential. I felt as if my abilities were on trial, and I did not have someone to guide me. My fear was raging all through the process. To cover my fear and ignorance my pride blocked my ability to ask for help or find an experienced person to guide me. Rushing into solutions is one of my character defects. Born of fear, I want to slam an answer or solution into the question or problem in order to stop the distress of "not knowing".

What action can I take today regarding these issues? Between me and 5 intelligent siblings, everything all worked out to everyone's satisfaction, the tasks all got done, and quite elegantly. Today, I am committed to trusting the universe, and the Great Creatress. I commit to asking for Divine help and help from appropriate human sources. I am willing to have patience. Some things just need time to resolve.]

~ Closing Prayer ~

Thanking the Great Creatress & Her Holy Spirit for Love, protection,
& healing received this day,
Thanking the Akashic Beings of Light for guidance,
Thanking the Masters, Teachers, & Loved Ones for wisdom & direction.
The Divine Portal & the Akashic Records are now closed.
Amen. Amen. Amen.

CHAPTER 21

Transitioning Between States of Consciousness

Channeled by Anubis

Bringing Forth Soul Consciousness
Akashic Records Prayer
©Rev. Annie Bachelder 1/22/2022

~ Opening Prayer ~

1) By the Power of Divine Light within me
2) Come Holy Spirit! Spirit of Light!   Spirit of Truth!
3) For the highest good of all, throughout time, fill my heart with Divine Love as
4) I humbly ask permission to open the Divine portal to the highest realm of the Akashic Records for (LEGAL NAME).

5) **Akashic Beings of Light,** guide me to the deepest Truth of my being, releasing any blocks & restrictions to my abundance & highest good.
6) **Great Creatress,** assist me to fully embody my Soul's Light, to fulfill my Soul's purposes, & to heal any accumulated karma.
7) **Surround me** with the enlightenment & wisdom of my Masters, Teachers, & Loved Ones.
8) **Clearly direct** my perspective & actions to those that manifest my Divine Plan.
(Repeat lines 5, 6, 7, & 8 two more times, then say line 9)

9) **Free of all resistance, judgment, and fear**, I am now filled with Divine love & the Records are open.

Greetings and welcome from Anubis.

When your physical world is in a state of stress, and anxiety, crowned by grief, **Bringing Forth Soul Consciousness** reduces stress. Embodying your Soul's Light reduces the impact and influence of mass thought, lightens the load on the nervous and immune systems Not only does it lighten the impact on your individual body, embodying your Soul's Light helps other life forms adjust, as well. Truly, it is a Bringing Forth, a birthing process. It is a process of creating a new behavior response that allows humanity to become aware gradually, and to adapt by bits. For most people, to eliminate the transition state of **Bringing Forth Soul Consciousness** would be too shocking. Many would close down and automatically deselect the increased consciousness and unity being offered. Many would deselect it as too dangerous, unknown, and foreign. Evolution is a process of gradual change, and gradual adaptation, by design.

Two universal laws are that no energy is forever lost, and every Soul exists eternally. Thus, an abortion does not kill a Soul or person. It changes the timeline of Its physical appearance on earth. This is true of war and murder also. The Soul is infinite, unkillable, incorruptible. The physical personality that dies in war or is murdered simply releases physical form, changing back into pure consciousness and is reabsorbed by the Great Creatress, awaiting the next experiential incarnation. The Soul that created the personality that is killed in war or by murder has designated this to be so, has chosen this so-called end, and subsequent transition. The drama and the players are all part of the Divine plan, my dear. All part of the Divine plan.

The Divine plan is to assist you every step of the way in transitioning from worry, to trusting the process of living as your Soul, and linking with the Great Creatress.

"Transitioning" is a process. It is a condition that can be felt or known when straddling two or more states of being. You might feel it as you consciously shift focus between two very different, highly concentrated projects. You are shifting from one focus to another, and it requires you to consciously adjust, internally, what your mind, body, and spirit centers on. You may sense the state of transitioning as an opening in the back of the neck and head. It's as if your energy sensors are in process of moving to the next energetic link up. We suggest that you give yourself a moment to feel this condition. There is a brief opening in the head or back of the neck, which allows unformatted energy to become available.

Get familiar with it because the state of transitioning between consciousness happens all the time.

Transitioning is a skill to be mastered in its many forms. One might be transitioning from being a child into a teenager, a teenager into a young adult, an adult into an elderly person, an aged person into matter-less consciousness commonly known as Soul. One might be transitioning from work-life to home-life, from physically inactive person to exerciser extraordinaire. One might transition from fearful to confident, from holding back to stepping forward. From non-spiritual to spiritual. You might be transitioning from being wholly male or wholly female consciousness, to a blended and balanced form of both. You might be transitioning from a mathematics activity to a spirit activity. You might be transitioning between life and death and rebirth.

Transitioning between states of consciousness is necessary in the process of change. Transitioning as a process is evidence, the demonstration of your acquisition of increased consciousness.

Degrees of increased consciousness affect degrees of change, in your personality, and in your concepts about reality.

As Soul Consciousness increases, your experience of reality changes. What had been important may now be less so. What is now important is taking pleasure in your Soul, communing with Its Light, and experiencing Its expanded consciousness. What is important now is employing the Light of your Soul and Its consciousness to get things done, to accept or shift energy, to shape your actions and plans.

As you acquire increased Soul Consciousness, you feel less constricted by the physical world. You feel enlarged, more centered, more stable, and powerful. Your capabilities feel refreshed. In this process, you acquire familiarity with your Soul, gently transitioning your earth-bound consciousness to the wider or more precise options afforded you from the Soul level perspective. *(See chapter 7 on "How the Soul is Constructed".)*

The **Bringing Forth Soul Consciousness** Akashic Records Prayer opens your Akashic Records, illuminating your Soul level perspective, giving you access to the Akashic Beings of Light, and to the Akashic field. The Akashic, or Soul level, perspective is free of judgment, resistance, and fear. It releases you to embrace whole-heartedly, the broader view of your circumstances, choices, and relationships. This perspective allows you to see and know why your Soul chose these experiences as learning devices, as vehicles for your evolution, growth, and expansion, and in some cases, humility.

Through Bringing Forth Soul Consciousness you are transitioning from being a body-based personality to a Soul, awake, alive, and aware!

This process is akin to being present at the birth of a human child. Such an awesome event is inspiring. We thoroughly enjoy witnessing your ever-increasing appetite for acquiring and experiencing Soul Consciousness, for this is the main theme of incarnating at this time in human history. We wish to invest in you, to instill within you, our appreciation and encouragement for your participation in this process. The process never stops. Like you, we, too, are ever-expanding into greater fields of consciousness, adapting our reach, and reformatting our frequencies of love to fit the changing complexities. We too, are evolving and bringing humanity with us.

We suggest that you love and accept your transitions between states of consciousness. If you cannot do so in this moment, set the intention to do so. Set the intention to improve your acceptance.

Love all of them. As you become familiar with your Soul and Its consciousness, you will be more invested in your abilities allowing you to experience Soul Consciousness, you soften the rough edges of your process, and transition between states of consciousness without resistance. You streamline your learning and be less fatigued or bothered.

Your ability to accept change, and to adapt to change, will become a thought-free, seamless event, a smooth transition.

If you are reading or hearing this information, and it is making vibratory, energetic sense to you, then you can know and sustain your Soul Consciousness. Allow yourself to get the energetics first. Then allow your brain-mind plenty of time to grow new neural pathways, as your brain-mind is hard-wired into your physical body and your personality. Your personality is doing the best that it can to conceive of, and hold this energy, in its limited awareness. Your Soul will do the rest of the heavy lifting.

We bid you adieu for now.

[While editing this chapter on Transitioning Between States of Consciousness, I received an email from my mother that my elderly Aunt Lucie transitioned (passed away) that morning. One of her son's, my cousin, who had provided generously for her for many years, has a terminal disease. Automatically, I received this understanding: Lucie could not bear the pain of her son dying before her. Aunt Lucie has gone ahead to prepare the way (even though I strongly suspect my cousin does not believe in any conscious afterlife), and to rally the Receiving Angels to be ready for his transition. I pray she finds the happiness and joy she richly deserves in her new abode and that my cousin's eventual transition is sweetly welcomed.]

Please write your responses to these interactive questions.

~ Interactive Questions ~

What happens to your stress level when you recite the Bringing Forth Soul Consciousness Akashic Records Prayer?

How do your nervous and immune systems feel when you bring in your Soul's Light?

Name or describe the different states of consciousness are you currently transitioning between.

Describe your sense of the new neural pathways you are growing to accommodate your expanded Soul consciousness.

~ Closing Prayer ~

Thanking the Great Creatress & Her Holy Spirit for Love, protection, & healing received this day,
Thanking the Akashic Beings of Light for guidance,
Thanking the Masters, Teachers, & Loved Ones for wisdom & direction.
The Divine Portal & the Akashic Records are now closed.
Amen. Amen. Amen.

CHAPTER 22

Going South

Channeled by the Akashic Beings of Light

Bringing Forth Soul Consciousness
Akashic Records Prayer
©Rev. Annie Bachelder 1/22/2022

~ Opening Prayer ~

1) By the Power of Divine Light within me
2) Come Holy Spirit!   Spirit of Light!   Spirit of Truth!
3) For the highest good of all, throughout time, fill my heart with Divine Love as
4) I humbly ask permission to open the Divine portal to the highest realm of the Akashic Records for (LEGAL NAME).

5) **Akashic Beings of Light,** guide me to the deepest Truth of my being, releasing any blocks & restrictions to my abundance & highest good.
6) **Great Creatress,** assist me to fully embody my Soul's Light, to fulfill my Soul's purposes, & to heal any accumulated karma.
7) **Surround me** with the enlightenment & wisdom of my Masters, Teachers, & Loved Ones.
8) **Clearly direct** my perspective & actions to those that manifest my Divine Plan.

(Repeat lines 5, 6, 7, & 8 two more times, then say line 9)

9) **Free of all resistance, judgment, and fear,**
   I am now filled with Divine love & the Records are open.

173

Greetings and welcome from the Akashic Beings of Light.

You have a saying that goes something like this: "I totally went south on that." Your human implication, laden with self-judgment, is that you went unconscious, emotionally out of control, off-center, glazed over, irresponsibly numb, or negligently out of hand. We love to see you in this state.

[Annie is thinking of her favorite acronym for GOD: Gift Of Desperation]

When you are in this "going south" condition, there are stressors or upsets which need to be released, and this is exactly when we can most easily help you. When the triggers that reignite old pain, trauma, or other unhealed memories, We Akashic Beings of Light are here to assist you in coming to peace with such past experiences. We are waiting for you like a safety net made of Golden Light to arrest your fall. When you are "going south", embodying your Soul's Light and consciousness, and linking you with the Divine, places a soft landing of comfort and appropriate awareness that sets you free from such past tyrannies. We invite you to "go South" with purpose. We invite you to receive such moments of distress and disorder as opportunities to heal and shift your consciousness upward. We invite you, first of all, to actually **feel** the feelings that you are feeling, even the ones you are trying to escape. Know that We are with you, supporting you, all the time.

"Going South" is also a term used to mean going to a tropical location, a vacation spot, taking time off work, giving yourself a break. We are with you as you take constructive time off even if you have no idea what the agenda might be for doing so. We urge you to take your "vacations", even if it is only internally, where you make a conscious decision to relax, be unfettered, set aside your usual tasks, and let yourself recover your unique equilibrium. We suggest that you are actually rediscovering your new balance point, as imbalance is often the result, signaling that you are under significant stress and strain. In support of you discovering your new balance point, you may wish to use the exercise "How to Embody Your Soul's Light" (Found in Prayers and Invocations at the back of the book.) and when your entire body is filled with Soul Light open the bottoms of your feet as if they had trap doors. Allow your Soul's Light to continue flowing into Mother Earth's center, her balance point.

Notice how easily your Soul's Light attaches itself (and you) to the Earth's balance point. This is the new balance point you are seeking. Let that new set point stabilize. You may be heaving a sigh of relief as you fully arrive here. Relax. You are remembering that you, Your Soul, and Mother Earth are all in cahoots with the Great Creatress, and it is She who is in charge. Not you.

As you may be noticing, while you are experiencing yourself in various relationships, professional activities, and in many other roles, that you are extremely flexible and adaptable. We have been very pleased with your presence and state of being within these moments, seeing that you have brought yourself to them fully, without hesitation or withholding yourself. You have honored your inner truth and values and acted admirably. Your service as an example during these times has been duly noticed!

Going South. 'Going' means traveling, means leaving the location where you were tethered, to which you are no longer attached. As if you have been unleashed from your center, or that point you were assigning centering power to, as the point of security.

As you leave this perceived station, and release attachment, you are finding some freedom. This is much like when Annie gave herself permission to also ground upwards, in addition to grounding downwards into the earth. Significantly, you too, may be becoming aware of your connection in the upper realms, aware that you belong with Us, and with other Light Beings who have aided you in this lifetime, and in many other lifetimes. So, we say to you that in these times of sadness, upheavals, earth changes, discord, distress, and people dying, that it is most natural for you to ground upwards, to look for harmony and solace in the upper realms, or to find stability and peace by grounding yourself to Mother Earth's balance point.

Obtaining the clarity of the Akashic Records, being subsumed by the Akashic Records themselves, or anchoring, repeatedly, your center of being in these realms is the same as "going home" for many of you. When you catch yourself "going south", return to the Akashic Records to be refreshed, revitalized, and become realigned with your Soul assignment.

There are reaches of understanding and consciousness that belong to, and can only be reached by, "going south". Going a bit crazy gets your consciousness there, outdistancing your ego's grip on its idea of normalcy, and suddenly you are taken into the higher realms in a new way.

The Akashic Records are governed by three principles: Judge Not, Fear Not, and Resist Not. It affords all who study the Records, not to object or judge, how others find their way to, or through, an opening into unusual realities.

The Akashic Beings of Light are bringing a memory to mind, my befriending a manic-depressive man, and being willing to talk to him, remarkably, without fear or any judgment whatsoever.

It was 1974. I was 16, an attendant pumping gas at the Fairfax, California Chevron station, when the middle-aged man drove in and began unloading from his tiny Honda, a collection of books, an iron, some clothes, and other random belongings. He was lining up these items on the concrete outside of the front office windows, all the while talking to himself, or perhaps to the voices inside of him in an agitated tone. He was clearly distressed. I talked with him a while, pumping gas in between spurts of conversation, hoping to discover the nature of his distress. His alarm and disordered thinking had not changed, but I could feel him opening up to me. Eventually, I asked my boss if I could have the afternoon off to try and help this guy. I was a trusting youth and sensed no harm or danger from him. Perhaps that was due to my inexperience with mental health disorders. I had no previous experience interacting with anyone in this particular condition. We reloaded his car and went for a drive. I was surprised and very pleased that he let me drive! Talking along the way, I tried to understand him and to follow the energy of what he was saying. He was getting messages from the car radio, from his metal tooth fillings, and many of the messages were not kind. He was filled with anguish! We drove for a few hours around Napa and Sonoma that sunny summer afternoon, places where I knew the peaceful countryside and the roads well. (In the 1970s, the area was rural countryside with small family farms, acres of tall corn, tomatoes and cows in fields, not the stylish shops, fancy homes, and sophisticated wineries the area now boasts). Suddenly, it all became crystal clear to me and out of my mouth came the words, "I get it. You just want to be loved!" I don't know where that understanding came from. I don't know how I knew that except to say that it was such an obvious and basic human need that all humans understand and recognize in each other. And the man began crying in earnest, relieved to be heard, known, and seen. At the end of the day, we drove back to the Chevron station and he departed.

A few days later, I got into my 1958 VW cargo van, and I could feel that someone had been in it. The back normally contained only a carpet, a bean bag chair, an ashtray, and two homemade ceramic candle holders. Me and my pals used to get stoned in there between high school classes. We called ourselves The Space Cadets. When I got in back and I discovered a low box with a small stack of newspapers and a pristine white bakery bag with two Danish in it. I ate part of a Danish and threw the rest away along with the newspapers. Later, I discovered that the man with mental health issues had been sleeping in my van. I firmly told him he could not do that anymore. It made me feel weird, invaded somehow. Thankfully, he stopped sleeping in my van.

A few months later, having forgotten about the whole scenario, a lawyer came by the Chevron station to say that the guy had gone into the woods nearby and starved himself to death, leaving a will that left everything to me! Shockingly, the attorney said the man had a wife or two, and children from both marriages, one of which was guy my age who attended the same high school. The lawyer asked if I wanted the house, the tiny Honda, and all his worldly goods. I was thinking, "I can't take this family's home and contents! I don't want to own a house. Way too much responsibility. Nope. I'm young and fancy free and want to continue that way." I said no thanks. The lawyer asked if I wanted a painting or something to remember him by. I couldn't imagine him having a painting that I would like so I said no. Looking back, these were huge decisions for a teenager to make on the spur of the moment, in between pumping gas and washing windshields for customers.

The Akashic Beings of Light are showing me that I have always been open minded about unusual people with different mind sets, and perspectives. They are emphasizing that the ability to see through other's eyes and feel their feelings grants a keen sense of their reality. In this case, I got to feel another person's desperate need for love, acceptance, and kindness, despite their circumstances and appearance.]

Please write your responses to the interactive questions below.

~ Interactive Questions ~

Describe a time when you felt yourself "going south", and rather than run away from your emotions you completely felt your feelings, and naturally came through the experience with a refreshing new perspective?

Describe a time when you felt yourself "going south" (kind of going crazy) and you asked for Divine help, and you received the help/clarity/solution you needed.

Describe a time when someone else was "going crazy" and you received deep insight into the inner workings of another human being. What was the insight? How were you changed?

~ Closing Prayer ~

Thanking the Great Creatress & Her Holy Spirit for Love, protection,
& healing received this day,
Thanking the Akashic Beings of Light for guidance,
Thanking the Masters, Teachers, & Loved Ones for wisdom & direction.
The Divine Portal & the Akashic Records are now closed.
Amen. Amen. Amen.

CHAPTER 23

Anubis Speaks – Healing Past Lives

Channeled by Anubis

Bringing Forth Soul Consciousness
Akashic Records Prayer
©*Rev. Annie Bachelder 1/22/2022*

~ Opening Prayer ~

1) By the Power of Divine Light within me
2) Come Holy Spirit! Spirit of Light! Spirit of Truth!
3) For the highest good of all, throughout time, fill my heart with Divine Love as
4) I humbly ask permission to open the Divine portal to the highest realm of the Akashic Records for (LEGAL NAME).

5) **Akashic Beings of Light,** guide me to the deepest Truth of my being, releasing any blocks & restrictions to my abundance & highest good.
6) **Great Creatress,** assist me to fully embody my Soul's Light, to fulfill my Soul's purposes, & to heal any accumulated karma.
7) **Surround me** with the enlightenment & wisdom of my Masters, Teachers, & Loved Ones.
8) **Clearly direct** my perspective & actions to those that manifest my Divine Plan.

(Repeat lines 5, 6, 7, & 8 two more times, then say line 9)

9) **Free of all resistance, judgment, and fear,**
I am now filled with Divine love & the Records are open.

Greetings Dear Ones. This is Anubis and I greet you warmly.

In my lengthy service to humanity and to the various Gods of Egypt, I now serve the Great Creatress. I have comforted the multitudes in every state of being. Most importantly, I have safely escorted animal spirits and Souls on their journey to the afterlife. Please take full advantage of the heartfelt energies we, as a group, broadcast to you in this missive.

Thoroughly experiencing each and every moment involves feeling each and every emotion, that in the past, could have been ignored. We acknowledge the courage it takes for you to meet each moment's ever-changing menu of physical sensations, emotions, and thoughts. Sometimes it is necessary to go deep into these personal feelings and thoughts. At other times, a bit of detachment serves your purposes well, especially in discerning "mass thought" from personal thoughts. It is when you pile judgment upon judgment, that you begin "sinking into overwhelm".

When your mind serves up memories of terror, damnation, pressure, disappointment, and discord, we say, "let the slide show begin". Be sure to have your pressure release valve (located in your crown chakra) in the open position. Be prepared to release every thought and feeling as they flow through and out of you. Embody your Soul's Light and consciousness. Connect with the Great Creatress and Her inexhaustible supply of Love. The images and feelings can easily appear, and fade, in the Light of your Soul. Let them arise and dissipate without judgement. Observe the show. Observe the way your mind presents narrow memories drenched in fear or denial. It is imperative that you remind yourself frequently, **what you are seeing or sensing is a memory. It is not happening now**.

An enhanced reaction to a memory may be happening now, yes. However, the original event is not happening now. Also, you are not the person that you were at the time of the original occurrence.

The universal energy has changed, and it is no longer necessary to wade through all the minute details of past lives to grow new neural pathways that are unencumbered by a current life memory, or unwanted and unnecessary past life influences. A brief description of the past life is enough to match up with your commitment to release and to heal.

That's all it takes for the clearing to happen naturally. The emotional heat source (usually shame, blame, anger, and/or fear) is neutralized.

When the energy shift happens, the past life or the current life event, has no point of attachment. The past life, or current life trauma, no longer serves as supposed protection, or as the knee jerk reaction that stimulates inappropriate action. Homeostasis is restored because the emotional and mental charges are neutralized. It is at this point that you naturally come to peace with a past life, or a current life trauma. You can love yourself unconditionally and the new neural pathways are established. Your software is updated.

Exercise: Healing an Undesirable Past Life

(It is essential that your Akashic Records be open for this exercise so that you receive the Akashic perspective, the Soul perspective.)

1. Begin by embodying your Soul's Light and the consciousness within that Light.

2. Follow your Soul's Light as it pours into your body, filling every system, structure, and cell in your body.

3. Your Soul's Light spreads all the way down your toes and out the bottom of your feet.

4. Ground your Soul's Light in the center point, the balance point, of Mother Earth.

5. Your Soul's Light is so brilliant, so strong, that it glows beyond the confines of your physical body. It makes a cone of Light that both infuses you and surrounds you. It holds you steady.

6. Ask your Masters, Teachers, and Loved Ones to show you a past life that is ready to be released.

7. Your Masters, Teachers, and Loved Ones are directing your attention to a place in your body that holds an undesirable past life. Get a sense of this location and the energy of the past life in question.

8. Make your consciousness very small. Small enough that you can enter the interior of your body at the location where the past life has been stored.

9. It is as if you entered a room in another time, another place. Look around. See what is there for you to see. Trust your sense of knowing. Your Masters. Teachers, and Loved Ones may point out things, people, and circumstances that fill in the details.

10. Using your "sense of knowing", notice whether you are male or female, strong or weak, the clothing you are wearing, your social status, the time period, and your emotional state.

11. Who else is involved? What are their chief characteristics? How are they involved? Are they familiar to you?

12. Ask your Masters, Teachers, and Loved Ones why this past life is being shown to you?

13. Ask them what is the most important aspect of this past life for you to know?

14. Ask your Soul how this past life helps you evolve?

15. Ask your Soul why this past life is ready to be released?

16. Become aware of your Soul's Light melting, dissolving, and releasing any past life attachments to your body. The sticky, dense energy becomes light, misty, and effortlessly flows out of your energy field.

17. Confirm that your willingness matches the release of the unwanted effects of this past life.

18. Confirm also that the new neural pathways are established.

19. Your Masters, Teachers, and Loved Ones are supporting you, assisting in the evaporation of the past life and any residual energy is removed from you.

20. Thank your MTLO's for their love and support. Thank your Soul.

21. Let all that go. Gently bring your full attention easily and effortlessly back into ordinary reality. Make written notes about your experience.

The value of understanding past lives is in knowing that the circumstance that caused it no longer exists. Your detachment while viewing past lives serves as a gauge of how much you have changed, how much you have evolved. The present moment experience of your Soul's Light and consciousness frees you from the past as it combines with the knowledge that your past life emotional and mental condition was an ineffective protective device that no longer serves your highest good in present time.

The undesirable effects of a past life may be similar to how your ancestors were trying to protect you from experiencing that level of hurt, pain, humiliation, frustration, and suffering ever again. That is fine as far as it goes, but true protection is embodying your Soul's Light and consciousness, open-hearted, in the present moment, where the infinite Light does the work of healing, rebalancing, and realigning your human self with the evolving perfection of your Soul. The renewed experience of Soul connection, linked with the Great Creatress, sets the new vibratory benchmark in current time, and the energy of the past is released.

This is true also about the release of old belief systems, family programming, and societal conditioning. Societal conditioning is a thing in the air. It is mass thought consciousness. You are surrounded by this conditioning. It is nearly inescapable. All the rules and regulations are encapsulated by the word "normal" for your family and culture. You breathed it in and breathed it out. You eat, sleep, and have your being in the soup of societal and cultural conditioning. In the past, you constantly trued yourself to this conditioning.

It can be freeing to realize that many feelings and associated thoughts are created by mass thought, mass unprocessed emotional energy, generated by repetition of old programming.

Embodying your Soul's Light and consciousness updates your energetic frequencies, and lovingly detaches you from the past, including mass thought and societal conditioning.

Unfortunately for most, the effects of mass thought and the state of mass consciousness are constant. An antidote to this trap is to embrace your Soul's consciousness, experience your connection to the Great Creatress, and continue **Bringing Forth Soul Consciousness**. It provides a level of detachment, of observation, free of judgment, condemnation, and categorization. From the Soul consciousness perspective and the perspective of the Akashic Records, you can lovingly observe with detachment the goings on in human life that formerly tied you to the repetitious chaos, the pain and hunger, the effort and struggle, and the predictable game of revenge involving the victim and dominator.

The Light of your Soul activates compassion for yourself, and others, even while it acts as a buffer to worldly pain and strife. Your Soul's Light and consciousness grounds your experience in the present moment.

Understand this: Earth life is rigged so that you have the opportunity to experience the highest healing possible at any given moment.

At this point, We urge you, encourage you, to merge your personal will (your self will) with Divine Will so that your thoughts, feelings, instincts, and actions are a working part of the activity of the Great Creatress on Earth. *(Please see the Exercise: How to Align Your Self Will with Divine Will at the end of the book.)* As Annie says, "Surrender and join the winning team". Yes, please do surrender. You will enjoy the ride.

We bid you adieu for now.

Please write your responses to these interactive questions.

~ Interactive Questions ~

Embodying your Soul's Light and consciousness, practice letting your thoughts and judgments arise and dissipate for 3 minutes. Set a timer. How does that feel?

Ask your Soul or your Masters, Teachers, and Loved Ones, "Is what I am thinking and/or feeling sourced in mass consciousness or my consciousness?"

What distinguishes thoughts that are actually yours?

What identifies certain thoughts as mass consciousness?

What identifies certain feelings as mass consciousness?

Ask your Masters, Teachers, and Loved Ones to show you how to merge your self-will with the Great Creatress' Will. Note here how that looks, feels, and changes your energy.

Ask your Soul or your Masters, Teachers, and Loved Ones to show you how to surrender to the Great Creatress' love and care. Note how that looks, feels, and changes your energy.

~ Closing Prayer ~

Thanking the Great Creatress & Her Holy Spirit for Love, protection, & healing received this day,
Thanking the Akashic Beings of Light for guidance,
Thanking the Masters, Teachers, & Loved Ones for wisdom & direction.
The Divine Portal & the Akashic Records are now closed.
Amen. Amen. Amen.

CHAPTER 24

Writing Your Soul's Divine Plan, the Akashic Perspective

Channeled by the Akashic Beings of Light

Bringing Forth Soul Consciousness
Akashic Records Prayer
©*Rev. Annie Bachelder 1/22/2022*

~ Opening Prayer ~

1) By the Power of Divine Light within me
2) Come Holy Spirit!   Spirit of Light!   Spirit of Truth!
3) For the highest good of all, throughout time, fill my heart with Divine Love as
4) I humbly ask permission to open the Divine portal to the highest realm of the Akashic Records for (LEGAL NAME).

5) **Akashic Beings of Light,** guide me to the deepest Truth of my being, releasing any blocks & restrictions to my abundance & highest good.
6) **Great Creatress,** assist me to fully embody my Soul's Light, to fulfill my Soul's purposes, & to heal any accumulated karma.
7) **Surround me** with the enlightenment & wisdom of my Masters, Teachers, & Loved Ones.
8) **Clearly direct** my perspective & actions to those that manifest my Divine Plan.
   (Repeat lines 5, 6, 7, & 8 two more times, then say line 9)

9) **Free of all resistance, judgment, and fear,**
   I am now filled with Divine love & the Records are open.

Greetings and a blessed welcome to ALL from the Akashic Beings of Light!

We are in receipt of Annie's objections to the topic, today. They sound like this: "I can't write about my Soul's Divine plan. I won't be objective. Why me? Can't someone else write about my Divine Plan and show me later, on day when I feel more powerful?" We Akashic Beings of Light are unaffected by her personality's imagined limitations. They do not impede our plans for this topic nor Annie's ability to channel our words and energy.

As previously mentioned, the Akashic Beings of Light, working in concert with your individual Masters, Teachers, and Loved Ones are here to validate your Soul given powers, your authority, and your Soul consciousness. Most of all, We validate the fact that you comprehend our message, both energetically and as written words.

Many of you have sought to serve in the highest way possible, and it is your Soul's plan to utilize your human limitations, illnesses, struggles, addictions, and relationships, to guide you along your path of service. So, we say to you, set aside your perceived obstacles. Embody your Soul's Light. Align with your highest state of being, commune with your Akashic Masters, Teachers, and Loved Ones in your Akashic Records. Soothe your personality with remembered moments when We served you, healed you, guided, and informed you. Know that we continue to be a consistently loving influence in your lives. Consider that you are where you are because your Akashic Masters, Teachers, and Loved Ones assisted you, lifetime after lifetime, despite your perceived limitations.

The Akashic Records always meet you
where you are now.

Hence, it is through your objections and your resistance that we begin the conversation about the Akashic Perspective of Writing your Soul's Divine plan.

We remind you that in the Akashic Records all time is present time,
and this shapes our explanation of such a daring topic.

With every thought, response, and action at any given moment you are writing your Soul's Divine plan. Thoughts, responses, and actions build on the past, continually altering your Soul's Divine plan. There is not one plan cast in stone that is your destiny. However, there is a basic energetic pattern, your Soul's blueprint, your essence, established at the time of your Souls' inception, which steers your general trajectory and sets the Soul's theme for many of your lifetimes. As beliefs and ideas are adopted, adapted, and discarded, experiences are recorded and integrated, so your essence energy pattern is refined. Beliefs, experiences, and choices create new possibilities and choices that contribute to the development of your Soul's consciousness and the unfolding of your Soul's Divine plan.

Free will to choose, and how you experience the consequences of your choices, shape your Soul's Divine plan. All these elements blend to create a rich experiential soup from which the Soul selects and reselects, lifetime after lifetime, all moving you toward deeper and deeper Oneness with the Great Creatress.

At a certain point of evolution, the Soul ascends and eclipses Oneness, merging with the infinity of Creation completely changing its nature, purpose, and service role. But that is a book for another time.

Every Soul, formed from a spark of the Great Creatress' original Light, has several objectives written into Its Divine plan.

One Soul objective is to rejoin Her Divine Light and all-encompassing consciousness. Human healing from misunderstandings of concepts, traumas associated with ancestral lineage, illnesses and injuries, misuse and under-use of power, the belief in separation, and the ability to love, are steps toward that objective.

Annie's objections and resistance are another convenient demonstration of how a human limitation, or "character defect", as Annie would call it, are elegantly employed as learning devices. During the planning stages of this, and all your lifetimes, your Soul volunteered to experience various limitations, character defects, conceptual misunderstandings, and uses and misuses of power. The Soul invites other specific Souls to play certain key roles in Its Divine plan for each lifetime. That is why relationships are significant in your Soul's evolution. The Soul often has a specific theme or themes to be played out during a particular lifetime or series of lifetimes, often through various relationships.

We use Annie as our example because her current life has been a constant series of greater and greater healing. From childhood earaches to dashed hopes of being a mother, to alcoholism and disability due to multiple sclerosis – all these and more have been profound demonstrations of healing, physical and spiritual restoration, and continuous expressions of her Soul's Divine plan. Each healing was sourced in a subtle spiritual nudge, urging her to turn inward toward her Soul and the Light for solace, healing, and direction.

All these experiences, and these healings, have left their imprint on Annie. However, for her, they have been barely noticeable, sometimes undetectable, as if they were a series of unconnected short stories happening to someone else.

This is characteristic of the Soul's Divine plan, operating in the background, silent, subtle, surreal.

The strongest theme operating through Annie's life is healing. Were it a book, we would title it "Yes, You Can Heal from That." She has done so. She hardly feels the extraordinary theme, or the fact that she is being utilized as an example of one possible, positive outcome of many potentially disturbing elements.

We will enlarge on some of these subjects, in deference to our readers, and because Annie has requested it.

Often, the Soul sets up a specific experience, or series of experiences, to prove a point. In Annie's case, it is truly to explore the question "How far can healing go?" Which, of course, begs the question, "Is there a limit, an ultimate end, where healing stops?" We assure you that there is no limit to healing.

In an ever-expanding Universe, ends are merely transformations.

The Soul uses absolutely everything available in the human experience pool to refine its ability to share consciousness with you and with the Great Creatress. To further Its evolution, the soul uses healing – or **not healing** – the human, depending on the Soul's plan for this lifetime.

Another, as we will show, is teaching and evolving through the utilization of a weakness, deficit, or character defect. Another way of looking at so-called "character defects" is that they are symbols of resistance to change.

Beneath every instance of resistance is a fear asking to be healed.

For example, Annie's initial resistance to writing this chapter was clearly expressing her fear that she would be unable to accurately transmit the words that would explain her Soul's Divine plan. So far so good. Her initial resistance is also because her personality does not recognize the profoundness of what has been healed in her. We love her attempts at humility, however, today, We favor an unrestricted flow of words and energy with her as the central example. Here again, her lack of recognition of **how much** and **what** has been healed could be seen as ignorance of the obvious. Viewed as a demonstration to others, it is very clear.

Beneath Annie's resistance, is the fear that to clearly see the enormity of the gifts of healing, received over and over again, might engender the sense of a debt owed, or worse, attracting too much attention. We suggest she allow these feelings to arise. Remember Matt Kahn's saying, "Feeling is Healing". Her Soul would not have chosen her personality and her body to have these experiences of illness, addiction, and healing if she was not up to the task of seeing it through to a very uplifting resolution. And her Soul has been correct. She **has** been able to fulfill the task. When she allows herself to have and release these fleeting feelings, what surfaces in its place is inextinguishable gratitude.

Some of Annie's resistance goes back to the original fear she had when she began channeling in 1988, "What if this information is simply my imagination or just plain incorrect?" Well, you humans do tend to find fears more credible than the evidence of thousands of channeled sessions! A similar fear can spring from self-doubt that says, "channeling for yourself is the hardest". We suggest you dear readers, and Annie, release that right now. Release it like a tadpole of a thought that was, never to grow into a full-sized frog.

Of course, We use your imagination to its fullest! To have Our message received and integrated, we must be very creative in outrunning your inflexible brain-minds. Just as your human self defends your perceived limitation, so we must look for other ways to speak to your deepest, true self, to your original spark of Light, to Your Permanent Atom of Light©.

And when you set aside your fears and place your awareness into Your Permanent Atom of Light© or your Soul's Light and consciousness then Our message becomes very understandable. *(see "Exercise: Your Permanent Atom of Light" in the chapter titled Prayers, Invocations, and Exercises at the back of this book.)*

It is forever surprising to us that human beings default to being "less than equal" in skills, knowledge, and experience. An inferiority complex is merely an inaccurate comparison and stresses the opportunity to generate an equality complex.

[Imagine saying to my friends, "I have an equality complex." Feel into that statement. Is there a TED Talk in that statement? "I have an equality complex" is a perspective changer.]

Even better is the statement, "I operate from a platform of equality of being, as a place from whence to spring forth". Inferiority and inequality are simply another misunderstanding to lovingly release, as you would release an item of clothing that has fallen to bits.

There was a time when Annie felt awkward about stating out loud that she had healed from MS. As with many expansions, she had to let herself grow into it. As she stands in the Light of this truth, it has come to be, is reinforced, and continues to be so. Thus, she has returned to her place of equality regarding her health.

Your health reflects embracing yourself as the Light of your Soul in action, another result of embodying Soul's Light and consciousness.

[I have the distinct sense of 'Ha-ha! We Told You So!' as the Akashic Beings of Light return again and again to the topic of this book.]

A chronic health issue may also be the result of your Soul's Divine plan unfolding, using health as a way of teaching you to love yourself unconditionally.

[Personally, I was afraid that if I let myself really believe in my total healing from multiple sclerosis, and was somehow proven wrong, I would be

relegated to the pile of fraudulent healers that have gone down throughout time immemorial. Perhaps even worse than being relegated to that ignoble group, is that I would be f*%king disappointed AGAIN! I have repeatedly experienced disappointment that has been wrenching, heartbreaking, and it is truly rugged territory. However, with the help of the Akashic perspective, I see that I have always come through disappointment stronger, more vitally alive, and more committed to my path of healing and spiritual expression than ever before. Therein lies the diamond in the mud, folks. Triumph over tragedy. Another instance where my Soul consciousness has become greater than my human consciousness.]

The Akashic Beings of Light resume. "Healing" is a ubiquitous concept. It applies equally to a scratch, a gunshot wound, a mental illness, a physical illness, an emotional event, or a trauma. Like an iceberg, the visible evidence is only the smallest measurement of the actual healing. Healing is an inner process, perhaps even, a never-ending process, as we all rejoin the Great Creatress in One consciousness.

Our main subject is **Bringing Forth Soul Consciousness**. This is inextricably involved with healing of the human self as it rejoins Soul consciousness. This is a great part of the Soul's Divine plan. This is why we are forever telling you, that you will benefit in all ways by experiencing and incorporating your Soul's Light and consciousness.

Healing is evidence of the Soul evolving. Healing resolves dilemma's set by the Soul as obstacles and objectives in Its Divine plan.

Every time you link heart to heart with your Soul, you gain wisdom, compassion, and vision. For every moment your Soul links with you, both you and your Soul access greater realms of consciousness.

Consciously linked, you and your Soul gain increased privileges to your Soul's assigned seat in the Great Creatress' infinite lap, and increased connection to all that the Great Creatress has created.

The more you embody your Souls Light, the more you can incorporate Our message. Infusing yourself with your Soul's Light conditions you to being at home in your human self, your body, and in the execution of your Souls purposes here on earth.

This is part of the Soul's Divine plan. Embodying your Soul's Light and consciousness brings triumph over obstacles that would have flattened you in the past. Embodying your Soul's Light and consciousness allows instantaneous releasing of old experiences.

For all that you release, your Soul occupies more energetic space in your body and consciousness.

Your Soul has an obvious influence upon, and connection with you. There is less human mental static interfering with your experience, and the execution of your Soul's purposes. You are more frequently inspired from a Soul level. Your past traumas seem like old movies that do not affect you anymore, they no longer swallow you up in emotional turmoil. Clearly dear Readers, you are motivated now, nearly exclusively, by Soul purpose, rather than by expired beliefs, misunderstandings, or irrelevant ancestral influences. You are more present and current in your relationships. You are known now as you truly are. Your age and wisdom suit you. This is evidence of the Soul's Divine plan in action.

As you come to peace with the most hurtful people, situations, and past events you are polished to perfection as a human and as a Soul.

In closing, we offer this: It is by reviewing and acknowledging your growth, the changes, and transitions you have successfully navigated over time, you see clearly how your Divine Plan has neatly unfolded. Not a scrap or word has been wasted in this unfolding. You are contentedly patient as you wait for inspiration about what is next to be revealed. And it is with joy and the confidence of complete assimilation that you perceive this magical review, rather than with resistance, fear, and judgment.

After all, joy is the true measure of a life well lived!

[*For the sake of continuity, I will describe some of the healing I have been through. The Akashic Beings of Light are referring to my earliest memory of the painful earache I had at age two. It was night and my older brother and sister were observing hesitantly off to the side. Crying loudly and fighting my mother's efforts, she laid me on our humble living room couch, a raised mattress with matching bolsters, the covers of which she sewed herself. Using an eye dropper, she dripped hot oil into the effected ear and immediately the canal opened, relieving the pressure, allowing the infection to clear.*

The Akashic Beings of Light are also speaking to the fact that I had 3 tubal pregnancies, the first one at age 17, nearly killed me. Just to keep the tally correct, several years later I discovered I was pregnant on Friday and miscarried on the following Monday. A few years later, married to my first husband and desiring a family, I consciously tried to become pregnant. The second and third tubal pregnancies were only 5 months apart, making recovery from these major surgeries longer and slower. Unable to bear my own children, we arranged to adopt a baby soon to be born to the placid 18-year old nephew of my husband's best friend and the nephew's resentfully pregnant 15-year old girlfriend. Disregarding the adoption attorney's advice against proceeding, we went forward with the adoption. The limited way I saw things, this was the last baby on Earth, and it was for me! I couldn't conceive (no pun intended!) of anything else. The day the baby was born I was allowed to visit the birth mother in the hospital and to feed the newborn boy. The hospital staff and the birth parents even let me fill out the birth certificate and name him. Michael Adrian Heggen. Astoundingly, this tiny newborn was released into my care on Christmas day. I felt like a criminal as I was leaving the hospital with the baby. Walking down the hospital corridor, I expected to be intercepted by the staff woman walking toward me, saying, "That's not your baby!" Somehow, she sensed my inexperience and offered to come out to my car where she securely hooked the baby into the unfamiliar car seat – FACING BACKWARDS IN THE BACK SEAT – where I couldn't see him! My face has always betrayed my feelings and my eyes must have been as wide as saucers. How could that possibly be safer than up front where I could check on him??? I nearly got into a wreck driving home craning my neck trying to see him in the back seat! Arriving at the house, I collapsed on all fours on the new gray carpet, arched protectively over the baby, like an unearned Christmas present, crying in breathless wonderment that I had escaped detection.

On an unseasonably warm January day about a month later, I was in the backyard with the baby enjoying the sunshine. My husband came out with a pained and confused look on his face. The 15-year-old birthmother unexpectedly appeared at our front door, flanked by two policemen, to take the baby back forever. The birthfather waited in a small car with mismatched fenders, a car they purchased with our non-refundable $10,000 given them for this "transaction".

*Years later I found out that the **birth mother's mom** wanted the baby, not her. The family history was clearly being repeated. Just as in the birthmother's life, her mother being too young, or somehow disinclined, the baby was raised by the grandmother. Now the baby I named was being raised by his grandmother and the birthfather. The birthmother was rarely seen.*

It was an unfathomable loss for both my husband and I. Our marriage to instantly unraveled like Kleenex in water. I could not understand my husband's anger about having to give the baby back. I was drowning in inconsolable grief. I remember standing in the peach glow of the newly painted hallway staring into the painstakingly folded sheets and towels in the linen closet talking to God. "Ok, God! I get it! I am not going to have a family. So, what do you want me to do?" Within two months, I bolted, leaving my husband with the house and moved to Washington State, attempting to out-run my grief and disappointment. Soon after, strangely enough, I learned to channel. So, this is how the Light gets in?

Three years after giving the baby back, I was diagnosed with multiple sclerosis, beginning a physical and emotional rollercoaster ride with exacerbations and partial recoveries every few years until I became disabled. Ten years after the MS diagnosis, I left my second husband, who had become my "using partner". My alcoholism and drug addiction became unsustainable. I wanted to be sober. Six months later I surrendered, joined AA, and got the needed help that redirected me to a path of physical and emotional healing, spiritual growth, and fulfillment. I became disabled with MS but I was a better person, daughter, friend, and AA member. A decade into my sobriety, amazingly, I was healed of MS. Looking back at what healed me, every day I was reading deeply spiritual books, meditating and channeling, exercising, and was impeccably disciplined about following a strict diet and daily herbs prescribed by my Traditional Tibetan Physician.

I no longer take any western medications for MS and all signs of the disease have been gone since 2011.]

Please write your responses to these interactive questions.

~ Interactive Questions ~

Describe three physical, mental, or emotional experiences which have been healed in you?

Describe a situation where disappointment has brought you to healing?

Describe a loss or a disappointment that galvanized a Soul purpose in your Life?

"Beneath every instance of resistance is a fear asking to be healed." Describe a personal example of this.

~ Closing Prayer ~

Thanking the Great Creatress & Her Holy Spirit for Love, protection, & healing received this day,
Thanking the Akashic Beings of Light for guidance,
Thanking the Masters, Teachers, & Loved Ones for wisdom & direction.
The Divine Portal & the Akashic Records are now closed.
Amen. Amen. Amen.

CHAPTER 25

Being of Service

Channeled by the Akashic Beings of Light

Bringing Forth Soul Consciousness
Akashic Records Prayer
©Rev. Annie Bachelder 1/22/2022

~ Opening Prayer ~

1) By the Power of Divine Light within me
2) Come Holy Spirit!   Spirit of Light!   Spirit of Truth!
3) For the highest good of all, throughout time, fill my heart with Divine Love as
4) I humbly ask permission to open the Divine portal to the highest realm of the Akashic Records for (LEGAL NAME).

5) **Akashic Beings of Light,** guide me to the deepest Truth of my being, releasing any blocks & restrictions to my abundance & highest good.
6) **Great Creatress,** assist me to fully embody my Soul's Light, to fulfill my Soul's purposes, & to heal any accumulated karma.
7) **Surround me** with the enlightenment & wisdom of my Masters, Teachers, & Loved Ones.
8) **Clearly direct** my perspective & actions to those that manifest my Divine Plan.

(Repeat lines 5, 6, 7, & 8 two more times, then say line 9)

9) **Free of all resistance, judgment, and fear,**
I am now filled with Divine love & the Records are open.

Greetings and welcome from the Akashic Beings of Light.

Please embody your Soul's Light and consciousness as We suggest that you release the following old ideas and pictures associated with Being of Service.

To be effective in re-embracing this topic you must first release the ineffective and confusing connotations that humans and various cultures have attributed to Being of Service. We offer the distinction between servitude and being of service. Annie has many past lives as examples of service and servitude. We trust some of them will remind you of similar past life experiences or current associations.

In one past life vignette, during the early formation of the United States, she was a bellicose man passionately banging his fist upon a local pub table, saying, "By God, I shall be no man's servant!". Now, embody your Soul's Light. Please release the energy of resistance and opposition contained within this past life.

Another past life memory was in approximately 500AD, as an excessively submissive and obsequious servant woman. She resentfully made herself smaller, lower, than those she served while hating her masters, whom she blamed for her life circumstances. She overestimated her value and barely concealed her harsh judgment of those she served. Please, embody your Soul's Light and consciousness, and forgive all involved, releasing the judgment and resentment of this past life.

Release this next past life as an ambitious priest, during early Elizabethan times. A self-proclaimed "Servant of God", he vociferously self-flagellated in vain, attempting to destroy the sinful, lustful cravings of his physical body. He felt shamefully unworthy of God's favor for which he hungered endlessly. He felt God's judgment was the cause of his unsuccessful aspirations to rise in power and influence in the Royal Courts. He was ineffectual despite his endless plans, imaginings, and scheming. Embodying your Soul's Light and consciousness, actively forgive the man, the circumstances, the participants who thwarted his schemes, and the beliefs of the time. Release the vestiges of shame, sin, ambition, disappointment, and scheming. Release the energy of the past experience of thwarted ambitions in the name of service to God.

There also was a past life as a Samurai warrior and protector, a devoted vassal, who selflessly defended his Overlord, the Overlord's land, the villagers, and the principles of Bushido that he believed brought honor to his consciousness and actions. He experienced great disappointment in this life, and scant recognition for his sacrifice of personal pleasure, family, safety, and security. Embody your Soul's Light and consciousness. Release the past and all disappointment associated with service without recognition in this past life.

We urge you to release all old vestiges of servitude as shown in movies and on TV. These servants eventually turn on their benefactor. These are the falsely humble, over-ingratiating, two-faced, unintelligent, Hollywood stereotypes. These examples are overly simplistic, and are about power, self-interest, and manipulation, not service. Embody your Soul's Light and consciousness and release that programming. Let it go.

In truth, truly Being of Service adds to your self-respect and increases your independence.

For many of you, in past (and current) lives, playing "second fiddle" to employers, spouses, lovers, children, and elderly parents has been intriguing and edifying. In these roles you are offered the opportunity to observe dispassionately, seeing where details needed handling while those you served were in the spotlight. You observed the triumphs and the crushing humiliations. Playing second fiddle was an opportunity for you to make the preparations, maintain the support structures, and the background elements that allowed others to shine their brightest. The difference was that no recognition or special mention of your services were required – and that is where you learned to be independent. There is true service in this instance.

The servant has exceptional powers of influence, depending on how well the servant performs her duties, or whether ineptly or with conscious neglect. A true servant can make the whole production soar to great heights. A servant can also be middling good, or sabotage unmercifully.

From the standpoint of *Bringing Forth Soul Consciousness* this is very valuable. Some use servitude to climb the social ladder, as with upper military roles. Some use the role of servant to prop up others who are supposedly their 'betters". Some use the role to learn true leadership of a group of servants. This is true with warriors and generals. Some choose servitude to have something to fight against, to provide support of their "cause". The "cause" is usually an attempt to gain freedom for themselves and others they consider "their fellow downtrodden". Some choose philanthropic service to give back, or share with others, in gratitude for their abundance and the gifts received.

The foregoing are simply examples; none are better, more desirable, or more instructive than the others. They are simply growth inducing experiences the Soul uses to aid Its evolution in the exercise of power, support, domination and victimization, kindness, and cruelty.

We, the Akashic Beings of Light, support you in embodying your Soul's Light and consciousness, releasing all pictures, beliefs, and old experiences of servitude and Being of Service. Let the Light of your Soul and your intrinsic connection with the Great Creatress replace the old with fresh, new perspectives, and understanding of Being of Service.

These images, largely past tense, often from past life experiences, serve as reminders to release the past as you receive Our Messages.

Detachment and release of the past allows you to invite the Great Creatress to reside in your very being, to work in and through you. You gain a full partner as you invite Her to inform your very being, to direct your thoughts, and inspire your manifestations.

The Great Creatress is not an oppressor or dominator, as you may have been taught by human experiences with power and authority.

On the contrary, She is a wise and capable promotor! She knows every atom and cell in your body. She understands your character. She knows your strengths, gifts, and talents. She assists your Soul in planning a powerfully transformative and effective life. She assists you to fully inhabit, embody, and claim your Soul's Light and consciousness and all the gifts received from doing so.

Being of Service to the Great Creatress, you trust Her to help you live at full potential while you act on Her wisdom, living in harmony, demonstrating Her miracles.

Being of Service to others as a channel, healer, or spiritual Guide, you make a space within you for your service to flow, neither neglecting nor rejecting yourself, neither enhancing nor minimizing yourself. You open a clear space within for Her Divine Presence as We Akashic Beings of Light influence your words, inspire gestures, offer visions, and enlarge your perceptual understanding. This is a "Both/And . . . " proposition, which naturally creates the third, or fourth, or fifth point of view. You are both fully conscious of your whole self, sensing the energy, and are fully connected while you **describe what you are receiving**. You and all involved benefit from every moment spent in connection with Our expanded Consciousness. There is no cost to Us or to the channel, only gain. This is an example of Being of Service.

If you are new to this, we suggest you experiment with making an interior receiving vessel for your Spirit Guides energy within the trunk of your body, gently compressing your personality to the sides around this receiving vessel. You may find that adjusting the volume and speed of what you are receiving by imagining a numbered knob at the base of your spine. Or adjust the knob to a lower setting when doing everyday tasks where psychic (or dare we say cosmic?) reception is not required. Energetically, open the back of your head, neck, and heart to allow your Guide to enter, and to work through you, with full access to your knowledge, experiences, memories, voice, vocabulary, body sensations, heart, and energy sensing abilities. You are placing your body, mind, memories, and energetic sensing in service of greater good, for yourself and to help others.

Being receptive to your Spirit Guides and to Us, you are Being of Service to the Akashic Beings of Light. We are devoted to the Great Creatress, disseminating Her Love and Light. In your service to us and to the Great Creatress, you will always be respected, uplifted, expanded, instructed, enhanced, validated, and you may even be healed through Being of Service. As you are Being of Service to others, you are given the energy shifts and profound love that flows from Us, through you, to those around you. This is truly Being of Service.

Being of Service is a higher calling than ambitiously seeking notoriety, fame, or fortune. Embodying your Soul's Light and consciousness, you and the Akashic Records serve as a bridge of love from your heart to the Great Creatress and to humanity. The natural outpouring of Light, energy, and love that flows through you as the bridge is your reward. The clarity of Our enhanced perspective is exceptionally educational as it teaches you to accept and love yourself, and others, unconditionally. This enhanced experience, the enlarged consciousness, and voluminous Love are what brings you back to this form of Service again and again. Even if you do not channel for others directly, the experience of enhanced Love and Light radiate outward from you so that others might also receive it.

Mind you, being ambitious is not wrong. Ambition often serves as a demonstration of the pitfalls of overcharged, egoic, or misaligned ambition and lack of self-care. Being ambitious and desirous of fame and notoriety at any cost is the way some Souls serve the greater good. An easy-to-see example is as powerful a demonstration as is the opposite, especially in your televised world. The Great Creatress may authorize a Soul plan offering the example of egotistical, self-centered fame. This example entertains with illusions, gesticulating grandly, while spouting empty promises. In a world of contrasts, this counterbalances the numerous quiet examples of selfless, humble servants who feed the hungry, clothe the poor, and share their abundance. The latter, for many of you is the "spiritually correct" example of Being of Service. That is simply an assessment based on your personal values, reflecting your Soul's path, themes for the lifetime in question, and Divine plan.

We remind you that the Great Creatress blesses all without reservation. She loves all without limits or judgment, and so can you.

Herein is the "Both/And . . . " or the "Expand to Include" proposition we are so fond of offering. The "Expand to Include" option allows the extreme comparisons and illustrations, as well as the "in between extremes" examples of Being of Service.

As Souls with ever-evolving consciousness, as Divine creations expressing the infinite choices of the Great Creatress, you all will experience, and have experienced, many versions of this paradigm called Being of Service.

Each of you serve the Great Creatress through your Soul's Divine plan in the way and manner that is individually suited to you and is yours to fulfill.

Annie's Akashic Records reading and channeling clients are drawn to her for the specific qualities of Light and consciousness that she emanates. The students and clients that you teach will be drawn to you for the unique experiences, abilities, and growth processes you exemplify. Any struggles with illnesses or relationships and the triumphs of healing and growth that you experience fuel and demonstrate your particular evolution as a Soul in service to the Great Creatress. Hence, without even consciously trying to do so, you Serve the Divine. Without knowledge of your Divine plan or Souls purposes you exemplify the Great Creatress' grand purpose.

Each of you has specific talents, skills, and abilities that demonstrate Soul paths consistent with your experience. These skills match your Soul agreement to serve the Great Creatress. These abilities serve the highest good and evolution of those who are drawn to your example.

Naturally, who you are, at each moment, is of service to your friends, family, clients, and students, and hence, to the Great Creatress who oversees everything. This is how your Divine plan plays out and how you express the myriad qualities and possibilities of the Great Creatress. This is how you, as a Soul, approved by the Great Creatress, planned your current life to be. Your current life, your aspirations to express your gifts, talents, and abilities are how you, as a Soul, express Being of Service.

We thank you deeply for your time and attention to these important matters. We bid you adieu for now.

Please write your responses to the following interactive questions.

~ Interactive Questions ~

Ask your Masters, Teachers, and Loved Ones to show you a past life of service. Describe the details of time, place, circumstances, others involved, and the emotions you are receiving. Ask your Masters, Teachers, and Loved Ones why this is important to your Soul Consciousness.

Ask your Masters, Teachers, and Loved Ones to show you a past life where you, or someone close to you, exemplified a misunderstanding between servitude and Being of Service. Describe your emotions, body sensations, visions, and sense of knowing. Ask your Masters, Teachers, and Loved Ones why this is important to your Soul Consciousness.

Now, ask to be shown a life in between physical embodiments, where you were in training with the Angelic Healing Conclave, or Light Beings, or a similar Consciousness group that serves the Great Creatress.

Describe the higher purpose of your education with this group, your emotional state, your consciousness, and your sense of knowing about what is revealed.

~ Closing Prayer ~

Thanking the Great Creatress & Her Holy Spirit for Love, protection, & healing received this day,
Thanking the Akashic Beings of Light for guidance,
Thanking the Masters, Teachers, & Loved Ones for wisdom & direction.
The Divine Portal & the Akashic Records are now closed.
Amen. Amen. Amen.

CHAPTER 26

A Discussion of Gender

Channeled by Anubis under the Auspices of
the Akashic Beings of Light

Bringing Forth Soul Consciousness
Akashic Records Prayer
©*Rev. Annie Bachelder 1/22/2022*

~ Opening Prayer ~

1) By the Power of Divine Light within me
2) Come Holy Spirit! Spirit of Light!   Spirit of Truth!
3) For the highest good of all, throughout time, fill my heart with Divine Love as
4) I humbly ask permission to open the Divine portal to the highest realm of the Akashic Records for (LEGAL NAME).

5) **Akashic Beings of Light,** guide me to the deepest Truth of my being, releasing any blocks & restrictions to my abundance & highest good.
6) **Great Creatress,** assist me to fully embody my Soul's Light, to fulfill my Soul's purposes, & to heal any accumulated karma.
7) **Surround me** with the enlightenment & wisdom of my Masters, Teachers, & Loved Ones.
8) **Clearly direct** my perspective & actions to those that manifest my Divine Plan.

   (Repeat lines 5, 6, 7, & 8 two more times, then say line 9)

9) **Free of all resistance, judgment, and fear**,
I am now filled with Divine love & the Records are open.

Greetings and welcome from Anubis.

Annie is asking why there has been a push for her to adopt a female gender for "The All That Is" or "God" as we have done in utilizing the terms the "Great Creatress" "the Divine" with the pronoun "She".

The Universe is largely a space of birthing, a giant uterus, if you will. For a moment, please allow the metaphor to hold for the purposes of this discussion. Annie became aware of this essential fact while learning the Aramaic language version of the "Our Father" prayer in which the translation from Aramaic to English refers to the Divine as "Birther". The language Jesus the Christ spoke was Aramaic and in the Aramaic version of the "Our Father" prayer, there are no fatherly or male gendered references. There are only female or neutral gendered references. The male god came about after many translations of the prayer, by men who spoke Latin and Greek languages which preferred powerful titles to be male. **Please forgive them**. They were simply expressing the values in accordance with agreed upon terms of the times and geographic locations.

Our purpose in addressing the Divine as "the Great Creatress" is that it acknowledges Her all-encompassing creative and procreative, universal power, Her love, caring, life affirming qualities, and abilities. Doing so allows all of us to access to Her in a Holy, nurturing, and intimate way. A deeply personal way. Addressing the Divine as the Great Creatress starts you on the path of acknowledging the rise in power, the presence, peace, and healing values of the Divine as Feminine. This begins the process of equalization of the genders, of balancing the duality of the powers of gender, on the way to neutrality, and universality beyond duality.

As in the previous chapter, you may find your preconceived notions of powerful females need to be released. Images of strong, powerful females have been presented to you as testy, spoiled, selfish, power-hungry, and fickle, irrational, and need to be released. Please give yourself permission to release all old, inaccurate, insulting, derogative, and prejudicial references. Most of these are based in and the result of the effects of cultural histories. In the west, the influence of Greek mythology has shaped your impressions of powerful women as stormy, thoughtless, unjust, and self-centered.

Please release the old concepts and make room for new understanding of the Divine Feminine that includes (but is not

limited to) infinite love, care, awareness, ever-present goodness,
limitless abundance, life-giving, and Divine authorization and
sponsorship of your gifts, talents, and abilities.

In the process of finding balance between male and female in a 3-dimensional world where duality and opposites are the dominant reality, there are few other options or descriptors. As you explore expanded dimensions of reality, you will encounter the limitations and conflicts in your language that are set by either/or, black/white, male/female, good/bad, all-or-nothing parameters. Realize, Dear Reader, that you and your culture are steeped in this version of reality and, by the 3rd dimension's very nature, your choices of male or female are in constant opposition with each other. This tension of opposites is balanced by evolving into inclusion of 4th or 5th dimensional realities, both of which present a fuller array of choices from which to select. Along the way, you are creating new terms that express options not limited to male or female, good or bad, right or wrong, etc. New terms express neutrality, Both/And, and your culture's attempts to be inclusive of nonbinary individuals and other nontraditional groups.

You may have the sensation of awkwardly forcing yourself to say "Great Creatress" instead of the traditional male-invoking term "God". Until recently, especially in the western Judeo/Christian cultures, this was simply not the norm, not the societal, and linguistic habit.

You are receiving, digesting, and assimilating an enormous wave of
female energy. Your language skills are struggling to express these
new options.

For a time, you may feel it is an "act of will", a conscious effort, to use the term Great Creatress. However cumbersome it may feel at this moment, we promise that you will adapt. One could always use the term "the Divine" as we have done in preparing Annie for this transition.

In the process of adjusting to the term the Great Creatress, you are
laying the groundwork for the rise of women around the Earth to a
balance of power, to the higher consciousness and appreciation of
Mother Earth, as She reasserts Herself in human awareness. You
are opening to the distinct harmony of feminine strength, authority,
vision, life-affirming, and holistic consciousness.

The embarrassment and shame Annie has felt in introducing the new title is related to the desultory term, "ball buster", that men in the 1970's and 1980's used to negatively categorize powerful women, women who stood up to men. As you have observed in politics, the act of accusing others to dominate opponents has been quite popular. This only exists in a 3D climate framed by opposites, where no 3rd, 4th or 5th option readily exists without the conscious act of will to bring it into focus.

Trail blazers, such as yourself, are providing that act of will. You feel you are pushing the river, fighting the tide, forcing a change into existence. Well, my dears, this is exactly what happens when a new consciousness is birthed!
That is how new habits are created.

There are growing pains as the narrow opening is made wider through increased consciousness and use. The energetic opening now exists and is utilized by growing numbers. The chamber's entryway continues to enlarge, and more are drawn to it. All are warmly welcomed by the Divine change Herself! Many relieved Soul's will find solace and deep relief in the enfoldment, the all-inclusiveness, of the Great Creatress.

This great wave of feminine energy now exists.
and it brings its current to the fore. This energy wave highlights those who resist the equalizing of gender powers in which a simple change in language, and inclusive perception, threatens old concepts.

Annie is asking, "At what point do we abandon, altogether, the reference to gender when relating to God/Goddess/The All That Is?" We answer in the affirmative: Anytime you are ready. The Divine is in the universe of No Time and is already prepared to receive you.

Further, the English language, as do most languages, assigns gender to things, people, and places. Ships are considered female. Flowers have male and/or female components for pollenating. Electrical components have a male or female connective ends. Traditionally, names for offspring, pets, and places are associated with gender, although this line is becoming increasingly blurred. It is evolving at a radical (for Earth) rate and names are the first flexible edge in which to bend. Human identities, sexual and otherwise, are shifting. It looks like a revolution to some, especially when fear and resistance are the dominant response. The shift toward female equality and away from male dominance is another step toward "expanding to include" 3rd, 4th and 5th options. Opening to fourth and fifth dimensional realities is how you expand beyond the limits of dualistic either/or gender assignments. After all, each of you has female and male characteristics that assist you in your daily life.

You are steeped in gender.
This is because duality most often results in two genders and is part of the way Earth life has been designed. It is up to humanity to enlarge their consciousness allowing for more options.

We encourage learning about the instructive rare species on earth that self-pollenate, are hermaphroditic, or that can their change gender to guarantee the survival of the species. Spend time exploring the vast realms of consciousness where different social structures are revealed, and other life forms introduce themselves that are not bound by 3D/Earth limitations such as gender. There you will be introduced to new, non-gender-based consciousness, roles, and social formats. This kind of exploration will give you practice in perceiving lifeforms beyond gender, encompassing a greater whole that is becoming possible for your brain-mind to acquire.

Use your Spiritual Heart to embrace
expanded concepts beyond the world of duality.

Conceptual walls that separate take time to break down. Some resistance is expected. For the moment, we suggest you allow yourself the over-compensating swing to the opposite side of male sky gods, to the Divine as Female Goddess. Simply understand that at this date and time in herstory you are in process of expanding to include new options to gender as they are revealed by the upcoming generations. It is they who are pushing the envelope for you.

It may be simpler, more accurate even, to call the Divine deity "Love".

We bid you adieu for now.

Please write your responses to the following interactive questions.

~ Interactive Questions ~

In your daily life, loosely track how many references to gender occur in an hour, or a day. What do you notice?

Describe how the current gender format works for you.

Describe how the current gender format limits you.

What names for the Divine feel right to you? Why?

What is needed so that you can forgive centuries of ancestors for diminishing females?

What is needed so you can forgive much of humanity for assigning Divine and Earthly authority to males?

In what ways are you experiencing the "giant wave of female energy entering the planet"?

~ Closing Prayer ~

Thanking the Great Creatress & Her Holy Spirit for Love, protection, & healing received this day,
Thanking the Akashic Beings of Light for guidance,
Thanking the Masters, Teachers, & Loved Ones for wisdom & direction.
The Divine Portal & the Akashic Records are now closed.
Amen. Amen. Amen.

CHAPTER 27

Prayer

Channeled by the Akashic Beings of Light
under the Auspices of the Great Creatress

Bringing Forth Soul Consciousness
Akashic Records Prayer
©Rev. Annie Bachelder 1/22/2022

~ Opening Prayer ~

1) By the Power of Divine Light within me
2) Come Holy Spirit! Spirit of Light! Spirit of Truth!
3) For the highest good of all, throughout time, fill my heart with Divine Love as
4) I humbly ask permission to open the Divine portal to the highest realm of the Akashic Records for (LEGAL NAME).

5) **Akashic Beings of Light,** guide me to the deepest Truth of my being, releasing any blocks & restrictions to my abundance & highest good.
6) **Great Creatress,** assist me to fully embody my Soul's Light, to fulfill my Soul's purposes, & to heal any accumulated karma.
7) **Surround me** with the enlightenment & wisdom of my Masters, Teachers, & Loved Ones.
8) **Clearly direct** my perspective & actions to those that manifest my Divine Plan.
(Repeat lines 5, 6, 7, & 8 two more times, then say line 9)

9) **Free of all resistance, judgment, and fear,**
I am now filled with Divine love & the Records are open.

Greetings from the Akashic Beings of Light!

Welcome to all who have a voice, to all who have ears to hear, and to all who are developing their skills with prayer.

Prayer is our topic of conversation with you today. Occasionally, We feel your need for some uplifting and playful energy and information. As such, we turn your attention to the Akashic Prayer you use to gain entrance to the Akashic Records, and which aligns you to your Soul, shifting your perception. It is often said that prayer is talking to the Divine. We assert that opening your Akashic Records amplifies your ability to receive Her response.

Prayer offers many options.
- Some days prayer is giving yourself permission to talk to the Divine about your feelings, thoughts, questions, intentions, and hopes.
- Some days prayer is how you let yourself consciously think the things you are already thinking underneath the busy-ness of the activities that fill your life.
- Some days you are pleading for forgiveness, love, and relief from mental, physical, or emotional pain.
- Some days your prayers are attempts to shift your attention to a higher plane, to a topic or an energy wave that matches your spiritual aspirations.
- Some days your prayers are ways of shifting your experience to one of a higher level of pleasure.
- Some days your prayers are flailing about when you feel you are drowning in negative mind chatter.
- Some days are prayer-by-rote days. Your heart and mind are not in it, and you are simply going through the motions hoping to convince yourself of your sincerity.
- Some days you prayerfully list your gratitude's, hoping the words will remind you of all that you are, and should be, grateful for.
- Some days, you're staunchly doing "the right thing", "acting as if".
- And some days, your prayers submerge you deeply within the Great Creatress' presence and you commune with Her.
- As Annie says, "Sometimes the magic works. Sometimes not so much."

There are moments when prayer is a pure expression of limitless inspiration. This happens when the prayer opens your heart wide, free of obstruction to connecting with your Soul and the Great Creatress. These are the days that you find most inspiring and uplifting. These are the days when you feel you are exploring new territory from the expanse of raw consciousness itself. These are days when you are know you are clearly receiving the Great Creatress' messages to you.

Prayer is a doorway to a new energetic pathway, to high vibration, that specifically produces contact with the Great Creatress as a repeatable experience.

Some of these prayers are the way you have been taught to create the inner change that you are instructed to create. Here we are referring to Alcoholics Anonymous prayers that help you realize that all your self-centered, self-will fueled, attempts to manage life have been misdirected. Maybe, just maybe, asking for Divine Help and Intervention will pull you through and beyond the quagmire of the past, or the present moment. So, you pray. You pray, crossing your fingers, hoping it works.

You take the spiritual pill and hope it will relieve the physical ill. This is a conscious act of will, of Trust in the Great Creatress. Trust leads to Faith.

[Annie interjects, Dear Goddess, must we discuss trust and faith in the same sentence? It's too much!]

Trust that a Divine One actually exists. Trust that this Divine One cares enough to listen to a mere mortal in distress. Trust that this Divine One could and would intercede on your behalf. Trust that the Divine One is benevolent toward an imperfect mess such as yourself. Trust that you can leave the spot you are rooted to, frozen by fear, and release the thoughts, concerns, and feelings to this invisible Divine Presence. Trust that the Divine will sort out your tangled thinking and solve your problems in ways that are healing and beneficial for all. Trust that there is a Divine One that has the overall picture and plan in hand and is not befogged by guilt, trepidation, resentment, and remorse! Trust that this Divine Being has your best interests at heart, for truly, no other humans have this grand perspective and selfless intent.

So, it seems we are discussing prayer as an act begetting faith. Prayer that begets faith in the Great Creatress, or the Divine of your understanding.

Prayer truly is an acknowledgement that your humble human mind is unable to produce the desired effect upon your inner dialogue, your perceptions, your actions, circumstances, and relationships with others.

Prayer is surrendering yourself and your personal agenda to the greater good as designed by the Great Creatress. Recognize that you, too, are a receiver of the greater good.

Annie's favorite acronym for G.O.D. is "Gift Of Desperation". Much as in chapter 22 on "Going South", we welcome – even relish – your defining moments of desperation when we are allowed to bypass your childish ego-mind that normally says "Be gone! I don't need your help. I can do this by myself!" Regardless, your prayers are legitimate attempts to consciously surrender to your innocence and ignorance of the Divine's infinite power.

*Prayer is standing before the Great Creatress, offering yourself.
"Here I am. Take me. Show me. Use me. Create good things with me.
Help others through me.
I offer myself entirely, freely, and
with eyes wide open."*

That being done, you go about your day, wash the dishes, do the laundry, and pay your bills.

Prayer is one way to empty the mind of words. This prepares you to receive, to listen, to hear instructions for the day, to know you are sitting in the lap of the Divine. This is what charges your physical energy and raises your vibrational frequency. Listening to the Great Creatress lifts you out of the mud and the mire of repetitive, boring old beliefs, fears, and thoughts that do not add to your aliveness. Prayer opens you to receive the Light and wisdom of your Soul, and to receive the Great Creatress' love and support for you. As you receive Her Divine Love, your needs are met. All your problems wither into nothingness. Peace descends upon you like a warm blanket on a cool evening.

We are particularly gentle with you because humans are still growing past the need for force. We demonstrate that gentleness and Light works effectively by being the example, through demonstration.

We wait until the opening arrives,
it always arrives after a dive,
When the time is right,
you give up the fight.
We send in the Light.
A light so bright
It illuminates the night.
A light so pure
it makes you feel demure.
A light so clean
it feels like a dream.
A Light so fine
It makes you re-align.
A Light so alive,
You can only thrive.
A Light so full
You feel the pull.
A Light so healing
It rights your reeling.
A Light so strong
You follow along.
A Light so highly sourced
You feel the force.
A Light so familiar
It is beyond linear.
A Light beyond good and bad
It removes everything sad.
A Light beyond difference
It melds you in its reverence.
A Light so whole
It resonates with your Soul.
A Light so fine
It can only be Divine.

Be assured, we are listening. The Great Creatress is listening. We have heard your prayers. Be assured, Love, validation, healing, and consciousness as Light, has been generated and surrounds you with each of your prayers.

For now, we bid you adieu.

Please write your responses to these interactive questions.

~ Interactive Questions ~

What has your experience of trusting the Divine shown you?

Give an example of trust in the Divine leading to faith.

Ask your Masters, Teachers, and Loved Ones to show you a past life where faith in the Divine resulted in what you, at that time, considered a bad outcome. Describe the circumstances, the time, who was involved, and what was at stake.

Ask your Masters, Teachers, and Loved Ones to help you release any residual energy from that past life. Describe how the MTOL's accomplish this and how it feels as your MTLO's make this happen.

Ask your Masters, Teachers, and Loved Ones how you can "Lighten Up" about your spirituality?

~ Closing Prayer ~

Thanking the Great Creatress & Her Holy Spirit for Love, protection, & healing received this day,
Thanking the Akashic Beings of Light for guidance,
Thanking the Masters, Teachers, & Loved Ones for wisdom & direction.
The Divine Portal & the Akashic Records are now closed.
Amen. Amen. Amen.

CHAPTER 28

Overwhelming Peace

Channeled by the Akashic Beings of Light

Bringing Forth Soul Consciousness
Akashic Records Prayer
©*Rev. Annie Bachelder 1/22/2022*

~ Opening Prayer ~

1) By the Power of Divine Light within me
2) Come Holy Spirit!   Spirit of Light!   Spirit of Truth!
3) For the highest good of all, throughout time, fill my heart with Divine Love as
4) I humbly ask permission to open the Divine portal to the highest realm of the Akashic Records for (LEGAL NAME).

5) **Akashic Beings of Light,** guide me to the deepest Truth of my being, releasing any blocks & restrictions to my abundance & highest good.
6) **Great Creatress,** assist me to fully embody my Soul's Light, to fulfill my Soul's purposes, & to heal any accumulated karma.
7) **Surround me** with the enlightenment & wisdom of my Masters, Teachers, & Loved Ones.
8) **Clearly direct** my perspective & actions to those that manifest my Divine Plan.

(Repeat lines 5, 6, 7, & 8 two more times, then say line 9)

9) **Free of all resistance, judgment, and fear,**
I am now filled with Divine love & the Records are open.

Greetings and welcome from the Akashic Beings of Light.

There is no greater place to be than where you are now. Sense the ground under your feet. Sense the moment. Alive with breath and the steady beating of your heart. Sense your desire to be at one with the moment. Set aside any resistance you feel. Just BE in this moment. Acknowledge the love you have flowing through you, the tender sensations of caring about, and honoring of, your experience of this moment. Continue to breathe deeply while your shoulders relax. Simply BE for the moment. Nowhere to rush to. No transitioning from one role to another, to force into place. Feel into the deep peace of the moment. This moment. Here. Now. Lean into the now that stretches forever outward in all directions. Release yourself from a box, a form, a role, a task, bound by doing. Feel. Breathe. Pulse. Float.

Allow yourself to place all your concerns into the hands of the Great Creatress. Let yourself float on the moment like a flower in a quiet stream, flowing peacefully onward to a distant destination. Be slow, lay low. Grant yourself the gift of this peace. Nowhere to be and nothing to do. Simply be in the stillness. Let any feelings float up to the surface. A lot of relief. A hint of sadness. Not serious or overtaking. Feelings coming and going, flavoring the moment. Release the demands you put upon yourself. Put down your walking stick. Soften your focus. Let all things that are present for you here be equal, none better or worse, none requiring action or greater attention. Breathe into the soft focus. Loosen the ties that have bound you. Ease up on pressing yourself forward. Relax. All is well. Let go of getting a jump on the next task or problem. Let others be in charge for a while. You get to be. Just be. No requirements for the moment. Revel in the peace. Stretch out in the peace. Soak it up. Absorb all you can of this peace and steadiness. Breathe it into your interior. This peace comes from within you. It always exists within you. When you abandon your cares, giving them to the Great Creatress, this peace is what arises naturally, easily, effortlessly. This peace is who you are. This peace is the ground of your being. No more and no less than any other relevant act or state of being, this peace is who you are. Revel in it. Absorb so much peace that you overflow with peace. Exude it. Radiate peace. You have plenty.

This peace is what is experienced after death. This is the reception you receive after releasing the body. Feel the natural lifting of gravity that has pulled on you for so long. The gravity that has tethered you to the planet.

Notice that even here, in this moment, you have free will to choose. You can be overwhelmed by peace or overwhelmed by doingness, or overwhelmed by love, or overwhelmed by grief and emotions. All of these options can exist within this one moment. Equally present, equally powerful, and potent. However, you, in this moment are choosing peace. Be present to this Soul quality within you.

Let it restore you, calm you, cradle you in safety. Let this moment stretch on into infinity. It is the peace that offers itself to you whenever you need it. You can fall into this peace. It is yours! Embrace it as if it were your pillow. Pull it to you, shaping it to your liking, forming it to that perfect comfort you know so well. Surrender to this peace like a child innocently surrendering to sleep. Drifting off effortlessly. No thoughts. No deeds. No plans. This peace is a part of who you are, at heart, deep within.

And from this place, you experience the greater reality of your existence as a Soul, as peaceful Soul consciousness, a part of the whole of creation. Embody your Soul's Light now, while there is no fight in you, while there is nothing to force, nothing to command, nothing to oversee, nothing to manage. The details are quietly corralled for the moment.

Be grateful for this delicate moment of simply being. A true Sunday morning moment. Of Peace. Of joining the Great Creatress and All That Is. Resting in the bosom of Her embrace. Look around your interior and know that all is well. All unfolds according to Her timing. Surrender and be overwhelmed by Her peace. This is the peace that surpasses all understanding. It is peace felt in the heart. Peace in the mind. The ego is silenced for a blessed moment, and it is restored to balance in this peace. No resistance. No argument to win, no point to prove. Just be. Just be. Dissolve into the breath. Dissolve into your heartbeat. No identity. No individuality. All is all. All is whole. Let this float down to the deepest part of you. Breathe it into the tip of the tailbone. Return at will. Know that you are invited to enter this expansive chamber, as often as you like. Choose it. Be it.

We bid you good day for now . . .

(There are no interactive questions included in this chapter.)

~ Closing Prayer ~

Thanking the Great Creatress & Her Holy Spirit for Love, protection, & healing received this day,
Thanking the Akashic Beings of Light for guidance,
Thanking the Masters, Teachers, & Loved Ones for wisdom & direction.
The Divine Portal & the Akashic Records are now closed.
Amen. Amen. Amen.

CHAPTER 29

Awaiting Divine Timing

Channeled by Anubis

Bringing Forth Soul Consciousness
Akashic Records Prayer
©*Rev. Annie Bachelder 1/22/2022*

~ Opening Prayer ~

1) By the Power of Divine Light within me
2) Come Holy Spirit!   Spirit of Light!   Spirit of Truth!
3) For the highest good of all, throughout time, fill my heart with Divine Love as
4) I humbly ask permission to open the Divine portal to the highest realm of the Akashic Records for (LEGAL NAME).

5) **Akashic Beings of Light,** guide me to the deepest Truth of my being, releasing any blocks & restrictions to my abundance & highest good.
6) **Great Creatress,** assist me to fully embody my Soul's Light, to fulfill my Soul's purposes, & to heal any accumulated karma.
7) **Surround me** with the enlightenment & wisdom of my Masters, Teachers, & Loved Ones.
8) **Clearly direct** my perspective & actions to those that manifest my Divine Plan.

(Repeat lines 5, 6, 7, & 8 two more times, then say line 9)

9) **Free of all resistance, judgment, and fear,**
I am now filled with Divine love & the Records are open.
Greetings and Welcome from Anubis!

Divine Timing, for humans, appears to be highly complex, uncontrollable, and terribly frustrating. Let us discuss self-will and Divine will, and how they can work together harmoniously, resulting in your ability to function efficiently and effortlessly in accordance with Divine Timing. We remind you that the Great Creatress created everything, including self-will and Divine will. Remember also, that She utilizes everything to good purpose in executing her Divine plan, and this supports your Soul in fulfilling Its Divine plan.

Release your personal agenda of forcing a preconceived result into existence. Surrender instead and harmonize with the energy that is already present. For many decades we have been transmitting to Earth the energy of new solutions born on frequencies of harmony, healing, and love for all life forms.

You will find relaxation awaiting you here. As you release your human agenda and walk, hand in hand, with the Divine, you will find the peace, possibility, and openness that is available to you in each moment. Herein lies another opportunity to develop Trust in the Divine.

Awaiting Divine Timing is an exercise in releasing personal will, also known as self-will, in favor of the dynamically inventive and interactive Divine Will. Divine Will always loves and supports everyone, and all life forms. There are no winners or losers. There is simply the NOW moment, filled with healing, love, and life.

Self Will

You might recognize the characteristics below and heed them as a warning.

In its uncooperative form self-will will be pushy, brittle, driven, and demanding others to be different than they are, requiring this and that to be happy, and needing to be treated as special. Self-will steps on the toes of your nearest and dearest. Self-will is often based in fear. Fear of not getting what you want, or someone else getting what you want at your expense. Self-will, by design, is limited and cannot conceive the grand scheme of the Great Creatress. In a duality-based world, self-will takes sides and insists that its side is the only correct side. Self-will injures as it presumes superiority. Therefore, unconscious inferiority, condescension, and judgment are its companions.

Undisciplined self-will is fueled by the insatiable ego's consuming fire.

Self-will is a function of the old paradigm that "everything comes into existence by the sweat of one's brow", through enormous personal effort. Self-will leads with a blind eye to its bulldozing effect on others. Self-will covers up the fragile fear and inadequacy lurking beneath. Self-will causes physical pain through its pushing matter forward like Sisyphus forever pushing the rock up hill. Self-will is a narrow view, and takes not the advice of the wise ones, friends, or concerned observers.

Now, to be fair, there are good reasons, that you have self-will. Self-will gets things done especially in survival situations. Self-will is persistent, and creates an opening, releasing the creative pressure of a Divine idea, well formed, to be executed in present time. Self-will can be the cause of action whose energy is ripe for the taking and is like a dam releasing its flow. The action taken, begets more action within that flow. Self-will seizes the moment and incorporates the resources available to support and further the cause undertaken. Self-will, expressed as self-discipline, performs the tasks required for fulfillment of Divine right action. Self-will may be necessary to implement your Soul's purposes, especially if you feel that the action required forges new energetic pathways and thought lines.

Consciously employed, self-will can be an expression of faith in action.

Self-will may be the way that a problem is exposed for deeper review (such as a character defect), how the deeper Truth is revealed. Self-will may be how the Great Creatress stirs up the status quo in your life and moves your attention and energy into other fields of endeavor.

Self-will may cause the mistake, the error, that eventually becomes the gift inside the problem.

We offer an example of self-will resulting in Divine Will through Annie's relationship with M.

Three short months into the relationship, M wanted he and Annie to get married. Annie agreed, and unconsciously swept any hints of doubt under the rug. This action forced the cracks and fissures in their relationship to grow and demand investigation. Annie willingly dove into marriage attempting to protect M from his fears of Annie leaving him. Annie also wanted to ensure this painful prospect would not happen. In deciding to marry, Annie had to overlook what she was feeling, namely, that M was running away from something in himself, not running toward her. In that situation, Annie felt she had to take an action that protected both of them from their own feelings of discomfort, confusion, and most especially fear. Annie feared losing M, feared the loss of sex, being taken care of, and the safety of being in a committed relationship. Annie had concluded at that because of her disabling multiple sclerosis, "M was the last love on earth for her". M had long been a caregiver for those with disabilities and accepted absolutely Annie's disability due to multiple sclerosis. It made this hardworking, entrepreneurial African American man in a community of whites, a true hero. He found Annie attractive and valuable. These facts were not lost on her. Although unspoken, Annie was also proving to herself that she could overcome racial differences with love and could be accepted by M's family and church culture, however awkward for all involved. Annie later learned that the self-will and fear-driven decision to marry overrode the fleeting need for a larger conversation about what M felt his role as a husband entailed and what Annie felt her role as a wife entailed. This left unsaid what each wanted from, and brought to, the relationship. As a sober person for 8 years, Annie had glossed over M's history of relapse and addiction, ignoring facts that M revealed quite openly.

They had a wedding ceremony five months into their relationship. Six months after the wedding M relapsed, disappearing for three or four days. This caused a fissure to become a chasm, unbridgeable in the end, and ensured their breakup.

This is an example of "what you resist persists!"

Annie stayed in the marriage for another 3 years. It was for her, a doubt-ridden, slowly eroding relationship. Both were resisting the loss of the other as they were growing apart. The loss came to be and could not have been otherwise.

Remember: What you think about the most, manifests the easiest.

This relationship was the swift and seamless execution of a Soul contract between them that was made many lifetimes ago when both were stolen Africans, transported over rough seas in the bowels of a soggy slave ship from Africa to Louisiana. At that time, the two of them made an agreement to stay with one another regardless of the suffering. The Soul contract we based on the agreement "it is better to suffer together than suffer alone". In that past life, the binding elements (the need for protection from suffering) kept them safer together than apart. When the need for suffering as a learning device, and the complex binding elements (surviving slavery) were eliminated, as they were in their current lifetime, the need for one another (masquerading as love) was neutralized in both their consciousnesses, and the relationship naturally floundered. The Soul lessons of self-will masking insecurity and the misunderstanding of dependency as love, was accomplished.

> ### *The gift for Annie within this self-will driven period was that she rapidly matured and stepped fully into her destiny.*

Annie grew into herself. She suddenly stopped fearing her destiny as a channel and spiritual teacher, and no longer feared her own authority and refocused her attention on fulfilling her Soul's purposes. She committed to publicly sharing her gifts, talents, and abilities and ceased using the relationship to insulate her from the world. She learned to register what she is seeing, to acknowledge what she is feeling, to perceive facts clearly, and to speak the unspoken message rather than operate on top of it. She learned to ask the tough questions, the questions that might cause temporary discomfort now, but would be truly painful later if left to fester unspoken.

She learned that she must listen to and trust her inner wisdom. She also realized that she is always loved by her Soul and the Great Creatress. That no person, place, or thing can provide the sense of security she has when she consciously, and overtly, loves, trusts, and respects herself and trusts the Divine to help her fulfill her dreams and Soul purposes. She understood that the outer world reflects back to her in direct proportion to her inner experience.

She learned too, that Divine Timing is a thing to be honored! When the exact moment to leave the relationship arrived, Annie was entirely free to go. The barriers of doubt, fear, and insecurity dissolved. All the doors and windows of opportunity were suddenly wide open. Entirely intact, she confidently walked through them into a bright and fulfilling life and future. She waited for Divine Timing for 3 years. When it arrived, all the details of where she would live, with whom, and how she would do her work were already worked out.

Therefore, self-will is action personified.
Divine Will is the wisdom and timing of the action.

Divine Will

Divine Will knows the play, its players, and the hidden motivations that make up the complex web of interactions with other humans. Divine Will is far seeing and considers the far-reaching effects of, and on, others. Divine Will makes use of the ripples of changes that happen down the line. Divine Will, rightly related, lifts a small action from mundane into Divinely inspired. Divine Will utilizes everything and all of you – spirit, body, mind, emotions, history, and circumstances. Divine Will is intimately familiar with your Soul's purpose and your Soul's constant evolution. Divine Will causes harmony and alignment with your Soul and the Great Creatress so that right action flows forth, even from the most desperate situations.

You experience Divine Will as energetic flow,
the unwavering guidance, and expanded consciousness
of the whole tapestry.

Consciously harmonizing your self-will with Divine Will tames the negative effects of self-will in a similar way that Aikido uses the attacker's inertia to the defender's benefit. Divine Will utilizes your self-will's driven determination to fulfill your Soul's purposes. Divine Will turns regretful mistakes into valuable currency for substantial change. Divine Will supplants the personality's self-will much as exchanging an under-powered engine on a large boat for a far larger engine. All the while, allowing the human to stand at the wheel, hair blowing in the wind, sun shining on her smiling face, believing she is in control.

Alignment with Divine Will releases vast stores of forward
momentum manifesting your Divine plan and your Soul's purposes.

Exercise: How to Align Your Self-will with Divine Will

1. Begin by taking 7 deep inhalations with forceful exhalations.

2. Notice how centered and stabilized you now feel.

3. Embody your Soul's Light, bringing it all the way down through your body from your 8th chakra down to the bottoms of your feet.

4. Your Soul's Light extends in a cone all around you.

5. Ground yourself up to the Great Creatress and down into the balance point of Mother Earth.

6. Allow yourself to receive the steadiness of this double grounding.

7. Become aware of your 3rd chakra, at the apex of your ribcage. This is the center of your self-will.

8. Your self-will extends out from your 3rd chakra like an energetic rope whose fibers seek connection with other humans and with the Great Creatress.

9. Imagine the Great Creatress' Divine Will as an energetic rope end dropping into your viewing screen from above.

10. She is extending Her Divine Will to you and your self-will for connection in the 3rd chakra.

11. Get a sense of Her Divine Will fibers opening and receiving your self-will fibers.

12. You may even feel the Divine Will fibers winding into and around your self-will fibers, blending together easily.

13. You are now connected to Her Divine Will like an infant in the womb is connected to the mother through the umbilical card.

14. Her Divine Will fibers tenderly enter your 3rd chakra blending the two ropes neatly into one woven energy rope.

15. Take a few deep refreshing breaths remaining connected.

16. Observe as Divine Will gently moves around the interior of your body.

17. Where inside your body does Divine Will go? What other parts of your body seem most receptive to blending with Divine Will?

18. Notice how Divine Will is interacting with your brain at the hippocampus and the amygdala..

19. The Great Creatress is harmonizing with your brain's learning and memory centers.

20. Allow yourself to receive Her Divine Will and Divine life force for you and your Soul.

21. Let the energy of this gift flow all around your body from cell to cell.

22. Take another 3 deep breaths encouraging the free flow of Divine Will energy throughout your body.

23. Notice the Light of your Soul in and around you.

24. Thank your Soul. Thank the great Creatress.

25. Place your right forefinger on the center of your left palm creating a memory file of this experience for future use.

26. Take a deep breath and return to ordinary reality refreshed and relaxed.

Divine Will is loving yet firm in its clarity. Divine Will is much simpler than self-will. Divine will is direct, whereas self-will is cagey, secretive, and covert. Self-will works alone, while Divine Will works in a cooperative manner. Divine will is overt, operating in plain view, so ever-present it is background rather than foreground. Divine will requires subordination of self-will, which at first, may feel risky and awkward. Divine Will requires a new way of seeing, a new perspective that ascertains the guidance already in place. Divine Will is flexible providing an abundance of suitable choices. For choose, you will. And choose, you must.

Choice is the name of the game.
Why you choose what you choose are elements to master.

Choosing is about laying out a number of options in plain view. Not just the dualistic, "either or" choices. Be open to the artistic, off path, magical possibilities that may exist.

Choosing is best done with your Akashic Records open so that you
include your Soul's perspective. You can ask the Akashic Beings
of Light or your Masters, Teachers, and Loved Ones to help you.
You can also ask the Great Creatress to reveal the choices she has
already brought you and why She chose these options for you.

Divine Will aligned with personal self-will produces more than a third choice. The combination naturally produces choices that are conducive to achieving the greatest good for the greatest number. Many choices achieve the desired result through a variety of routes.

Harmony results from allowing your self-will to align with Divine Will. Aligning your self-will with Divine Will eases stress, clarifies actions that serve your Soul's purposes, and reduces the angst produced by operating on self-will alone.

Aligning self-will with Divine Will steers you in an optimal direction, toward an inspired end. It is not an end as much as a pause in the continuance.
For, in truth, there simply is no end.

Instead, there are various levels of refinement. Refinement of choices, refinement of connection with the Great Creatress and her Divine Will, refinement of higher purposes, refinement of who is served in the greatest way.

Awaiting Divine Timing is like waiting for a peach to ripen, for the flavor and sweetness to fully develop, and the stone easily is removed.

In summary, we have self-will leading the parade, marching, staff in hand, knees lifted high with each step, intent on having its way, assuming that all the marchers behind her are in step with her lead.

When aligned with, and guided by, Divine Will, self-will eventually results in an easier, more inspired journey, and ensures that the human is in the middle of the pack, playing her part in the Divine Drama.

Self-will, humbly aligned and motivated by Divine Will, promotes fulfillment of ALL Souls' Purposes.

Divine Will presides over all and lovingly lays the groundwork for Divine timing. Divine timing occurs when energy is ripe for action, all the details seem to have sorted themselves out and are lined up so that the action produces the highest result, with the least effort.

And the journey goes on. We bid you adieu for now.

Please write your answers to these interactive questions.

~ Interactive Questions ~

Describe a situation when you were overtaken by self-will and how it worked out.

Describe a time when you were Divinely motivated and inspired to act. How did that situation work out?

What are the hallmarks of your self-will in action?

In what settings are you prone to operating from self-will?

What are the hallmarks of Divine Will as the operating program in your life?

How do you Await Divine Timing in your life?

~ Closing Prayer ~

Thanking the Great Creatress & Her Holy Spirit for Love, protection, & healing received this day,
Thanking the Akashic Beings of Light for guidance,
Thanking the Masters, Teachers, & Loved Ones for wisdom & direction.
The Divine Portal & the Akashic Records are now closed.
Amen. Amen. Amen.

CHAPTER 30

Self-Doubt and Disappointment

Channeled by The Akashic Beings of Light

Bringing Forth Soul Consciousness
Akashic Records Prayer
©*Rev. Annie Bachelder 1/22/2022*

~ Opening Prayer ~

1) By the Power of Divine Light within me
2) Come Holy Spirit! Spirit of Light!   Spirit of Truth!
3) For the highest good of all, throughout time, fill my heart with Divine Love as
4) I humbly ask permission to open the Divine portal to the highest realm of the Akashic Records for (LEGAL NAME).

5) **Akashic Beings of Light,** guide me to the deepest Truth of my being, releasing any blocks & restrictions to my abundance & highest good.
6) **Great Creatress,** assist me to fully embody my Soul's Light, to fulfill my Soul's purposes, & to heal any accumulated karma.
7) **Surround me** with the enlightenment & wisdom of my Masters, Teachers, & Loved Ones.
8) **Clearly direct** my perspective & actions to those that manifest my Divine Plan.
   (Repeat lines 5, 6, 7, & 8 two more times, then say line 9)

9) **Free of all resistance, judgment, and fear,**
   I am now filled with Divine love & the Records are open.

Greetings and welcome from the Akashic Beings of Light.

Self-doubt and Disappointment have many influences on you, which we will explore today. We will begin by exploring self-doubt and let that lead us to exploring disappointment.

In preparation, please do not be too harsh with yourselves when feeling self-doubt or disappointment. Self-doubt is yet another way that the Soul pulls you closer, offering you security, safety, inclusion, and connection. It is your connection with your Soul, of course, that we are most focused upon. Again, We encourage you to embody your Soul's Light for the duration of this discussion. Alignment with your Soul calms the personality, clears the vision, and neutralizes stressors that disturb your peace of mind. Embodying your Soul's Light securely connects you with the Great Creatress, calming you as well.

Let us lovingly remind you, that you are born of love and light, held in a constant stream of love by all the Beings of Light, and you are fostered in your evolution by the infinite points of finer consciousness and Light that exist throughout all time. This is how We love and support you. Open your Spiritual Heart and receive our offerings.

Being thusly prepared, you are ready to address these two subjects.

Self-doubt begins when you are quite young. Beginning when a parent or caregiver said, "Watch out!", the adult's fear is projected onto you. Fear, as you already realize, is the most irresponsibly used, and corrosive, emotional energy. When parents, teachers, and elders become fearful, this is registered in the young human as "your survival is in jeopardy" or more emphatically, "you're going to die!". These anxiety-ridden predictions are broadcast loudly and clearly with varying levels of emotional charge at a time in life when you are testing out new skills and trying all kinds of new things with your body. It is a worthy concern, for instance, when a child climbs a tree without considering the strength of the branch, or the ability to hold on securely to the branch. It is only much later in life that you translate this survival alarm into loving concern. This may occur when you have a child or a pet for whom you are responsible.

Self-doubt has some "early rebel" energy to it. You may express it as being unapproachable. Self-doubt may be a form of resistance. It may be the reluctance to dive in, to swallow a concept wholesale, or buy into it, without engaging your discernment. Self-doubt can also be the intuitive "let's wait and see." Self-doubt may be the indicator that wholesale acceptance without due diligence means that you are preparing to give your power away, or to over-ride, or compromise your inner values.

You may be interpreting your "BS meter" pinging in the red zone as self-doubt.

Self-doubt can function as the expression of reluctance to join in with a new group of people until you have a clear sense of what is acceptable behavior and what is not. In this case self-doubt is self-protective. Self-doubt may make you feel as if you are relegated to the "observers only" sidelines.

Self-doubt occurs when you are uncertain whether an action or direction you are considering furthers a Soul purpose. Your personality questions, "Is this plan Divinely inspired? Or am I making a grave mistake? Or simply wasting my precious time?"

Self-doubt is a symptom of shyness, lack of confidence, of wanting to fit in. Take a moment to realize that you already fit in, quite perfectly, with your very own Soul and the Divine who created you!

We are talking about being comfortable with who you are, in full acceptance of yourself, exactly as you are, fully aligned with your Soul.

Self-doubt has a way of slowing down the decision process so you can determine your truth. You may need to ask for time to consider, or reconsider possible actions, options, or points of view. Slowing down may be the way fear appears, usually associated with familial or ancestral programming, causing hesitation, second guessing, especially when stepping forward into unknown territory. When you are in the midst of a change, or are considering making a change, you may experience the sensation of being held back at the edge of the highway. It may be that your ancestors, and perhaps you also, suspect launching into the "new" is ill conceived and will be worse than the "old", despite your ambitions.

Desiring change and manifesting it requires vision, courage, and confidence.

It requires the willingness to be Divinely led.

First, get comfortable with the change you are consciously consider-ing. Allow yourself to grow into it. Play with creating various visuals and vignettes that represent the new you, and the new situation you desire. With your Akashic Records open, ask your Masters, Teachers, and Loved Ones what they recommend? You are free to ask them how self-doubt pertains to the change you are planning? Is this a Soul purpose? Then, measure your readiness to go forward. You may be awaiting Divine timing.

Are you ready, or not, to act?
Does your energy go up or down when you consider an action?
Are you experiencing fear?
Excitement? Enthusiasm? Caution? Dread?

Do you have to decide right now, or do you have a window of time before a decision or action is required? Energetically, it is best if you take action only when the energy is ripe, when the energy has set up enough to sustain action. Otherwise, it is better to be patient and wait. The idea will still be alive when Divine timing gives you the go-ahead. If not the action will have lost its luster and your attention will be elsewhere.

Self-doubt may be what causes you to revise, refine, recalibrate, and realign with the Divine any proposed action. There may be necessities pushing you toward readiness, for instance, a new job that provides you with the income and benefits required to better sustain yourself and your family. There may also be false starts when the timing is not yet ripe for action. You may have interpreted the delay as your self-doubt, even if it was caused by forces outside your control.

Self-doubt can be a slippery element as it is often
fueled by what you do not want and what you are running
away from.

Consciously create what you do want by identifying, feeling, visualizing, and "pre-experiencing" yourself and others reaping certain rewards. Immersing yourself in what you do want, especially what you want to feel, is a far more potent way to proceed into manifesting the new.

Immersion in visions and feelings of what you want
gives your ancestors a way to adapt to the changes that they,
themselves, have asked you to create for the entire ancestral line.

"Owning" that which you want to create aligns this creation with how the universe works and is a magnetic attractant in creative endeavors. It will cause your holdbacks, such as self-doubt, to surface for inspection, healing, and release. Self-doubt is often interwoven in this process.

The antidote to self-doubt is trusting your Soul and the Divine,
an even more challenging topic! Remember, self-doubt is your Soul
inviting you to embody Its Light and receive love, comfort,
and courage.

The price of admission is placing your trust in the Great Creatress and your Soul. This begets the possibility of disappointment. Herein lies the source of your distrust. Who among you wishes to invite disappointment? Let's investigate disappointment for a moment. Consider writing your responses to these questions:

- How many times have you been mildly disappointed?
- How many times have you experienced deep disappointment?
- How many times have you recovered from disappointment?
- What conclusions did you draw from experiencing disappointment?

Here we remind you that you have experienced disappointment many times, and none of these experiences has killed you. Many of you have had past lives where disappointment was a major theme. This has caused you to fear disappointment and to take drastic self-protective measures to avoid the feeling entirely. Forever.

We are here to tell you that you are made of stronger, more vital stuff than disappointment could ever tear down or destroy. From our Akashic perspective, disappointment burnishes your multi-faceted Soul into the gleaming diamond that it is. Disappointment may be the only way your Soul is able to get you to shift focus, direct your attention and your creative intentions, in a more successful direction.

Often, we Beings of Light reach you during episodes of self-doubt and disappointment. These may be the only opening your ego will permit that affords you safe introspection and consequent healing.

Self-doubt and disappointment have inspired many desperate prayers for self-improvement, direction, healing, and adjustment of circumstances. Self-doubt or disappointment has been the key opening new doors of perception, of creativity, and of prayers for redemption, and communion.

Employing Self-Doubt has been the way many have exercised power over others, for misdirection, and redirection, to leverage the advantage of one person or one group. Long has it been used to "keep others in their place", to repress whole groups, in the name of business, government, and religion. You may have experienced this when someone with more authority than you said:

"Don't be too sure of yourself",

"You don't know what you are doing",

"You don't know what you are saying",

"You're not old enough, smart enough, important enough, intelligent enough to know what you are talking about",

"Do this and we'll all pay",

"You'll go to hell for that",

"You'll make me go to hell for this",

"This hurts me more than it does you",

"You're taking food out of the mouths of my children",

"You are responsible for making me feel ___",

"You're no good,"

"You're no good at anything,"

"You're messing this up for everybody,"

"You people are all ___"

"You never ___"

"You always ___"

"Only bad people do that, think that, say that,"

"Only good people know ___"

"You'll never amount to anything,"

"You always screw things up and I have to fix them."

Release any personal identification with self-doubt as the predictor of future success. Substitute your magnetic Soul's Light as a measuring stick.

Exercise: Blessing Self-Doubt and Disappointment into Nothingness

1. Refresh your Akashic Records by repeating the whole prayer once.

2. Now, take three deep breaths, releasing them forcefully and completely.

3. Use your exhalations to aid in releasing old energy.

4. Embody your Soul's Light.

5. Surround yourself with your Masters, Teachers, and Loved Ones. Allow yourself to receive their loving support.

6. Expand your consciousness and connect with the love, authority, and power of the Great Creatress. She, too, is helping you in this process.

7. Ask your Masters, Teachers, and Loved Ones to help you to whole-heartedly bless and release your limiting history of self-doubt.

8. Whole-heartedly bless and release the unwanted effects of self-doubt throughout time.

9. Whole-heartedly bless and release any self-doubt that no longer serves you.

10. Whole-heartedly bless and release the lifetimes where self-doubt was the obstacle that defeated you.

11. Whole-heartedly bless and release every shred of unwanted self-doubt as it evaporates from you, like steam disappearing in the air.

12. Whole-heartedly bless and release all self-doubt that has been stored in your memory throughout the centuries.

13. Know that everything you bless and release is raw, unformed energy by the universe.

14. Take three deep cleansing inhalations followed by forceful, clearing exhalations. Notice how this refreshes your consciousness.

15. Whole-heartedly bless and release all memories of disappointment in this lifetime. Use your breath to aid this process.

16. Whole-heartedly bless and release all disappointment you experienced in past lifetimes.

17. Whole-heartedly bless and release all disappointment that you experienced while in your mother's womb.

18. Whole-heartedly bless and release all disappointment experienced by your mother, father, and your grandparents.

19. Whole-heartedly bless and release self-doubt and disappointment like steam dissipating in the air.

20. Whole-heartedly bless and release others misuse of your self-doubt for their selfish gain.

21. Whole-heartedly bless and release others misuse of your disappointment for their selfish gain.

22. Whole-heartedly bless and release all self-doubt or disappointment that may briefly appear through reading or seeing images depicting repression and control. These are not you.

23. Whole-heartedly bless and release your past until it is nothingness, until it is completely neutralized.

24. Whole-heartedly bless and release the past in service of your neighbors, your cities, your counties, your states, and all the countries everywhere on Earth.

25. Whole-heartedly bless and release the past in service of Mother Earth.

26. Whole-heartedly bless and release the past until you are no longer separate from the Great Creatress. Until you are neutral space. Pure consciousness. Until you are the Great Creatress.

27. Take three slow, deep, relaxed breaths as you calmly, gently, gracefully re-enter ordinary reality.

28. Thank the Great Creatress and your Masters, Teachers, and Loved Ones for their love and assistance. Thank your Soul, too.

29. Roll your shoulders and open your eyes.

Allow Healing Light to penetrate the space in your body where Self-Doubt had kept you operating in a limited and underpowered way. Allow the Light to repair the damage of the ages, to repair the family formatting that has hindered you. Allow your Soul's Light in the 8th chakra to fill the space between it and the crown chakra. Then allow your Soul's Light to flow throughout your body. Even as we speak these words, even as you read these words, you are updating your own Light and creative energy.

You are giving yourself the freedom and
the courage to choose to venture forward.

It may feel safer to begin with small actions, leading to greater endeavors, as you develop trust and confidence in your Soul and the Great Creatress' infinite love and support for you.

Flashes of the past that support self-doubt may occur. Without self-judgment, embody your Soul's Light, knowing these flashes no longer hurt or control you.

You are driven by the Light of your Divine Soul to reach higher, to source yourself within the auspices, the power, and the authority of the Great Creatress. You are receiving a hand up, restoring you to equality. You are receiving new orders to go forth and be productive, free of fear, judgment, and resistance. You are being authorized by the Divinity of your Soul to live, present in this moment, steeped in freedom and Light, energizing your creations, and your path forward.

Live as your Soul would have you live.
Love as your Soul would have you Love.

Step into the Light. Step into your freedom. This is your freedom to express yourself fully, unreservedly, creatively. Let the whole-hearted blessing and release of self-doubt and disappointment be your ticket into the new. Let the Light of your Soul shine through you, illuminating your next steps forward.

You, your Soul, and the Great Creatress are now,
and have always been, yoked together in creative alignment, forging
the path forward, step by step.

Your Soul is ever confident and never doubts you
or the Great Creatress. Your Soul trusts the Great Creatress to
lead you both to your highest and best good.

Build the small structures that eventually become the bridge, the mansion, the legacy of your Soul's purposes. In these you will find fulfillment of your desires and the evidence of your contributions to others. These are the gifts that heal, uplift, and launch others on their paths to freedom and Soul fulfillment.

We bid you adieu for now.

Please write your responses to the following interactive questions.

~ Interactive Questions ~

Describe a situation where you had overwhelming self-doubt. How did that situation work out?

Describe a moment when you misinterpreted your "BS meter" pinging as the red zone as self-doubt.

Describe a deep disappointment and how that affected your self-doubt.

Describe a moment when you felt inexorably pulled inward to trust your Soul or the Divine.

As you envision a specific change, describe your sense of how Soul Consciousness is influencing you, your feelings, and your action plans.

~ Closing Prayer ~

Thanking the Great Creatress & Her Holy Spirit for Love, protection, & healing received this day,
Thanking the Akashic Beings of Light for guidance,
Thanking the Masters, Teachers, & Loved Ones for wisdom & direction.
The Divine Portal & the Akashic Records are now closed.
Amen. Amen. Amen.

CHAPTER 31

Self-Judgment and Your Inner Critic

Channeled by Anubis

Bringing Forth Soul Consciousness
Akashic Records Prayer
©Rev. Annie Bachelder 1/22/2022

~ Opening Prayer ~

1) By the Power of Divine Light within me
2) Come Holy Spirit! Spirit of Light!   Spirit of Truth!
3) For the highest good of all, throughout time, fill my heart with Divine Love as
4) I humbly ask permission to open the Divine portal to the highest realm of the Akashic Records for (LEGAL NAME).

5) **Akashic Beings of Light,** guide me to the deepest Truth of my being, releasing any blocks & restrictions to my abundance & highest good.
6) **Great Creatress,** assist me to fully embody my Soul's Light, to fulfill my Soul's purposes, & to heal any accumulated karma.
7) **Surround me** with the enlightenment & wisdom of my Masters, Teachers, & Loved Ones.
8) **Clearly direct** my perspective & actions to those that manifest my Divine Plan.

   (Repeat lines 5, 6, 7, & 8 two more times, then say line 9)

9) **Free of all resistance, judgment, and fear,**
   I am now filled with Divine love & the Records are open.

Greetings and Welcome from Anubis.

We are delighted to assist you today as we discuss your inner critic and the intense self-judgment that ensues. We have heard many of you complain about being overly critical of yourselves and this is an excellent time to bring healing to this topic.

> *We suggest you soften your heart toward yourself.*
> *Soften your heart toward your inner critic.*

Soften the way you are judging yourselves and your productivity levels. We remind you that you are not machines designed to run at full throttle for twelve or more hours every day, seven days a week. This is simply impossible, untenable, and is a function of perfectionism. Soften your heart and realize that you have produced significant results. We are here to let you know that you will continue to produce good work, even though the previous outer pressures are largely eliminated, and your goals may have changed with time.

Pacing yourself has its place in this conversation. Also, acknowledging the current season and the planetary influences will help you to accept and adapt. At the time of this writing, in Annie's hemisphere it is springtime. Mother Earth is very busy birthing all manner of creation. The craziness you may be feeling is due to the spring push, the desire of so many species to mate, to procreate, to nest, to grow, to flower, and to fruit. So, pace yourself, Dear Ones. Observe, acknowledge, and ride the river of springtime energy. Let it carry you. Do not resist the flow as it is very potent, and resistance will only tire you.

We recommend doing the tasks that feel right to you, the tasks that flow most easily, at each moment. Be sure to get exercise and sunshine to balance your physical body with the great spiritual strides you are making with the energetic practices in this book. Exercise and sunshine will help you sleep deeply at night and blow off stress accumulated during the day. This will enable you to feel the calm clarity you so eagerly seek.

> *Do not pressure yourself. Bless and release any judgments you have*
> *made about your productivity and progress in any area of your lives.*
> *Pressuring yourself only backfires and causes the energy to work*
> *against you, dulling your creativity and receptivity to our message.*

Give yourself lots of permission. Permission to feel as if you are stitching the pieces together that you previously created along the way. Ask questions that involve and engage the help of your Masters, Teachers, and Loved Ones.

Comparison, a sneaky form of judgment, is not useful. You must allow yourself to be truly authentic and original in your own projects and creations.

Use this book as inspiration as it contains the energy of your entire spiritual support team, including the Great Creatress, the Akashic Beings of Light, the Akashic Records, your Masters, Teachers, and Loved Ones, and your own Divinely created Soul. This combination is a rare and powerful find. Allow yourselves to be educated and utilized as channels for your Soul's purposes, and for the Akashic Beings of Light, your Masters, Teachers, and Love Ones, and the Great Creatress to work in and through.

The perfect motivation is wanting to see a painting like the one you are now painting. Wanting to read a book like the one you are writing. Wanting to create a healing center or class that heals others the way you have been healed.

This motivation flows elegantly into your blossoming ability to channel Divine Light and to allow the Great Creatress to update you, to transform you, and to use you as She sees fit. Readers of this book are asking to be of service to others and to the planet.

Allowing yourselves to be utilized as an instrument for the higher good of all is a privilege. Each of you are the Instruments.
You want to play your part in the Divine symphony in the capacity for which you have been designed. Nothing more. That is fulfillment.

[To have my mission simplified in that way feels like a relief, a weight of responsibility lifted, the incessant perfectionists' need to know "what is next?" is silenced.]

You know you are on the right track if your projects, goals, and visions for being of service hold Light, expand your consciousness, support inclusion, and overall unity with your Soul and the Great Creatress.

Annie has noticed that both she and her clients feel positively gleeful when they follow their inner guidance, follow the suggestions of their Souls, or Masters, Teachers, and Loved Ones. They feel free, on purpose, and alive.

> ### *Your inner people pleaser, inner critic, and your perfectionist are happy, as well.*

You feel on track, useful, helpful, energized, and organized. This is why we have you open your Akashic Records before reading or listening to each chapter and responding to the interactive questions. The Akashic Records, your Akashic Records, exist on a Soul plane of consciousness, an environment free of judgment, fear, and resistance. Embodying your Soul's Light within your open Akashic Records grants you freedom from the personality's limited viewpoint, doubt, fear, and orientation toward merely selfish aims.

> ### *You can take any fears, doubts, and questions into your Records and receive practical and applicable guidance on what to do, how to handle any situation, and why your Soul chose these experiences as learning devices.*

> ### *When your inner critic, self-judgment, and perfectionist cause difficulties it is a reminder to embody your Soul's Light and expand your awareness to include the presence of the Great Creatress.*

When you occasionally forget to embody your Souls Light and link to the Great Creatress you'll become hungry for the Divine Light that soothes as it directs. Your self-judgment, inner critic, and perfectionist will gang up on you and be the only things you can hear. Instead of resorting to your human effort to control this, develop the habit of embodying your Soul's Light, link with the Great Creatress, and do any preparation on the energy planes first. *(see Chapter 12 on Masterful Manifesting)* Perhaps you'll choose to center yourself with one of the many exercises provided in the back of this book.

> ### *You can use self-judgment and your inner critic as your cue to embody your Souls Light, fill in the space between the 8th and 7th chakra's with Soul's Light, and allow your Souls Light to fill your entire body.*

(see Exercise: How to Embody Your Soul's Light in the final chapter "Prayers, Invocations, and Exercises".)

We invite you to call for Divine help. Call for Divine Light to enter you, surround you, and to direct you. Yes. Ask the Divine "What would You suggest I do now?" Willingly follow Its directive.

When you open your Akashic Records and do a reading for yourself, ask the Divine to help you, and open your channel wide so the Divine Light can enter you, flow through you, and hence, to all the people who are receiving Light as it ripples outward. Accept the information you receive. Even more important is to sense the energy you are receiving. Describe to yourself how the energy feels, the color, the vibration, any movement, or notable stillness in the energy. It is not for you to measure or evaluate. Simply receive. Simply receive. You are always doing the best you can at any given moment with whatever skills you have. Your job is to receive the information that the Akashic Records offer you. No matter what, your task is simply to take the love available in your Records and thoroughly receive it. That is all.

Look for the love.
The Akashic energy and the Light of your Soul will do the rest.
Allow yourself to be spacious and receptive.

Your inner critic is often at its loudest when you are over-tired and are trying to force your limited energy to match your human-mind-made "to do list".

And now, a little bit about perfectionism.

Your inner perfectionist wields a razor-sharp blade that can slice you to ribbons with her criticisms. She does not allow for human fallibility, or the need and ability to be flexible when necessary. She is attracted to formulaic answers that are supposed to produce predictable results. She tries desperately hard to fulfill the unfulfillable goals, and schedules. She is trying to create an image that is not authentically your own. An image that has been adopted from the outside, from television and advertising.

Your inner perfectionist needs to witness the image that arises from within and is powered by Divine Light. Otherwise she is insatiable and her bar only rises, never relaxing into whatever "level" is accurate for you in the moment.

Perfectionism is often driven by the Ancestors, especially those Ancestors who felt that "praise ruined the child while the rod of discipline perfected the child". Let us formally unchain these Ancestors from your caboose so that you (and they) travel freely. You can use the Akashic Prayer line at do this:

> **"Akashic Beings of Light, guide me to the deepest truth of my being, releasing any blocks and restrictions to my abundance and highest good."**

It is as if the handcuffs and shackles are unlocked, fall away, and you are free.

All life is a process, an ongoing, ever-changing process. Many of your projects reveal themselves in stages, requiring you to stop at certain points and declare the work good enough for now. The project needs to incubate until the next phase is ready. Then you revisit it later, perhaps many times, when you are refreshed and inspired, to revise, update, and polish the work. There is nothing wrong with that. Here we entreat you to reread chapter 29 "Awaiting Divine Timing" as you will fare better by waiting for the energy to set up, to be ripe and ready or action. This is when the task will nearly do itself.

Finally, we remind you that many thoughts, beliefs, and ideas that feel like "pressure to perform" are vagrant thoughts floating about in mass consciousness and the media. Many are directed to self-employed and sole proprietors as formulaic marketing plans promising "pie in the sky" results. Some are left over from incomplete experiences belonging to the Ancestors. They are not your thoughts, beliefs, and ideas. Mass consciousness thoughts, beliefs, and ideas distort your receiving a clear channel of energy and information. Embodying your Soul's Light, show the Ancestors your vision for your work in process. Show them how it helps you, the Ancestors, and other people, or other life forms. Show the bigger picture of what you are creating. Then show them your wrists, throats, and ankles without the handcuffs. Send the Ancestors love from your Spiritual Heart.

> **Bless and release the mass consciousness. Allow your discernment to kick in. Realignment with your Soul's purposes fills your consciousness. Detach from mass consciousness by remembering "These thoughts are not my thoughts".**

Bringing Forth Soul Consciousness and fully embodying your Soul's Light always permits the best expression of you. It clarifies and purifies the mission of fulfilling your Soul's Purposes. In the process, you have completely forgotten about your inner critic, self-judgments, and perfectionism. The pressures of mass consciousness are neutralized.

We offer an alternative if your inner critic remains the loudest part of your inner dialogue. Take a moment to treat your inner perfectionist or critic as an inner child. With your eyes closed, imagine all your emotions arranged around you as inner children. They are seated in children's chairs or on the floor. Notice the type and condition of the clothing, sex, and ages of your inner children. Ask your inner perfectionist or critic to raise her or his hand and introduce yourselves to one another. Ask this inner child to come and sit on your lap so you can hug, rock, and comfort it. Stroke your inner child's face and surround it with your loving patience. Continue to soothe your inner child until your inner child is calm. Ask your inner child what it is upset about. Listen attentively to everything it has to say. Ask if there is anything else it is trying to communicate. Say thank you, I understand now.

Show your inner child your vision of what you are creating, the person you are growing into, and your Soul's Purpose.

Ask your inner child to assist you in this mission. Show this inner child love and appreciation for its willingness to help you and to be part of your team. Release them. Repeat the process, if needed, with any other inner children.

For now, we bid you adieu.

Please write your responses to these interactive questions.

~ Interactive Questions ~

Describe how you feel when you "Soften your heart toward your inner critic, soften your heart toward yourself".

In what ways does interacting with your inner critic release the pressure to be perfect?

Describe what shifted when you used your inner critic's activity to remind you to embody your Soul's Light.

What thoughts are you discovering are not your thoughts but are mass consciousness?

What happened when you interacted with your perfectionist or critic as an inner child or inner children?

~ Closing Prayer ~

Thanking the Great Creatress & Her Holy Spirit for Love, protection, & healing received this day,
Thanking the Akashic Beings of Light for guidance,
Thanking the Masters, Teachers, & Loved Ones for wisdom & direction.
The Divine Portal & the Akashic Records are now closed.
Amen. Amen. Amen.

CHAPTER 32

Beauty

Channeled by the Akashic Beings of Light

Bringing Forth Soul Consciousness
Akashic Records Prayer
©Rev. Annie Bachelder 1/22/2022

~ Opening Prayer ~

1) By the Power of Divine Light within me
2) Come Holy Spirit!   Spirit of Light!   Spirit of Truth!
3) For the highest good of all, throughout time, fill my heart with Divine Love as
4) I humbly ask permission to open the Divine portal to the highest realm of the Akashic Records for (LEGAL NAME).

5) **Akashic Beings of Light,** guide me to the deepest Truth of my being, releasing any blocks & restrictions to my abundance & highest good.
6) **Great Creatress,** assist me to fully embody my Soul's Light, to fulfill my Soul's purposes, & to heal any accumulated karma.
7) **Surround me** with the enlightenment & wisdom of my Masters, Teachers, & Loved Ones.
8) **Clearly direct** my perspective & actions to those that manifest my Divine Plan.
   (Repeat lines 5, 6, 7, & 8 two more times, then say line 9)

9) **Free of all resistance, judgment, and fear,**
   I am now filled with Divine love & the Records are open.

Greetings and Welcome from the Akashic Beings of Light.

Today, we wish to talk to you about the value of Beauty, to explore and expand your appreciation for Beauty and what it offers you.

Beauty lifts you into a different state. Beauty comes in many forms. There are the external and the internal forms of Beauty. You have judgments about Beauty, especially those that occur when you compare yourself to another person's external Beauty. You say that Beauty is only skin deep. In that form, you are comparing your inner self to another's outer self, and automatically evaluating from that viewpoint. There are some erroneous assumptions in this automatic assessment.

When you notice Beauty in nature, a flower, a sunset, or a sparkling stream, you are taking in that Beauty. You naturally harmonize with it. There is no comparing or evaluating. You stop for a moment to absorb the vision, the colors, the sounds, the smells, the natural movement. Via your senses, you are engaging with that Beauty. You allow that Beauty enter your consciousness. You allow your consciousness be influenced by Beauty. You feel appreciation for that Beauty. You may even adore the Beauty, say in the graceful movements of a treasured horse, or a child at play.

In the appreciation of Beauty,
you momentarily become one with that Beauty.
You become a vibrational match to that Beauty.

All these feelings, these states of being, are what We feel for you as we observe you in your daily life. We observe without comparing or evaluating, We naturally harmonize with your state of being with our energy sensing capabilities. When invited, We engage with your ingenious physical design, and We marvel at your Soul's plan for you. We are amazed at your ability to screen out a myriad of unnecessary distractions, whether you are experiencing life at surface level, are moderately focused, or are singularly engaged with fulfilling your Soul's purposes.

We are sensitive to your needs for Beauty. We observe how Beauty
captures your attention and your respect. To that end,
We often add frequencies of Beauty to our transmissions.

We are aware of your appreciation for the Beauty of Mother Earth's inventions and adaptations. We are sensitive to your desire to create Beauty in art, to include Beauty in and around your home, and most importantly, to experience Beauty in your inner life.

Often, it is during a human being's last moments of consciousness that they remember the moments of extraordinary Beauty, they feel again their appreciation for a beautifully functioning body, and the Beauty of love and kindness. They remember dancing, laughing, gazing into a loved one's eyes, the Beauty of a baby. It is often during the last moments of their life that they realize that access to Beauty, creating more Beauty, and having beautiful experiences are useful, satisfying, and calming to the insatiably hungry personality consumed by acquiring money, power, and influence.

We support you in experiencing as much Beauty as you can during your embodiment. We assist you in experiencing beautiful inner and outer states in your quiet times, in your meditations, in your visual world, in your imagination,
in your daily life, and in your dreams.

Beauty soothes. Beauty stills the racing mind. Beauty captures you. Beauty fulfills a deep human need. Beauty is freeing.

Beauty stimulates change, intrigues the chatty mind, offers a different perspective, opens the imagination to alternatives. Beauty exists deep within the inner self. Beauty is often seen as an expression of the Divine.

Beauty relieves the monotony of the expected. Beauty awakens the spirit within. Beauty inspires creativity in recreating a vision, or through copying nature's offerings. Beauty exists to comfort you, to collude with you, and to focus you.

Beauty can be sensual, visual, stimulating to the senses. You describe experiences in terms of Beauty, such as we had a beautiful day. We watched a beautiful sunset. We felt the power of beautiful waves crashing against the rocks. The athlete's physicality and movements are beautiful. We felt the beautiful state of peace. We enjoyed a beautiful meal with many flavors from around the world. We swam in the beautiful waters. We beautified our home. We listened to beautiful music. We created beautiful treasures. We created beautiful memories. We beautified the landscaping with fragrant flowers and plants that attract and feed beautiful birds, bees, and butterflies.

We urge you to experience Beauty, to appreciate Beauty and to have more Beauty in your life. We seek to help you build and create more Beauty in your life in support of all the joy and fulfillment it brings you. Place yourself in beautiful situations. Make available your own Beautiful offerings.

Beauty is fulfilling and satisfying on so many levels.

We will see you in the beautiful energy planes of the Akashic Records and beyond!

Please write your responses to these interactive questions.

~ Interactive Questions ~

With your Akashic Records open, what do you notice about Beauty in your life?

Describe how you feel when you think about 3 beautiful things or memories?

What are you doing to add Beauty to your life and your surroundings?

How do you feel when you notice the Beauty of your own energy, your connection with your Soul and the Great Creatress?

Describe your experience of 3 beautiful experiences you've had in your Akashic Records.

~ Closing Prayer ~

Thanking the Great Creatress & Her Holy Spirit for Love, protection,
& healing received this day,
Thanking the Akashic Beings of Light for guidance,
Thanking the Masters, Teachers, & Loved Ones for wisdom
& direction.
The Divine Portal & the Akashic Records are now closed.
Amen. Amen. Amen.

CHAPTER 33

By All That Is Holy

Channeled by the Akashic Beings of Light

Bringing Forth Soul Consciousness
Akashic Records Prayer
©Rev. Annie Bachelder 1/22/2022

~ Opening Prayer ~

1) By the Power of Divine Light within me
2) Come Holy Spirit! Spirit of Light!   Spirit of Truth!
3) For the highest good of all, throughout time, fill my heart with Divine Love as
4) I humbly ask permission to open the Divine portal to the highest realm of the Akashic Records for (LEGAL NAME).

5) **Akashic Beings of Light,** guide me to the deepest Truth of my being, releasing any blocks & restrictions to my abundance & highest good.
6) **Great Creatress,** assist me to fully embody my Soul's Light, to fulfill my Soul's purposes, & to heal any accumulated karma.
7) **Surround me** with the enlightenment & wisdom of my Masters, Teachers, & Loved Ones.
8) **Clearly direct** my perspective & actions to those that manifest my Divine Plan.

    (Repeat lines 5, 6, 7, & 8 two more times, then say line 9)

9) **Free of all resistance, judgment, and fear,**
   I am now filled with Divine love & the Records are open.

Greetings and welcome from the Akashic Beings of Light. We offer you this experiential topic and chapter. Be certain to open your Akashic Records before continuing as your experience of the energy, your own Holiness, and Our messages will be heightened..

By All That Is Holy. This includes all that is, does it not? Is there anything created by the Great Creatress that is not Holy? Is there anything about you that is not Holy? Anything about you that is outside of the Great Creatress' blessed creative, healing reach? All That is Holy is everywhere. All that is Holy is inside of you. All that is Holy flows through you at this very moment. You are created by the Great Creatress. It is by Her Holy grace that you live, breathe, and have your being. It is by her Holy design that you are perfectly suited to serve your Soul so that your Soul evolves into ever increasing unity with the Great Creatress.

Unity is Holy growth, Holy Spirit in action, Holy transformation at its best.

Exercise: Becoming Conscious of All That is Holy

1. Take 7 deep, refreshing breaths. Inhale to your fullest point. Slowly and thoroughly exhale.

2. You can experience all that is Holy in your Permanent Atom of Light©. Locate it somewhere in the trunk of your body.

3. Place all of your consciousness inside of that very tiny yet powerful, brilliant spark of Light within you.

4. Sense the Holy energy within the exuberant Permanent Atom of Light. Sense the life packed within it ready to explode into your complete Soul.

5. You might find all that is Holy by embodying the Light of your Soul.

6. This too, was created in Holiness by the Great Creatress.

7. As you embody your Soul's Light you realize it is sustained in Holy Grace by the Great Creatress.

8. You might experience All that is Holy in the depths of your breath as you let yourself simply be.

9. No demands. No requirements. No effort. No muscling anything. No forcing.

10. Just breathe and be.

11. All that is Holy is within you. It is always there. Like an old friend.

12. Kind, patient, accepting. Yes. You know that Holiness, don't you?

13. Sense that Holiness in you. It is perfectly alive and well inside of you.

14. All that is Holy has you, and you have it.

15. The distinctions between you and Holiness are becoming quite blurred, aren't they?

16. Play with that blurriness. Put your attention where both you and all that is Holy reside, in peace, in comfort, in total ease. Rest there.

17. Breathe in that overlap of you and all that is Holy, and you find there really is no difference.

18. You belong to one another. Your essence is made of all that is Holy.

19. This is the strength of your heartbeat, the constancy of your blood flowing, the depth of your breath.

20. This overlap is the Spirit that lives within you that we are calling your Soul, that we are calling the Great Creatress, that we are calling all that is Holy.

21. There simply is no division. All is All. You are in it, part of it, filled with it, surrounded by it, enamored of it, and it is enamored with you.

22. By All That Is Holy, you are that. And that is you. By All That Is Holy. Created in pure innocence. Created divinely.

23. When you die, you transition from being encased in a body to being purely All That Is Holy. You become non-substance. You exist only as consciousness. Soul Consciousness. You transition into Holy peace. You leave the drama, exit stage left. No bow. No curtain call. No standing ovation. Simply released into peaceful All-ness. We are here to welcome you.

We bid you adieu for now.

(In this chapter We are not asking you to respond to any interactive questions.)

~ Closing Prayer ~

Thanking the Great Creatress & Her Holy Spirit for Love, protection,
& healing received this day,
Thanking the Akashic Beings of Light for guidance,
Thanking the Masters, Teachers, & Loved Ones for wisdom
& direction.
The Divine Portal & the Akashic Records are now closed.
Amen. Amen. Amen.

CHAPTER 34

The Power of Story, Past Lives

Channeled by Anubis

Bringing Forth Soul Consciousness
Akashic Records Prayer
©Rev. Annie Bachelder 1/22/2022

~ Opening Prayer ~

1) By the Power of Divine Light within me
2) Come Holy Spirit! Spirit of Light!   Spirit of Truth!
3) For the highest good of all, throughout time, fill my heart with Divine Love as
4) I humbly ask permission to open the Divine portal to the highest realm of the Akashic Records for (LEGAL NAME).

5) **Akashic Beings of Light,** guide me to the deepest Truth of my being, releasing any blocks & restrictions to my abundance & highest good.
6) **Great Creatress,** assist me to fully embody my Soul's Light, to fulfill my Soul's purposes, & to heal any accumulated karma.
7) **Surround me** with the enlightenment & wisdom of my Masters, Teachers, & Loved Ones.
8) **Clearly direct** my perspective & actions to those that manifest my Divine Plan.

    (Repeat lines 5, 6, 7, & 8 two more times, then say line 9)

9) **Free of all resistance, judgment, and fear,**
   I am now filled with Divine love & the Records are open.

Greetings and Welcome from Anubis.

This recounting of one of Annie's past lives demonstrates the power of the Soul's story. Along with the story line, the characters, and the obstacles overcome, underneath, there is a subtext showing the reader or listener the value of having their own Soul's story told as it is in your Akashic Records. As Readers imagine themselves in the consciousness of the various past life roles, the reader or listener plays the role, taking on the personality, qualities, obstacles, strengths, and perspective of the character, as well as the motivations and justifications for actions. This ripples out energetically influencing mass thought to varying degrees, depending on the breakthrough authority and power that the story conveys. That is why it is impactful to share your personal stories of challenges surmounted and creative innovations picked up along the way. This is the Soul speaking, influencing you, validating you, and assisting others.

What the reader relates to, and **can see themselves being** in the role, are ways the Soul communicates Its goals, Its agenda, Its lessons, and Its support. The story, and your story, demonstrates how your human personality is attempting to come to peace with, and unconditionally love, in themselves and in others. As you come to peace with these events and people, this is how your Soul and the human you become more unified with the Great Creatress.

Each breakthrough moment of coming to peace adds another lustrous layer of compassion to the Soul's Light.

Over many lifetimes, layer upon layer of experience, learning, and testing new conclusions and behavior, expands your consciousness. This increases your capacity to love, so that compassion, connection, understanding, and acceptance reign. That is why time spent in the loving embrace and the familial glow of the Great Creatress during meditation is essential to your growth in embodying your Soul's Light and consciousness.

Learn to see yourself as a Soul engaging in fulfilling your Soul's agenda in your daily life.

What you desire to experience is added unto you and your life unfolds with expanded consciousness and more intimate connections with others. Challenges to old, rigid thought, and cultural beliefs become nudges to release and allow further Soul consciousness and exploration.

Codification and over-dependence upon structure works against creativity. The kind of creativity that kicks against the stall to break free, to explore unhindered, discovering the next breakthrough, the next invention, the next innovation, and the distant horizon.

Many of you came into your current life to have
as many personal and spiritual breakthroughs as possible.

The Akashic Records reveals the story of your Soul purposes,
and how your Soul has created settings that spur growth and
evolution.

The Records reveal how your Soul has chosen a specific mother, father, time, and social setting as the incubator of Its new ideas, behaviors, and Its challenges to old forms and beliefs. These human connections and the settings all contribute to pressures that spur you toward unconditional self-love and unconditional love for others. The Soul is using all these details to pour Its energy into material form, to carry on evolving, cycle after cycle.

The Akashic perspective is always the long view, the multiple lifetime
view, the Soul growth view. This is communicated on waves of love
and compassion.

Past Life – Annie's Introduction to Anubis

Annie and Anubis have traveled a mighty road, suffered, and surrendered to Divine Will as the force and source of all good. Through many millenniums together, you have grown into a sane, positive, productive person. You have grown into one who expresses the Light within and without. Along the way, the energy in the Light has been tempered in accordance with what you could assimilate and radiate at the time. You perceive the brilliance of Anubis' Light as profound because you can subsume and reflect this volume and intensity of Light.

Let Us tell the story of how and where Our work with you began.

You have been subtly asking about the image you received of 12-year-old twins, one female and one male, peeking around the corner of a pyramid in ancient Egypt. You both were in service to the Priest who embodied the spirit of Anubis during embalming ceremonies. This is when you first became consciously aware of Anubis and began your deliberate connection to this particular Being of Light.

The twins operated as one identity, intrinsically knowing that there were circumstances where a female could enter a location or environment without suspicion, or when a male could best accomplish the task. As youths, the two of you could move about largely undetected. As twins, you could maintain greater consciousness than as "separates", as you called the other humans. Your shared identity and consciousness gave you a stable balance of female and male energies and perceptivities. These capabilities were not lost on the embalming Priest who embodied Anubis, who employed you. In fact, the Priest secretly felt that you twins made his work more connective and effective than when he worked alone. He never let on about this convenient fact because he felt that it would diminish his power, status, and authority in your eyes and in the eyes of the community in which he served as head of the embalmer's guild.

In the positions of "Fetch and Hold" the two of you secured a steady supply of cats, papyrus paper, rocks, soils, plants for colorful paints, herbs, gauze, and various oils used in embalming. What was most compelling for the female twin was the procedure of channeling Anubis. When the twins squeezed themselves into a dark corner to observe silently and unobtrusively, their presence was entirely forgotten.

As spells were cast, and spirits of the dead conjured, the twins sensed quite clearly the energies and the nature of the spirits invoked. The filters common to humans in current times were not present. The culture of ancient Egypt was far more alive with the spirits commonly found in nature, in plants, animals, the water, the weather, sun, moon, and stars.

After a time, the male twin learned the Priest's system of writing using symbols and characters that conveyed the invocations, compounds, and recipes he used. The male twin became obsessed with writing down as much as he could. He taught the female twin to read the symbolic writing so she could check for accuracy the healing ointments and herbal cures the local healers gave out. Some of these healers were uneducated, untrained, and inexperienced. Their ignorant cures were more "snake oil" than beneficial, and some were downright harmful. In this way, the female twin served the people of the region, ensuring that poisonous combinations and uselessly inactive ingredients were avoided. Many women in the area were saved from disaster through ingesting bad combinations or giving family members the wrong prescription. As the female twin's success grew, her popularity widened. She was known for humbly substituting poor quality or inappropriate herbs with better choices, often at her own expense.

When the twins were adults, the male twin died in a boating accident on the Nile. The old Priest (who, by the way, was Annie's father in her current lifetime) eventually became elderly and was failing, the female twin ultimately took on the role of Priestess to Anubis, the first female in Egyptian history to do so. Much recognition was given to the anomaly, some of it threatening and judgmental, even though her work was of the highest quality. This is one of the strongest lifetimes where Annie, in her current lifetime, learned to be circumspect in calling attention to herself, as some of the consequences were hurtful and damaging. At one point, her right hand was amputated by jealous priests, to punish her and reduce her powers. This only heightened her awareness of energy, strengthening her conjuring, spells, her healing abilities, and embalming skills, making them more potent. Her work eventually became the "industry standard", as you would now say. Reluctantly, the loss of her hand forced her to employ and mentor two junior assistants, one male and one female, to aid her in two handed procedures. She trained them in her methods, passing along her knowledge for the benefit of future generations. As you can imagine, it took some experimenting to finally connect with suitable assistants who had the consciousness, innate interest powered by ability, and integrity needed to excel in this most important and rather public role.

This past life is the source of Annie's inner setting that draws her toward herbs rather than modern pharmaceuticals, and to acupuncture rather than surgery. This past life is also the source of some of the health issues she has experienced in her current life regarding digestion and a broken right wrist.

Dear Readers, We bid you, at this moment, to surround with love, all your physical ailments and discomforts that occur in present time.

> *Release them to the Great Creatress. Be free, dear Ones, and effort not*
> *in all you do, for We are assisting you with healing at all times.*

Annie honors Anubis by being the conscious channel for us. Anubis is part of Annie's assemblage of Light Beings, voluntarily assisting her and those for whom she channels. To all Our Readers, please pay homage to the other Beings of Light who have walked the path before you, and prepared the way for you, making your life full, richly satisfying, and far reaching.

We bring this story to your attention to inform you that as a Soul, you live multiple human lives interspersed with equally important un-embodied lives. All these experiences add to your essence in layers of luster and iridescent colors like an oyster generating a pearl. Whether it is a physical human life on Earth, or a period of study and practice in other consciousness dimensions under the tutelage of Masters of Light, energy, and consciousness, each life is lived from where you left off in consciousness.

In some past lives, the details are not important. However, the overall energy, theme, and the qualities learned and expressed, are of interest. In the story of Annie's past life just recounted, our Readers can see how, in past lives, you learn to love and appreciate both female and male perspectives, female and male body types, and the story lines of females and males. Our Readers learn how to breakthrough traditional walls separating the sexes and separating the social classes. Most of all, you learn through experience, and through attempts to apply your learning for the higher good of all.

As the female twin, Annie knew that caring for females equaled caring for all family members because it was largely, but not exclusively, the females who produced meals, and cared for the sick and the elderly. As the male twin, there was an unspoken social point of view that males were educated to their station in life, within in their social class, so that they could become teachers, family heads, and government ministers. So, of course, the male twin became that which was expected of him and then some, through his symbolic writing and the documentation of spells, conjuring's, and herbal concoctions.

Annie also learned to connect with and channel Anubis. This is a consciousness skill she carried with her from that time forward. In other lives she connected with Angels, Forest Sprites, and Fairies, Norse Goddesses and Gods, or other culturally acceptable Spirits. Annie learned the joy of working with others toward a common goal, and to work in partnership as twins with both women and men. Annie learned that partnership and groups make the work fun, doable, and allows others to bring forth their skills and make their unique contributions a part of the whole. Annie learned to share consciousness as twins which aids in channeling and doing readings. Annie learned that uplifting service to others was key to satisfaction in life and to fulfilling her Soul's plan.

We bid you adieu for now.

Please write your responses to the interactive questions below.

~ Interactive Questions ~

We recommend that you repeat the opening Akashic Prayer in order to perceive the answers to the following interactive questions. Read the instructions all the way through, then close your eyes and receive the answers to one question at a time. Make detailed notes.

Ask the Akashic Beings of Light to show you an informative past life. Assume that what you are perceiving through your sense of knowing, your physical sensations, images, words and phrases, flashes, and intuitions are the correct information.

- Please describe in as much detail as possible the setting, the personalities present, the time in history, the feelings, the actions, and why this past life is being shown to you.
- Are you male or female? What tells you this?
- Where on Earth are you located?
- Or are you in between embodiments? Or on another planet or star?
- What is your social status?
- How are you dressed?
- Are you inside a building that you can describe?
- Describe any other details that flesh out the vision, sensations, and sense of knowing that you have about the past life.

- What is the higher purpose of the past life you are being shown?

- Why is it important?

- What were the important lessons learned?

- How did you learn them?

- Start your descriptions with the words, "I get the sense that . . . " or "It feels as if . . . " or "It seems like . . . "

- Keep asking the Akashic Beings of Light, or your Masters, Teachers, and Loved Ones if there is more that you can know about this past life?

- Ask your MTLO's to help you release everything from the past life that no longer serves you in present time.

- Thank the Akashic Beings of Light for their assistance and close your Records.

~ Closing Prayer ~

Thanking the Great Creatress & Her Holy Spirit for Love, protection, & healing received this day,
Thanking the Akashic Beings of Light for guidance,
Thanking the Masters, Teachers, & Loved Ones for wisdom & direction.
The Divine Portal & the Akashic Records are now closed.
Amen. Amen. Amen.

CHAPTER 35

Resistance, Judgment, and Fear, Ancestral Healing

Channeled by the Akashic Beings of Light

Bringing Forth Soul Consciousness
Akashic Records Prayer
©*Rev. Annie Bachelder 1/22/2022*

~ Opening Prayer ~

1) By the Power of Divine Light within me
2) Come Holy Spirit!   Spirit of Light!   Spirit of Truth!
3) For the highest good of all, throughout time, fill my heart with Divine Love as
4) I humbly ask permission to open the Divine portal to the highest realm of the Akashic Records for (LEGAL NAME).

5) **Akashic Beings of Light,** guide me to the deepest Truth of my being, releasing any blocks & restrictions to my abundance & highest good.
6) **Great Creatress,** assist me to fully embody my Soul's Light, to fulfill my Soul's purposes, & to heal any accumulated karma.
7) **Surround me** with the enlightenment & wisdom of my Masters, Teachers, & Loved Ones.
8) **Clearly direct** my perspective & actions to those that manifest my Divine Plan.
(Repeat lines 5, 6, 7, & 8 two more times, then say line 9)

9) **Free of all resistance, judgment, and fear,**
I am now filled with Divine love & the Records are open.

Greetings! We are the Akashic Beings of Light.

"There is no place like home." Your home is where your heart is, and we encourage you to activate your Spiritual Heart as you partake of the information and energy of this chapter. *(Please see chapter 11 "Your Spiritual Heart".)*

Resistance, judgment, and fear are the underpinnings of self-centeredness.

Self-centeredness interferes with your connection to your Soul and to the Great Creatress. These three emotions, or states of consciousness, are so tightly compressed that they rigidly perpetuate all kinds of character flaws, faulty thinking, distorted perspectives, and erroneous conclusions. We fault you not for experiencing them, as they supply contrast, and illuminate certain choices.

To transform these feelings, first, you must be in acceptance of these feelings.

This an inescapable part of Earth life. You must feel them fully. Take them to your Spiritual Heart much as you would a fussy child needing your attention. Fussy children are very persistent and so are resistance, judgment, and fear. We do not fault you for having these experiences. We suggest being kind to yourself and not criticize yourself for having them. Instead of resisting and blocking these feelings, look at them kindly, in a detached way, and say hello. Acknowledge these feelings as if you are taking attendance in class. Thoroughly look at each feeling as if meeting it for the first time, acknowledging the feeling, and gathering facts.

Let us examine how these three emotions operate in your energy, awareness, and life experience.

Resistance. One of Annie's favorite sayings is, **"What you resist persists."** In other words, resistance begets more resistance. You'll end up tangled in resisting your resistance. Physically, resistance implies tension. Digging in your heels like a donkey that refuses to move in the direction you choose. You may experience tightening in your body, your breathing becoming shallow. You may have the sensation of your jaw clamping down and biting back your words. Physically, your body is alerting you to a trampled boundary, a conflict, frustration at not getting "your way", or a breach of safety. Or you may be experiencing a moment of extreme, or hardened, inflexible self-will. Your inner child may be saying, "I don't wanna and you can't make me."

> ***"Hold on there one moment!"***
> ***is resistance's message.***

When the body signals resistance, fully embody your Soul's Light. Soul Consciousness can lovingly interact with you. Imagine your Soul saying,

"What's the problem, honey?"
"What's the danger?"
"What feels off?"
"What do you need?"

Have this conversation whenever your sensory warning system signals you, whenever you feel "triggered". When you greet resistance without argument in this gentle manner, you're able to receive helpful answers, and an energy shift. Your attitude of gentle curiosity invites your willingness to come forward so you can apply the information received. Connected with your Soul, you initiate a new response pattern that brings your Soul and physical self together in cooperative unison, conscious alignment, for your highest good, even in difficult moments.

> ***Resistance may indicate that the energy has not set up sufficiently for action to be taken on a task, or for an event to materialize on the earth plane.***

> ***If the energy for action has not yet set up, patience is indicated. Your Soul may be asking you to grow in some way that allows you to truly receive and accommodate that which you desire to manifest.***
> ***Or something better!***

Using the "Of Course treatment" is helpful. Saying to yourself, "Of course, I feel resistance. Of course, I am balking. Of course, I don't want to ___. Of course, I feel ___". Name each feeling you have in quick succession using the "Of course" format. This allows you to acknowledge and feel each feeling while neutralizing the emotional charge.

The "Of Course treatment" is one of the fastest processes We recommend for acknowledging your feelings, changing your energy, your perception, or your experience.

Thank you, Dr. Linda Howe, for introducing Annie to it.

Judgment. When judgment kicks in, often humans will catch themselves being judgmental toward others and then castigate themselves for being judgmental. This pattern creates the classic "double bad syndrome". Judging yourself for being judgmental digs a hole twice as deep out of which you must now climb. Here we advise letting yourself out of what Annie calls "the judgment jail". *(See Exercise: Release Yourself From Judgment Jail BELOW and at the back of the book.)*

Your Soul neither judges nor condemns you.
Neither does the Divine.

We suggest asking yourself in what way have you judged and compared yourself?

Another popular saying is, "If you can spot it, you got it." In other words, "That which I accuse others of doing, I also do." **[Think: forgetting to use turn signals while driving.]** Here we have the great ego leveling. Just balanced, factual, information. This is self-appraisal in a very neutral fashion. When you notice that you are judging yourself or others, embody your Soul's Light, filling in the gap between Soul chakra and crown chakra. *(See Exercise: How to Embody Your Soul's Light at the back of this book.)*

Feel your Soul's Light in your heart.

Silently say to yourself, "I forgive myself." Or "Forgive me." Then begin again. Notice that we list "forgiving yourself" before "forgiving others". This is because as you forgive yourself, so you fill your forgiveness bank account, and you have more wherewithal to forgive others. The rigidity of judgment softens, and you become more flexible. Annie was known for her self-judgment, cruelly punishing herself so that any punishment others might impose would be far less painful than what she had already inflicted on herself. She was trying to prepare herself or "to beat others to the punch".

Exercise: Release Yourself from Judgment Jail

1. Breathe deeply 7 times, inhaling into your low belly first, then filling your upper chest. Exhale forcefully and completely. You may have to push out the last bit of old air.

2. Now feel the relaxation that automatically follows.

3. Embody your Soul's Light. Notice that your consciousness changes from busy mind to relaxed, quiet mind.

4. Bring to mind a moment where you judged another person.

5. Without judging yourself for doing this, notice how fast your mind raced to judgment.

6. Know that your mind is designed to judge, to assess, to evaluate, as a preprogrammed survival mechanism.

7. Your mind is designed to name and classify dangers. That's its job.

8. Rather than resisting this programming, notice that you are choosing to have a different experience right now.

9. Ask yourself, "What are my options?"

10. The road to freedom is through acceptance, and through "expanding to include" that part of you which automatically judges.

11. Feel how your body relaxes when offered the option to accept your pre-programmed response to the other person. Now expand to include the whole scenario, judgment, and all.

12. Your Soul's Light gets brighter and larger in this state of relaxation. See if you can now feel, or sense, the presence of the Great Creatress.

13. Recall another occasion where you judged yourself intensely.

14. Feel the judgment in your body, your mind, and your heart.

15. In your inner mind you may be seeing, or feeling yourself trapped, as if in jail, the judgment jail.

16. Accept fully for this moment, that this is your experience when you judge yourself. Sit in this feeling for a moment. There will be a point where the sensations of judgment loosen and lift.

17. Stay with your experience.

18. Look at the bars that make up your judgment jail. You may feel the shackles around your wrists and ankles falling off.

19. The bars fold down or dissolve. You easily step out into freedom.

20. Take a moment to forgive yourself and anyone else involved.

21. Gently accept your new experience, accept the softening in your heart, and accept the friendly tone of your inner voice.

22. Thank your Soul. Thank the Great Creatress.

Go on about your day.

Fear, of course, is a powerful component of situations involving resistance and judgment. Fear often hides and disguises itself behind resistance and judgment.

Fear may be the sensation of your Ancestors pulling back your reigns to slow those of you who are on a faster growth path than your forebears. Oddly, it was your Ancestors who selected you to be the front runner, blazing the trail that they would later follow.

When this is the case, use the following exercise to clear the old programming and initiate a new era.

Exercise: Clearing Excessive Ancestral Influences

1. Take 5 deep cleansing breaths to refresh and organize your energy.

2. Embody your Soul's Light until your Light extends beyond your skin and you're ready to add in your connection with the Great Creatress.

3. Get a sense of two lines of ancestors forming behind you.

4. Notice whether the ancestral line behind your left shoulder are from your mother's or your father's line?

5. Converse with these ancestors, exploring the fear programming that began with them. Simply gather facts and examples of the kinds of fear that were promoted in the ancestral line.

6. What time in history did this pattern of fear begin?

7. Ask your ancestors, what was the original danger?

8. Which of your ancestors began this fearful reaction?

9. How did it personally serve this ancestor at the time?

10. How was a fearful reaction helpful to the ancestral line?

11. Why are they afraid for you now?

12. How are they trying to help you?

13. It's time to release the old energy pattern. Simply let the old energy leave your breath, your body, your consciousness.

14. Ask your MTLO's for assistance if you need it.

15. Notice how your energy shifts as your release the old programming.

16. Acknowledge that you accepted your ancestor's nomination to be the trail blazer leading the whole line to a better future.

17. Take a moment to form a new agreement with your ancestors so that you, and those who follow you, have greater freedom to explore, to grow, and to take big, confident steps forward, for the good of the whole ancestral line.

18. Show or describe to the ancestors the higher purpose of your intentions and activities.

19. Show them what your Soul wants for you.

20. You may need to take a firm leadership stand and tell them they are no longer in charge of your spiritual growth. As agreed, when you designed this life, they are to follow your lead.

21. Ask for their cooperation and support in experiencing a life of achievement which the ancestors previously felt was too risky, daring, or beyond your capabilities.

22. Let this shift in energy settle into your consciousness and body.

23. When that feels complete, thank your ancestors, your Soul, and the Great Creatress for a job well done.

Spiritual transformation of blockages is always at the heart of our message for humanity. Hence, we offer two of Annie's favorite acronyms for Fear:

Future Events Already Ruined
or
Feeling Excited And Ready

Feel the energy of these two statements. In the first acronym you can feel the fear of the future. The second acronym clearly transforms the former into excitement and readiness. Whenever you feel fear, embody your Soul's Light, then ask which acronym best fits your situation? Ask that any residual fear be released now. Let yourself open to the excitement you are experiencing.

We bid you adieu for now.

Please write your answers to the following interactive questions.

~ Interactive Questions ~

You just did two exercises. What was the issue that involved judging yourself?

How does it feel to be released from judgment jail?

What ancestral fear was presented in the second exercise?

How are your ancestors responding to your leadership?

What are you resisting at this time?

How are judgment and fear involved with your resistance?

~ Closing Prayer ~

Thanking the Great Creatress & Her Holy Spirit for Love, protection, & healing received this day,
Thanking the Akashic Beings of Light for guidance,
Thanking the Masters, Teachers, & Loved Ones for wisdom & direction.
The Divine Portal & the Akashic Records are now closed.
Amen. Amen. Amen.

CHAPTER 36

The Value You Bring to Your Soul

Channeled by the Akashic Beings of Light

Bringing Forth Soul Consciousness
Akashic Records Prayer
©*Rev. Annie Bachelder 1/22/2022*

~ Opening Prayer ~

1) By the Power of Divine Light within me
2) Come Holy Spirit! Spirit of Light!   Spirit of Truth!
3) For the highest good of all, throughout time, fill my heart with Divine Love as
4) I humbly ask permission to open the Divine portal to the highest realm of the Akashic Records for (LEGAL NAME).

5) **Akashic Beings of Light,** guide me to the deepest Truth of my being, releasing any blocks & restrictions to my abundance & highest good.
6) **Great Creatress,** assist me to fully embody my Soul's Light, to fulfill my Soul's purposes, & to heal any accumulated karma.
7) **Surround me** with the enlightenment & wisdom of my Masters, Teachers, & Loved Ones.
8) **Clearly direct** my perspective & actions to those that manifest my Divine Plan.

   (Repeat lines 5, 6, 7, & 8 two more times, then say line 9)

9) **Free of all resistance, judgment, and fear,**
   I am now filled with Divine love & the Records are open.

Greetings from the Akashic Beings of Light.

Now that you have your Records open, We affirm that, as your Soul's precisely chosen human being, you bring immeasurable value to your partnership with your Soul and hence, with the Great Creatress. (She is always your ally.)

The value that you bring to your partnership with your Soul cannot be overestimated. Your Soul requires your participation and free will to evolve into greater oneness with the Great Creatress.

> *Your Soul has a deep need to grow, to experience,*
> *to expand, to evolve, to select and reselect,*
> *giving you many opportunities to exercise your free will.*

Your Soul requires your human participation to evolve. Out of nearly 8 billion possibilities, you were specifically chosen by your Soul as the perfect partner to execute Its purposes. Your personality, body, race, family, social status, gender, and geographic location were all consciously chosen by your Soul. You are the experience module for your Soul. This plan necessitates your human participation. *(Please see Chapter 7 on "How the Soul is Constructed).* Your Soul treasures you. Your Soul has never regretted choosing you as Its human counterpart. Your Soul is never too tired or too busy to attend to your needs and your questions. Utilize this partnership to your advantage regarding questions about love, health, wealth, career, and relationships.

> *Open your Records and communicate with your Soul and the*
> *Great Creatress. Maximize the opportunity to know and grow from*
> *question-and-answer sessions. Tap into these rich resources and,*
> *with practice, a slow drip of information becomes a waterfall.*

Contrary to popular notion, this side-by-side partnership is a two-way street, not a top-down power structure. You can communicate with your Soul. You do influence your Soul. You can enlarge your perspective through conscious inquiry in your Soul's Akashic Records regarding the details of the past, even past lives as we have explored in previous chapters. This inquiry positively influences your experience of the present and positively changes your future.

Changing or healing your perspective of the past and the present positively influences your how your future unfolds.

This changes your perspective, and makes your energy more flexible. Can you feel the energetic fabric of your Akashic Records shifting and adjusting as you take that point in? Through Akashic Records inner work, you'll discover that your Soul planned certain events to allow you to step out of being a victim of other's actions. This teaches you to love yourself unconditionally, and your perspective shifts significantly.

You may even discover that during your Soul's planning stage for your current life, your Soul asked another Soul (who loves you very much) to play the important role of "bad person" just for this purpose. This "bad person" is not at fault. They are merely acting out the part that, for your benefit, your Soul requested of them.

We often advise small shifts are as effective, and affective, in making changes in your life. For example, your Soul may determine that you experience a physical condition that requires specific care and tending of the body. This will allow you to slow down, and be present to your physical needs, to answer your Soul's call, and expand your consciousness upward. This will be accomplished as predetermined. If you choose to fight this condition, to resist this requirement for extra care and consciousness, you will experience the Universal Truth "What You Resist Persists". The probability is increased that your physical condition will deteriorate. Sooner or later, whether in this life or in another, your Soul's plan will outpace your resistance. You will surrender and turn inward toward your Soul, discovering your partnership with It, and with the Great Creatress.

Mind you, there are neither "gold stars" or "demerits" regarding your choices.
Simply the consequences of your choices.

You could choose to flow with this river of experience. You could respond calmly, objectively, from a place of loving Soul consciousness. You could listen to and love your body. Give it what it needs. You could offer your body unity instead of a fight, then you will experience another Universal Truth:

"That which you love harmonizes with the highest vibration available."

In your partnership with your Soul, should you choose to affirm your separateness, then it is so. Should you choose to affirm your connectedness, then it is so. Should you choose to affirm your neutrality, it is so. As a human, you will experience multiple permutations of connectedness beginning with one with one, then one with tribe, one with nation, and all the way to One with All. You experience this from the female viewpoint and from the male viewpoint. You experience this from the Child's perspective and from the Crone's perspective.

Every embodiment of your Soul's Light and consciousness enhances your Soul. Your Soul becomes more vigorous, evolved, refined, and potent.

Every embodiment of your Soul's Light and consciousness deepens your partnership and unity with your Soul. As you and your Soul unify, your connection with the Great Creatress is personified, and the Holy Trinity kicks in. You + Your Soul + Great Creatress = All. Or more accurately, as much Vast Love that your consciousness can accommodate at that moment.

As you are unified with your Soul, you communicate as your Soul. You can communicate with other Souls, and other Souls can communicate through you. This skill goes far beyond language. It can go beyond communication as you know it. It transforms into communion with the Great Creatress, and into Oneness, and beyond. This is what you bring to your partnership with your Soul. Endless potential. Infinite possibilities. Harmony with everything and everyone. A vehicle for expression of your Soul and the Great Creatress.

When you are Soul unified, you trust the Great Creatress. You experience Her compassion, love, and safety. In truth, you always have this safety, but your human mind may throw in some objections such as self-doubt, unhappy memories of the past, or religious training that muddies the water. If you pause and regroup, embodying your Soul's Light and consciousness, radiating your Soul's Light throughout your whole body, you can re-establish your unified state quite easily. This may be the way that your Soul causes you to practice **Bringing Forth Soul**

Consciousness. By now this simple process is nearly instantaneous and requires only a quick thought. *(See Exercise: How to Embody Your Soul's Light" at the back of the book.)*

Once you feel your Soul's Light, relax into Its love and care for you. Your Soul knows that fulfilling Its agenda for you requires all your capabilities and that you acquire new ones.

Many of you truly wouldn't have your life be any other way and that is exactly as it should be. You are harmonized in your partnership with your Soul. In this harmony, you are loved, appreciated, accepted, validated, encouraged as you continue your journey. In your Soul's embrace you are restored to sanity, rejuvenated, and filled with the necessary energy to continue.

Again, you can ask anything of your Soul, your Akashic Records, the Akashic Beings of Light, and the Great Creatress. You are welcome in all territories, categories, and arenas of knowledge. You were never meant to be kept in the dark, in ignorance.

You were created to be enlightened, educated, aware. That is part of your human development and the consequent evolution of your Soul.

So, ask away! Your questions are tremendously valuable devices that open to larger understanding, an enlightened perspective, a more loving, and accepting perspective.

Our intention is that each chapter of this book clearly delivers the message that you and your Soul are inseparable. That you are harmonized, consciously bonded, in a unique way, specific to your combined, integral being. You are loved and respected for your contributions and the parts you play in your own and others' lives.

It is from this perspective that we challenge you to uncover your deepest questions and to ask them in earnest. Perhaps the interactive questions below would reveal the most information in your Akashic Records.

We recommend that you ask these questions several times in separate openings of your Akashic Records and that you write down the answers.

Ask any subsequent questions that arise from the forthcoming information and write the answers to these as well. Then close your Records. Put this aside for a minimum of two weeks and then reread your notes.

We bid you adieu for now.

Please write your responses to these questions designed to help you master partnership with your Soul and your facility working in the Akashic Records. You can ask anything. You decide. Experiment with these questions.

~ Interactive Questions ~

Try phrasing your questions this way: "Please guide me regarding _____."

"What would my Soul have me do about _____?"

"Please show me how to love _____?"

"Why is ____ needed on my Soul's path?"

What small step can I take that fulfills my Soul purpose today?

What one thing heals (or strengthens) my body the most, at this time?

How does my Soul envision the next sequence of events within a specified amount of time (day, week, month, year)?

How does forgetting my Divine Origin help me evolve?

How does rediscovering my Divine Plan, piece by piece, lifetime by lifetime, help me?

What have I learned by giving away my authority, autonomy, and sovereignty, only to reclaim it over and over again?

How can I lovingly and effectively operate outside of the limitations of time and space?

Name the gifts, talents, and abilities that are most important to fulfilling my Soul's purposes.

How is my Soul utilizing the above gifts, talents, and abilities to forward Its objectives?

~ Closing Prayer ~

Thanking the Great Creatress & Her Holy Spirit for Love, protection, & healing received this day,
Thanking the Akashic Beings of Light for guidance,
Thanking the Masters, Teachers, & Loved Ones for wisdom & direction.
The Divine Portal & the Akashic Records are now closed.
Amen. Amen. Amen.

CHAPTER 37

Soul Connection

Channeled by the Akashic Beings of Light

Bringing Forth Soul Consciousness
Akashic Records Prayer
©*Rev. Annie Bachelder 1/22/2022*

~ Opening Prayer ~

1) By the Power of Divine Light within me
2) Come Holy Spirit!   Spirit of Light!   Spirit of Truth!
3) For the highest good of all, throughout time, fill my heart with Divine Love as
4) I humbly ask permission to open the Divine portal to the highest realm of the Akashic Records for (LEGAL NAME).

5) **Akashic Beings of Light,** guide me to the deepest Truth of my being, releasing any blocks & restrictions to my abundance & highest good.
6) **Great Creatress,** assist me to fully embody my Soul's Light, to fulfill my Soul's purposes, & to heal any accumulated karma.
7) **Surround me** with the enlightenment & wisdom of my Masters, Teachers, & Loved Ones.
8) **Clearly direct** my perspective & actions to those that manifest my Divine Plan.

   (Repeat lines 5, 6, 7, & 8 two more times, then say line 9)

9) **Free of all resistance, judgment, and fear,**
   I am now filled with Divine love & the Records are open.

Welcome from the Akashic Beings of Light. We offer a mighty welcome to all our readers and listeners. We are pleased to offer this message of loving connection, so please accept our heartfelt gratitude and acknowledgment. **Bringing Forth Soul Consciousness** with its attendant Soul Connection are required for you to be functional while expanding to include the shifts and changes that are afoot.

As always, it is our intention to speak directly to your Spiritual Heart. (Please see chapter 11 "Your Spiritual Heart" for more information.) Your Soul utilizes your Spiritual Heart as a listening, reception, and communication device. That is because Soul Connection is a function of the Spiritual Heart. The Soul loves you as a gentle parent loves a child, lovingly attending to the child's curiosity, fears, and falls. True Soul Connection, true Soul intimacy, happens in the Spiritual Heart. It is a worthy enterprise, a suitable topic for your keen consideration, and active incorporation to consciously receive and fully embody your Soul's Light.

We cannot advocate often enough, that the Soul desires connection with you for your highest and best good. Your life will be easier for it.

Your Soul desires to lovingly assist you, at all times, in all conditions, whether or not you feel deserving. Let us be unfailingly clear about this: There is no moment or condition in which your Soul does not desire to be consciously connected to you. There is no point at which your Soul is unavailable to you.

In this way, the Soul is energetically patterned in the likeness and function of the Great Creatress. In this way the Soul demonstrates its unconditional love for you. You can reprogram your own self-love, repatterning your self-concept in the likeness of your Soul, and hence, in the likeness of the Great Creatress.

We, the Akashic Beings of Light, and your Masters, Teachers, and Loved Ones all communicate with you through your Soul, through the Divinity of your Soul. By definition, this inherently includes your Spiritual Heart.

Becoming Soul Connected is very important in the process of evolution. Becoming Soul Connected allows you to grow into your appointed place **within** the Great Creatress. Your Soul uses all opportunities and mechanisms to direct your attention inward to It, so you can energetically merge with your Soul. This is required for you to feel complete. Soul Connection enables you to know your origins as **a creation** of the Divine and **a function** of the Divine.

Your Soul uses health, wealth, career, and relationships as doorways to your inner world.

Utilizing these ever-present and ever-active openings to connect with you, your Soul calls to your heart, revealing the spark of Light that you are. It's link through shared Light brings new knowledge and understanding. It fortifies your clarity of Universal Principles at work.

Like the Divine, your Soul cares not for your evaluations of worldly success, failure, right, wrong, good, or bad. These judgments are restricted by third dimension limitations.

Your Soul is inviting you to rise above limited reactionary viewpoints, to feast upon the rise in vibration and the elevated perspective that inspires aligned action.

Rest assured, the failures and traumas which many of you have endured, by design, eventually bring you into harmonious connection with your Soul's Light.

This method of using health, wealth, and relationships to draw your attention inward is somewhat repetitive. As you practice embodying your Soul's Light you will find, over time, the lumps and bumps on your path smooth out. Clarity is revealed from the fog of confusion and indecision.

We have explained that embodying your Soul's Light, the Soul pours Its shimmering life force energy into you, aligning and igniting the 7 chakras below.

As your Soul's powerful, healing, organizing Light travels through the body, your Soul caresses each organ, strengthening, healing, and balancing them, as it fills the entire body with Its glorious essence. This is a good practice. It stabilizes the body, unifies purpose, calms the personality, and prepares you to receive more of the Soul's love, care, providence, and guidance.

*There is a corresponding spark of Soul Light in each cell and
microorganism that make up your body.
Every one of these microorganisms, atoms, and the subatomic
components, that make up your physicality have volunteered to
participate in your Souls' physical presence and journey
here on Earth.*

[Annie is thinking "That makes me feel extraordinarily grateful!"]

As your Soul's Light moves throughout your body, the corresponding
sparks of Light brighten, joyfully acknowledging this profound and
complex connection.

*The Soul has exercised great discernment in choosing such willing
and essential components. The Soul orchestrates the dynamic event
that is YOU. Such is "the deepest truth of your being"!*

The Soul functions as the right hand of the Great Creatress regarding the
maintenance and fulfillment of the material world plan. This is another
reason that **Bringing Forth Soul Consciousness** and Soul Connection
are useful, practical, and timely. Long awaited shifts and changes are
resulting from the availability and quantity of increased consciousness.
Communing or sharing consciousness with peaceful Higher Beings via
inter-dimensional travel has increased. These become highly relevant
and necessary for fulfilling your Soul's purposes in the flow of events
and evolutionary processes. Increasingly, you are fielding more details
and complexities in navigation of your Divine plan and holding within
your consciousness "the unfolding bigger picture".

*"The bigger picture" becomes the flowing result of acceptance and
surrender to a state of never-ending change.*

Flexibility is required. Nonattachment is healthy for effective digestion
and assimilation of the state of never-ending change.

During a reading for a client in Goa, India, We Akashic Beings of Light
revealed that all 144 strands of DNA reside in the unique space between
chakra's 7 and 8. From there they are disseminated throughout the
body. The full complement of DNA strands were thought to be forever
lost at the fall of Atlantis. These DNA strands contain the formatting

frequencies of the original design of the human form. The Akashic Beings of Light always encourage embodiment of Soul Light so that the full complement of DNA is activated and put to proper use. (Annie has found the "Reconnecting Soul, 142 DNA Activation Cards" by Jean Adrienne to be consistently revealing about the nature and power of the formerly missing strands of DNA.)

Reclaiming this space and the DNA strands within is a process that happens over time. It happens most easily if you trust the process, trust the perfection of the DNA codes you receive, and actively utilize the information imbedded within them. There is much to be said on this topic. We are careful in selecting the most immediately useful, and transformative information, that paves the way for more details and energy in the telling. Patience with yourself is very helpful.

The Soul is deceptively simple. The Soul is the connection to the Great Creatress. The Soul is enhanced by the Permanent Atom of Light© that is the essence of Divine Light in humanly registerable form. Hence, the Soul, constantly linked to the Great Creatress, is the antidote to the feeling of separateness. The Soul is the receiver of the Great Creatress' continuously updated instructions, magnanimous growth, and is the compounder of life force energies as relates to the specific human. The Soul is a transposer of sorts.

The Soul is also deceptively sublime and must be treated with the respect it deserves as a daringly imaginative creation of the Divine.

The Soul is always expressing the bliss of serving the Great Creatress, servant to the exquisite Divine higher purpose, happily evolving, instructing the human, and healing the planet on the way.

The Soul is very close to the heart of the Great Creatress. The Soul is a favorite of the Divine. While it's difficult for your mind to accept, concurrently, the Great Creatress holds **all** creations with equal importance. The Great Creatress is fully aware of humanity's need to feel special, unique, and highly favored, and occasionally indulges those needs.

As an extension of the Great Creatress, the Soul effectively dispenses such sweetness.

The Soul carries out the Will of the Divine. Both equal and highly favored, this estimation is not a measuring stick for your personal value, or of the Divine's preferences. Humans are equally as important as the microcosm of single cell bacteria that perform your digestion. The Great Creatress sees the whole of all creation, rather than as separate, disconnected, individual parts. The Soul has a similar perspective, larger, and more wholistic than your personality's perspective, yet lithely focused on the task at hand.

> *Using the Soul's innate connective abilities,*
> *the Soul carries out the Will of the Great Creatress.*
> *Hence, connecting Soul to human, Soul to the Great Creatress, Soul*
> *to Earth, human to Earth, human to the Great Creatress, on into*
> *infinity. These connections form the Flower of Life pattern.*

Practice connecting with your Soul, filling in the frequencies of Soul Light in the space between chakras 7 and 8. Become familiar with the additional strands of DNA, one at a time. Notice the shape, the movement, the energy changes that ensue, and the locations in your body where the additional DNA automatically settle. Use your sense of knowing, your visual cues. Notice your physical sensations, and the change in your Soul's Light.

> *As the added DNA strands begin to function, you will notice a*
> *sharpness, a clarity to your vision and understanding. Your ability to*
> *comprehend the minutia combined with your comprehension of the*
> *grand vision of everything working together in perfect harmony will*
> *become enriched. You have always had this ability however, now, it*
> *will be an important aid in fully receiving the multi-layered energetic*
> *messages you get from Us and from your Soul.*

It is becoming evident that the increased Soul connection enhanced through the line 8 in your Bringing Forth Soul Consciousness Akashic Prayer that says, "Great Creatress, assist me to fully embody my Soul's Light, to fulfill my Soul's purposes, and to heal any accumulated karma" that the Soul is more readily available and that karma is becoming less potent an affect upon people's lives. The stain of karma is effortlessly lifted from the human in the presence of the Akashic Beings of Light and the embodiment of your beloved Soul Light.

Here we direct your attention to the fact that Soul connection and consciousness is on the rise, in general, with, and without, conscious embodiment of the Soul's Light.

This is what is meant when someone says, "the veils are thinning" or "the veils are lifting". Phalanxes of very high Light Beings have been transmitting Light to earth, and to Our Dear Readers, in support of this fantastic upheaval and rearrangement. Knowledge, Light energy, and vibration of consciousness are on the rise, as well.

Our Beloved Readers and many other energy workers, known and unknown, are some of the forerunners of this rise in consciousness, carrying the banner wide and high for all to see. As a group, you are testing this newfound connection in a variety of ways and in different circumstances. We could not be more pleased. We trust you to relate this message of acknowledgment to all involved.

We are aware that, unfortunately, the concept and existence of the Soul has been somewhat perverted through humanity's acceptance of incorrect translations of spiritual terms. A significant point of resistance to engaging with the Soul has occurred because of ignorance and erroneous religious training. Historically, the concept of Soul has been removed from human control, distanced, disempowered, displaced, and in many cases, completely eliminated. Historically, it has been presented to you that your Soul belongs to God/Goddess. Correct. But your Soul does not belong to you. Incorrect. You belong to your Soul and vice versa. Both of you belong to the Great Creatress. Meanwhile, religious teachings have implied that the human is responsible for the Soul, as if the Soul is an errant joy-riding teenager in need of discipline. Quite the reverse. Religions have given little enlightenment on the nature of the Soul, much less how to be responsible for, or to, your Soul. You are supposed save your Soul from the timeless ravages of hell through choosing to abide by religious rules, adhering to that religion even more than to your Soul, your family, or your spouse. Far too many unnecessary conflicts arise because of this.

We comprehend religions have tried very hard to help humanity, and have simply gotten off track over time.

We have no intention of becoming a religion. We earnestly are providing energy-charged information that continues the upward and expansive trajectory of the Soul consciousness, as an option and addition to religious teachings.

Taking Ownership of your Soul

As you take ownership of your Soul, you claim the Light of your Soul to be your Light. You experience the space between your 7th and 8th chakras filling with Soul Light easily, and this Light effortlessly fills your body. You feel the wholeness, the uniformity, and the connection with your Soul. You feel it physically, emotionally, and mentally. You feel the connection causing your consciousness to expand upward and outward. You begin to feel yourself encircled and infused by the presence of the Great Creatress. That which birthed you is present in your awareness as nurturing, soothing love, and infinite wisdom. As you are connected in this way, you become accessible to your Soul and to the Great Creatress. You are accessible by the great Creatress and receive Her bounty.

The Great Creatress and many High Beings of Light are fostering your connection, aiding in your Soul Consciousness, expanding your Soul connection. Fear Not. Settle into this level of expansion. Let it pulsate. Feel the augmentation. You are feeling the heartbeat of the Great Creatress. You can feel your umbilical cord connected to her Divinity. She is superlative and, together, the two of you are exquisite. Relax and feel this fulfillment.

This is unification with the Great Creatress, a key feature of 5th dimension of consciousness.

It spans into greater dimensions of consciousness, and you are free to roam. Your innate Divinity is no longer in question here. You are Divine, of course. Your entry here only happens when you are aware of and are settled into your Divinity. You are permitted here through your consciousness of your own Divinity. Soul Connection and consciousness are the gateway. The more you access these realms the more able you are to return, to explore, and to wander purposefully.

Eventually, there will be nothing to tether or limit you to the 3rd and 4th dimension. You will have outgrown the physical world as your environment.

With these explorations, you are gaining necessary skills and experiences that you bring back and work into your daily life and interactions with others. Inter-dimensional travel paves the way for others, much as the **Bringing Forth Soul Consciousness** Akashic Prayer transports you to the Akashic Records. As you groove the path with your consciousness, others will follow. They will find their own diverse experiences and options. This is not yet a path with great detail, however detail soon follows. It grows naturally out of your experience. What is important is your current, moment to moment experience.

Devote yourself to the experience of being wholly infused with your Soul. As such, you're naturally infused by the presence of the Great Creatress. Feel the fecund creativity here.

Feel Her promotion of all that is life, alive, and moving in this expansive Soul consciousness. The direct sense of life force energy is strong here. Let Her heartbeat pulse in you. Her heartbeat is your heartbeat.

You are inside of The Great Creatress, connected with everything She is, and all her creations. You are surrounded by effortless, weightless, space, freed of all need to control.

All is well. All was well, and all will be well. The time is now. In this now you find solace, comfort, rest. Her Divine presence is sweet, loosely embracing, supportive without limits.

We are holding this connection steady for you. This is a place of restoration, where the new is added unto you. The new can only be added to you in the sweet stillness of Her Allness. Let this pervade you. Let the Great Creatress' largess fill you with awe, and pleasant sensations.

Experientially, the 4th dimension is an incubator of sorts. It restores, rebuilds, refocuses, reinvents, relieves, removes, redirects, and repurposes your mission, recreating you in many amazing ways.

As you blend this with access to the 5th and higher dimensions, there are no demarcation points denoting the end of one dimension and the beginning of another. It is like traveling through a mist of multi-colored and varying vibrations.
None are better or worse than the other.

They simply are, just as you simply are.

The organic openness is safe, sound, free. There are no requirements here. Only beingness. Partake of the freedom here and drink deeply because it will fuel the next steps bringing into fruition your new projects as well as the next new inspirations to create.

Can you feel this book becoming part of the cells in your physical body?

Can you feel this book is completely unhindered, in accordance with your Soul? You are vibrating with it as your body agrees with the source of this writing. It suits your personality and your Soul.

Let your sincere appreciation for the vibration of words be elevated this day. Let yourself enjoy the dance of words in your consciousness as they shape themselves into descriptions, orations, pictures, and connect themselves one to another. Let the infinite supply of words needed to express your Soul's purpose swirl around you. The words are easy to select, easy to refine, easy to express, present for you to express in your own way. Your Soul, and hence, your body recognizes their belonging within you. Your body accepts the added skills, the added ability to heal, and to regenerate. Accept this beyond any mental imaginings or conflict. The Great Creatress is, of course, part of this project, as She is part of any undertaking, and sources the enormous motivation for this missive. The Great Creatress completes the complement of energies that are sourcing the words of our message.

For now, we bid you adieu.

Please write your responses to these interactive questions.

~ Interactive Questions ~

You have been developing and experiencing your Soul's Light and consciousness throughout this book. List three ways your experience has changed over time.

Becoming Soul connected allows you to grow into your appointed place within the Divine. Describe how your connection to your Soul and the Great Creatress has deepened?

How does your Soul demonstrate its unconditional love for you?

How has your Soul's unconditional love for you helped you to unconditionally love yourself?

What helps you to repattern your self-concept in the likeness of your Soul and in the likeness of the Great Creatress?

What is your Soul leading you to do now, to further investigate, and to reach for?

In what way(s) are you now being called to serve others?

~ Closing Prayer ~

Thanking the Great Creatress & Her Holy Spirit for Love, protection, & healing received this day,
Thanking the Akashic Beings of Light for guidance,
Thanking the Masters, Teachers, & Loved Ones for wisdom & direction.
The Divine Portal & the Akashic Records are now closed.
Amen. Amen. Amen.

CHAPTER 38

Soul Inspired Action, Creation, and Healing

Channeled by the Akashic Beings of Light

Bringing Forth Soul Consciousness
Akashic Records Prayer
©*Rev. Annie Bachelder 1/22/2022*

~ Opening Prayer ~

1) By the Power of Divine Light within me
2) Come Holy Spirit!   Spirit of Light!   Spirit of Truth!
3) For the highest good of all, throughout time, fill my heart with Divine Love as
4) I humbly ask permission to open the Divine portal to the highest realm of the Akashic Records for (LEGAL NAME).

5) **Akashic Beings of Light,** guide me to the deepest Truth of my being, releasing any blocks & restrictions to my abundance & highest good.
6) **Great Creatress,** assist me to fully embody my Soul's Light, to fulfill my Soul's purposes, & to heal any accumulated karma.
7) **Surround me** with the enlightenment & wisdom of my Masters, Teachers, & Loved Ones.
8) **Clearly direct** my perspective & actions to those that manifest my Divine Plan.

   (Repeat lines 5, 6, 7, & 8 two more times, then say line 9)

9) **Free of all resistance, judgment, and fear,**
   I am now filled with Divine love & the Records are open.

Greetings from the Akashic Beings of Light.

Five fundamentals of Soul Inspired Action, Creation, and Healing

- **faith,**
- **allowing,**
- **trust,**
- **listening, and**
- **acting on guidance received.**

We welcome you to this co-creative space, with you and your Soul as the prime creators. Open your Akashic Records and feel this creative medium. The Records exist at a Soul level plane of consciousness. Many ideas regarding fulfillment of your Soul's purposes come through your Akashic Records explorations.

> *The Soul level information you receive from your Akashic Records is always heart centered. You and your Soul are joined at the heart, your Spiritual Heart.*

Take a moment to **feel** deeply into the statement "You and Your Soul are joined at your Spiritual Heart". Feel the purity and goodwill emanating from your Soul. You and your Soul are joined at your Spiritual Heart, bonded together to fulfill your Soul's purposes, benefitting both your physical body and your personality.

Embodying your Soul's Light, the Light stimulates the third eye, activates the throat chakra, and infuses the Heart chakra. This energy pathway allows the Soul's wisdom to penetrate the brain, speech center, lungs, and heart. The energetic nudge causes the Light to spread through the lower chakras, legs, and feet. Your Soul's Light grounds at the balance point in the center of Mother Earth.

> *Grounding your Soul's Light into Mother Earth is a very stable and reliable stance.*

Notice that you're instantaneously linked into your pineal gland, deep within your third eye center. Clarity ensues. A spacious clarity that forms an infinite opening into the vastness of the multi-dimensional Soul realm, which includes, of course, the Akashic Records.

Yes, there is a Soul plane of consciousness. This realm allows movement between many dimensions for experiential learning of different kinds of expanded consciousness. The information is transported via Soul to your Spiritual Heart for sharing at the human level. This is a function of the Akashic field, also known as the Akasha at large.

Soul linking through the Spiritual Heart is how communication between Soul and Human occurs. It is often the best way to energetically link with other humans, with or without words.

Many would call it intuition; however, Soul linking is more precise, filled with concentrated energy and information. By becoming one with your Soul's Light, you acquire the consciousness of the Soul. In turn, the Soul gains access to greater dimensions of consciousness.

Human and Soul benefit equally and simultaneously.

It's not limited to a "top down" flow. Embodying your Soul's Light, you may wish to view it as open ended spirals of lifting energy moving gracefully upward and outward. Through the Heart-to-Soul link you are free to venture about, exploring vast space and the consciousness that exists there. Your Soul may even take you by the hand and introduce you to the various areas and dimensions.

From far out in the vastness, coming toward to you now, is a brilliant star, approaching indirectly, gently, respectfully, from the left side at about 10 o'clock. This star is the energy of the Akashic Beings of Light, here to merge with you. We are here to fulfill your request for assistance in the "matter of creation". For Us, this is humorous, because for you, the term "creation" always implies "matter", as in material things such as money, as evidence of your creative abilities. We remind you that you create many things, and experiences, in many ways.

You broadcast thought all day long and this creates magnetism, homeostasis, and repulsion. You broadcast images all day long. You broadcast thoughts and images, mostly of what you **do not** want, and a few of what you **do** want. Whether there is material evidence or not, has little to do with the truth of your idea of "matter".

The truth of your "matter" is that you are infinite energy,
expanding and contracting like breath,
formulating and re-formulating yourself,
and the "stuff" of your creations.

Matter is formed from raw energy, compiled from your thoughts, feelings, and images. Therefore, you deftly create from raw energy, consciously formed thoughts, fully experienced feelings, and images, which becomes matter. We recommend embodying your Soul's Light, and then consciously opening to your Soul influenced, and Soul sourced, thoughts, feelings, and images. You do this best when your Akashic Records are open to your Soul's energy and information.

Your Soul is always present in the forms created by your consciousness in action. Your Soul is reflected in the matter around you and the body you inhabit. Your Soul reflects your human thought forms, feelings, images, and the material things that came from them. The difference is that your Soul also provides the question, "Is that what you were wanting? Perhaps you would like to try again using my guidance." Your Soul is here to guide you in conscious creation of Its Soul purposes, which includes material forms, feelings, and thoughts.

The Soul is wholly in harmony with you, having chosen you out of the billions of bodies and personalities available on earth, creating on behalf of you, often creating **for** you, when your physical self is not able. For instance, Annie's Soul was quite active on her behalf, during the 10 years when you was "very ill with multiple sclerosis". All that stillness, all that quiet time, all that non-stimulation, allowed her sweet Soul to move about, largely undetected, creating (there is that word again!) a platform from which wellness could spring forth. A surprising amount of rearranging in her physical, mental, and emotional energy patterns was required for her to experience this miracle. Yes, she has permission to call it a miracle. She says the healing was slow, 20 years in the making, but that is human perception of time, mostly her perception of time wasted (a judgment), that puts limits on her miracle. Release that.

We didn't come all this way, with you,
to teach you limits.

Your culture does that exceedingly well. We came to you to share, to merge, to disengage and re-engage for the purpose of mutually expanded conscious experience that results in Soul Inspired Action, Creation, and Healing.

There was also the "matter" of faith involved in healing from multiple sclerosis.

We encourage Our Readers to develop faith: Faith in a friendly Universe. Faith in an understanding, kind and compassionate Divine who loves you. Faith that fills in the gaps in your knowledge. Faith in the moment. Faith that you are being guided and that all is well. Positively recognize how blessed you are.

Disabled with multiple sclerosis, Annie reclaimed her faith in Anubis through daily channeling and meditations with Anubis' guidance. It was thus that she quit eating wheat and sugar. It was thus that she co-created with her Soul, the resources that paved the turn-around in her health. She began the shift upward from a deep and unrestrained place of Soul congruence, truth, and trust. Faith inspired her to receive the urgent spiritual message to "resume active channeling for others and leading public guided meditations **now**". This message to act marked the positive change in her condition. This message to act marked the energy that spawned the Soul Inspired Action, Creation, and Healing.

The fundamentals of Soul Inspired Action, Creation, and Healing are faith, allowing, trust, listening, and acting on messages.

Annie sensed the urgency, which meant "Divine right timing". She took "right action" and has stuck with it. Meaning: no regrets and no turning back.

To turn back now would be a "dis-grace", for truly it would be turning her back on the Grace with which she has been showered.

Via Soul Inspired Action, Creation, and Healing, dear Readers, you become magnetic to **all those whom you serve**. Embodying your Soul's Light, you have an attractiveness that inexorably draws to you appropriate opportunities. This magnetism draws the fulfillment of your Soul Purposes to you. This is the time, Dear Readers, to be public, to show your true colors, to actively release your gifts, talents, and abilities upon the world without hesitation. You are alive, centered, powerful. You all are well-developed humans with Soul, and we would say, with style, as well. Your inner work will continue; however, the biggest difference is that now you are operating on a higher, broader, more potent frequency. A frequency to which We, as your cocreators, have added what we call "a sweep" to the uplift. As you channel your energy into projects that fulfill your destiny and your Soul's purposes, there is a noticeable upward flow.

We are calling it "a sweep" because your energy and consciousness are potent enough to sweep others into your flow, into higher energy, and higher spirit connections that are imbedded in you and the energy you radiate.

With you, We send out our combined clarion call to those Souls who most benefit from the example you set, from your experience, to come hither for Soul sustenance and joyful expression. In doing so, you are automatically Soul linking through your Spiritual Heart center with the Spiritual Hearts of the Souls that you most serve. *(see chapter 12 Masterful Manifesting)*

We hear your call, and we support your ongoing request to fully open to the Light, to be a **channel for the Light, in service of healing and harmony. And so it is.**

We bid you adieu for now.

Please write your responses to these interactive questions.

~ Interactive Questions ~

What are your "true colors" to be unleashed publicly?

Whom are you being drawn to help?

How are you being drawn to serve?

How do you see/feel/sense your partnership with your Soul and the Akashic Beings of Light taking shape?

How are Soul Inspired Action, Creation, and Healing being expressed in you?

The fundamentals of Soul Inspired Action, Creation, and Healing are faith, allowing, trust, listening, and acting on messages. How are each of these being demonstrated or amplified through you?

Describe an example of how Grace has been showered upon you.

~ Closing Prayer ~

Thanking the Great Creatress & Her Holy Spirit for Love, protection, & healing received this day,
Thanking the Akashic Beings of Light for guidance,
Thanking the Masters, Teachers, & Loved Ones for wisdom & direction.
The Divine Portal & the Akashic Records are now closed.
Amen. Amen. Amen.

CHAPTER 39

By the Power of Divine Light Within Me

Channeled by the Akashic Beings of Light

Bringing Forth Soul Consciousness
Akashic Records Prayer
©*Rev. Annie Bachelder 1/22/2022*

~ Opening Prayer ~

1) By the Power of Divine Light within me
2) Come Holy Spirit! Spirit of Light!   Spirit of Truth!
3) For the highest good of all, throughout time, fill my heart with Divine Love as
4) I humbly ask permission to open the Divine portal to the highest realm of the Akashic Records for (LEGAL NAME).

5) **Akashic Beings of Light,** guide me to the deepest Truth of my being, releasing any blocks & restrictions to my abundance & highest good.
6) **Great Creatress,** assist me to fully embody my Soul's Light, to fulfill my Soul's purposes, & to heal any accumulated karma.
7) **Surround me** with the enlightenment & wisdom of my Masters, Teachers, & Loved Ones.
8) **Clearly direct** my perspective & actions to those that manifest my Divine Plan.

   (Repeat lines 5, 6, 7, & 8 two more times, then say line 9)

9) **Free of all resistance, judgment, and fear,**
   I am now filled with Divine love & the Records are open.

Greetings and Welcome from the Akashic Beings of Light. We bid you a Divinely inspired day!

The power of the Divine Light grows within each of you ever more fully, ever more effectively, every day. We are highly aware of the Light within you, deep in the background largely unobserved by you, Our Dear Readers, even as it increases. Allow the Divine Light within you to prosper and flow through acknowledgment, access, and use. Let the power of Divine Light within you shine forth unobstructed, to touch the people and things that are important to you. Most of all, let the power of the Divine Light within you be connected vigorously to Divine source, the Great Creatress.

At some level of consciousness, each of you have already surrendered and joined the Light. You must have done so to be aware of your Divine origin.

Prior to incarnation in this life, many of you surrendered, and your willingness to be utilized in the execution of the Great Creatress' plan still stands. As if you could do anything else? Now embodied on Earth, your surrender lasts only as long as you can sustain active consciousness of it. When your attention turned elsewhere, your surrender reverted to self-will. We have good news for you all:

The energies have changed, and you are now free to surrender and to remain surrendered until such time as you consciously remake your pledge.

Now, your surrender today, yesterday, or yester-year, has become the platform on which you build your intimacy, trust, and reliance upon the Great Creatress. No longer alone on this journey, you have the ear of the Divine. You have Her Divine attention. You always have the Soul connection and access to Her wisdom. You are aware, now, of the durability of your connection with the Great Creatress.

You are aware of the layering of surrender upon surrender over time. You are aware of the constancy of your connection with the Great Creatress as it broadens and strengthens with frequent use.

Utilizing your Soul's Light and consciousness as your connection with the Great Creatress empowers this connection. The distance between you and the Great Creatress vanishes completely.

When you think of the Great Creatress, She is present with you. Doing so calls Her presence to you. She is offering Her strength and clarity so that you step forward with confidence into this moment and into all the moments that follow. No fear. You are experiencing increased trust in Her Divine direction regarding the highest and best manner in which to proceed in your day. (Please see the Great Creatress Invocation at the back of the book.) She has fulfilled her promise to eliminate the separation between you and provide stable, reliable, unfailing, smooth connectivity. She is faithful to you despite your perceived failings. Daintily at first, tentative, exploring blindly. You now know that each time you have reached for the Great Creatress she has strengthened you. She has received you instantaneously. It takes practice. It takes application of self-orientation toward Her High Authority, Her help, and Her Bounty. She delivers on her promise to fold you into her brood, keep you under Her wing, and include you in Her Oneness. A rich pleasure it is!

After all the stabs in the dark, groping blindly, seeking Her warmth, healing, and comfort, now it is a constant. Now it is sure.

You need not fear. You need not worry. You need not stress.

She is many steps ahead of you laying the groundwork of your path, while being uniquely in-step with you as you walk your path. We say to you, give your path the dignity it deserves! Honor yourself! Hallelujah! You have painstakingly applied yourself to creating a strong and steady bond with the Divine.

You surrender because it is your path to do so.

You have surrendered out of hope, out of desperation, out of simply following suggestions you picked up along the way. This is your journey, Dear Soul! This is your path, beloved Soul! You are sensing that your path could never have been otherwise. Everything that has transpired, even the so-called missteps and mistakes, have been required to create the diamond bright Light that is you.

We see you as your Soul. Your personality has been trained and honed, polished nearly to perfection. You are more often recognizing yourself as your Soul, rather than as your personality. You recognize and identify with your own interior Light. You recognize your Divine Plan in action. You recognize your belongingness as one of the Akashic Beings of Light as we meet in our circle. You occupy your assigned place within the group. Each of you recognizes that you are part of Divine Order, part of a team who has a great purpose. You are doing your part. You are fulfilling your Soul's Highest Purpose as Divine Light channels, healers, teachers, and guides for others with similar gifts, talents, and abilities, on their similar paths.

> **"By the Power of Divine Light Within Me"**
> **is a strong stance, a certain stance,**
> **a confident stance.**

Everything that each of you has been, done, and are doing, has led up to this. Much bravery, diligence, and persistence has been required. And because you humans love a good reward, this is it. A lovely, abundant life! A life of love and security and yet with enough challenges to keep you occupied (most of them spiritual, but, what isn't spiritual?).

Annie and all our dear readers, started with the spiritual kernels of Christ Light. You have gained much Light since then. Now you serve at the right hand of the Great Creatress, in the circle of the Akashic Beings of Light, and in partnership with Anubis! This is what we see, and you are tracking it all quite nicely as you read this.

To our readers and listeners: We welcome you. Your paths have been similarly difficult and yet Light-filled. That is why you are interested in this missive whose purpose is to buoy you as you go forward, to shine the Light on your next steps, to guide your attention, and hone your perceptions, and expand your sense of reality.

In honor of your imperfections, in honor of healing your wounds, we offer this human wisdom:

> **"Ring the bells that still can ring,**
> **Forget your perfect offering,**

There is a crack in everything.
That's how the Light gets in."
Leonard Cohen

Please write your responses to these interactive questions.

~ Interactive Questions ~

How has the Divine utilized your flaws to good purpose?

How has the Divine used your mistakes to promote your spiritual growth?

"She is many steps ahead of you laying the groundwork of your path, while being uniquely in-step with you as you walk your path." What thoughts and feelings does this statement arouse?

~ Closing Prayer ~

Thanking the Great Creatress & Her Holy Spirit for Love, protection, & healing received this day,
Thanking the Akashic Beings of Light for guidance,
Thanking the Masters, Teachers, & Loved Ones for wisdom & direction.
The Divine Portal & the Akashic Records are now closed.
Amen. Amen. Amen.

CHAPTER 40

Final Messages

Channeled by the Akashic Beings of Light, the Great Creatress, et al

Greetings and Welcome from the Akashic Beings of Light!

Many of you have intensely felt the sometimes confusing, sometimes blissful, climb to higher states of being through **Bringing Forth Souls Consciousness** and embodying your Soul's Light. Great shifts are upon us all now! From the perspective of the Akashic Records and the host of Beings of Light who are focused on the enlightenment of all humanity and the Earth, the shift upwards and outward in consciousness is ever increasing. You may be feeling this as a tightening around the crown of the head and forehead. You may be feeling this as a pit in the stomach, and as a sense of general restlessness (sometimes with temporary feelings of irritability). You may be feeling this as "Hurry up. Time's a-wasting."

In response to these experiences, we implore you to become aware of your beautiful Soul's Light pulsing and radiating in the Soul chakra. Notice that your awareness settles easily at this moment when totally centered within your Soul chakra, in your Soul's Light, and is mightily connected to your Spiritual Heart.

It is because your central processing functions have been transferred to a higher elevation.

We Akashic Beings of Light, along with your Masters, Teachers, and Loved Ones, and other High Beings of Light all stand supportively, encircling you, welcoming you to this higher state known as Oneness.

Our love, guidance, and support does not end here at the end of this book. Rather, our lavish support continues to include all of you, spiraling onward, outward, and upward, as together we travel shoulder to shoulder, often blending our individual Lights together into one powerful ray of Love.

As you go forward, moment by moment, day by precious day, we wish for you to recognize that the entire galaxy in your corner of this particular universe, is contained within your Permanent Atom of Light©. Your Permanent Atom of Light© is always with you, residing within your physical body, most likely secreted deep within the trunk of your body.

Your Permanent Atom of Light© is your unique energy signature, holding all that the great Creatress desires to have you manifest, as the spark of consciousness that is your Soul. Contained in the crisp, brilliant, diamond-like multicolored refractions of Light that is your Permanent Atom of Light© is all that was and has ever been created, sharply focused on you as an individual, and extending out to encompass the entire maximal space of the universe. It is a seed of your burgeoning Divinity.

Compressed in this tiny, powerful, expansive spark of Light is all the Light that ever was, allowing you to view and experience infinite volumes of consciousness.

This is why We say that you are equal to, and One with, the Divine. For in Her creativeness She designed each of you to be able to hold – to lovingly encompass – all Her creations. And thusly you are entitled to the same creative powers and the resultant responsibility for these creations.

One of the capacities of your Permanent Atom of Light© is that it can function as your cosmic traveling mechanism allowing your Soul consciousness to range far beyond the physical world, deep into many other consciousness dimensions. In this way you might experience other Consciousness Collectives, some embodied and many without bodies, learning how they communicate, structure their social groups, educate themselves, and demonstrate their higher purposes.

Another capacity of your Permanent Atom of Light© is that it can make your consciousness microscopically small, such that you can send it into your body to see what is happening at a cellular level, and to make changes accordingly. With a person's conscious permission, of course, you can use it as a healing device for others, to enter their body to view various structures and systems. You can also use your Permanent Atom of Light© to divine (read) the Akashic Records and the history stored therein.

Your Permanent Atom of Light© combined with your Soul Consciousness will be the next key growth module as you go forward. These two powerful elements of consciousness create an intentional, diligent, and effective discovery apparatus for decerning consciousness, individual human consciousness, or groups of humans, or the consciousness of earth elements such as crystals and cellular health. We stress the word "discern" as it allows differentiation of consciousness without the deprecating aspect of judgment.

We encourage you to explore this vast and diverse Universe of consciousness for its educational value and the advancement of enlightenment. We encourage your playful curiosity as you do so. For your Permanent Atom of Light© combined with the Light of your Soul – fully embodied – is a powerful ally. It can take you far into and beyond your earth life and your Soul's purposes. These two keys unlock the doors of perception, awareness, shared consciousness, and can link you to our Light as we bathe you and the Earth in it. Enjoy!

Greetings and Welcome from the Great Creatress!

Much attention, love and energy are continually being shared with you, both individually and collectively, as we tempt you with Divine Oneness, unity, and present moment purity. We call to you daily. We broadcast to you individually and collectively so that you ALL are sufficiently prepared for unified consciousness.

In your own preparation, assistance is given mostly to surrendering your personal programming and historical familial stories about the so-called nature of reality that you inherited from your Ancestors. Clear yourself of the past, happily discarding it as one would an outdated, ill-fitting suit of clothes, knowing that the weight of the past only slows you down. The past weighs you down when your joy is alight with uplifting currents of energy. You are not an agent of your Ancestors as much as you, Dear Readers, are My Agents, carriers who radiate and dispense Light, healing, and unity with the Divine Feminine.

You now have the key to the Akashic Records and what is known is recorded there for your illumination and the empowerment of your good works – works that assist your Great Creatress with the creation of our combined present moment, highest and best for all activities and plans. Together we are activating My Divine Plan to Illuminate All Consciousness, elevating all to equality and serenity. Join your physical selves, filled with the Light of your Soul, sparkling with your Permanent Atom of Light©. Join Me by blending with My Divine Light and Allness. This is the state which you hunger for, driven by your Soul, and only now fulfilled through rejoining Me as Divine Source. Ah! There it is. You have arrived. This is the moment and the state of consciousness you have craved and now you have it. Let every cell in your body experience it. Taste it. Smell it. Feel it. Sense it. Know it. This is your rightful place, here with Me. Here in me, in the womb of the Universe. Welcome. Home. You have my Heart.

From Reverend Annie

Allow me to thank all the Readers and Listeners of this book. Your attention honors your Soul connection. You honor the Akashic Beings of Light, and the Great Creatress. It has been a pleasure and an enormouos blessing to me to feel your consciousness as the audience, while I channeled this book. I bow to your courage, intrepid explorations, and good deeds.

Please, please, please stay in touch with me. Email me with your experiences of this material at AnnieChannels@gmail.com.

Join my Bringing Forth Soul Consciousness Members Portal where we study this book and receive guidance, as needed, from the Akashic Beings of Light, Anubis, and the Great Creatress. Visit www.AnnieChannels. com to become a member.

Every Wednesday I offer two free, live video events:

At 7:30amPT/10:30am ET on https://www.Facebook.com/annie.bachelder I lead a channeled guided meditation and report on the energy present for the week.

9amPacific/12noonEastern I channel answers to your questions written in the comments on the **Bringing Forth Soul Consciousness** private Facebook group https://www.facebook.com/groups/328360825953128 Become a member today!

Utilize my website www.AnnieChannels.com to

- · Schedule Akashic Records readings,

- · Schedule Anubis Channeling sessions

- · Schedule Divine Energy Healing sessions,

- · Schedule a Real Estate Reading

- · Schedule a Surgery Preparation Session

For digital downloads (suitable for framing) of book quotes, prayers, and affirmations please visit www.SoulSourcer.Etsy.com

Again, I bow in honor and gratitude to you.

Reverend Annie Bachelder

Bringing Forth Soul Consciousness
Akashic Records Prayer

©Rev. Annie Bachelder 1/22/2022

~ Opening Prayer ~

1) By the Power of Divine Light within me
2) Come Holy Spirit! Spirit of Light!   Spirit of Truth!
3) For the highest good of all, throughout time, fill my heart with Divine Love as
4) I humbly ask permission to open the Divine portal to the highest realm of the Akashic Records for (LEGAL NAME).

5) **Akashic Beings of Light,** guide me to the deepest Truth of my being, releasing any blocks & restrictions to my abundance & highest good.
6) **Great Creatress,** assist me to fully embody my Soul's Light, to fulfill my Soul's purposes, & to heal any accumulated karma.
7) **Surround me** with the enlightenment & wisdom of my Masters, Teachers, & Loved Ones.
8) **Clearly direct** my perspective & actions to those that manifest my Divine Plan.

(Repeat lines 5, 6, 7, & 8 two more times, then say line 9)

9) **Free of all resistance, judgment, and fear,** I am now filled with Divine love & the Records are open.

~ Closing Prayer ~

Thanking the Great Creatress & Her Holy Spirit for Love, protection, & healing received this day,
Thanking the Akashic Beings of Light for guidance,
Thanking the Masters, Teachers, & Loved Ones for wisdom & direction.
The Divine Portal & the Akashic Records are now closed.
Amen. Amen. Amen.

I and My Soul are One

I and my Soul are ONE.

I and my Soul are inseparable.

I and my Soul belong together.

I and my Soul walk hand in hand on the path of enlightenment together.

I trust my Soul to love me no matter what transpires.

I trust my inseparable Soul to stand by me.

My Soul has never, and will never, reject me.

Consciously linked, my Soul and I are clearly directed to the highest and best outcomes for our mutual benefit.

My Soul and I safely explore, grow, and expand together.

My Soul is my best friend and the keeper of my innermost gifts, talents, and abilities.

My Soul assists me with solutions, insights, and inspiration.

My Soul never abandons me in times of trouble.

My Soul aids in my healing, maturation, and supplies the courage needed to progress on my path.

My Soul actively draws me toward uplifting opportunities, experiences, and abundance.

The more I merge with my Soul the more healed and whole I am.

The more my Soul merges with me, the more we can accomplish together.

I more I identify with my Soul, the capabilities for achieving my aspirations increase.

The more I identify as my Soul, I experience fewer limitations, distractions, and obstacles.

The more my Soul becomes my human identity, I experience more peace, inclusivity, and harmony.

I now see through the loving eyes of my Soul.

I now experience through the expanded awareness of my Soul.

I now love with my Spiritual Heart, the heart of my Soul.

I now clearly hear and follow the wisdom and direction of my Soul.

I and my Soul are indivisible.

My Soul and I are one.

We are one with the Great Creatress.

Thank you, dear Soul. Thank you.

Great Creatress Invocation
©Reverend Annie Bachelder 7-28-2020

Oh, Great Creatress!

I invite your Divine and Holy Presence to flow through me now.

Opening my Spiritual Heart©, I receive the fullness of your gifts.

Perpetually aligned in Divine partnership with you, I offer my mind, body, and spirit in unity with Your Power and Purpose.

Surrendering all obstacles, Your pure Light flows gracefully through me.

Receiving your Divine instructions for this day, all thoughts, words, and deeds that most serve You arrive preformatted with Your Impeccable timing, love, and strength of purpose.

Inspire me to proceed in the direction and manner that You prescribe.

Born of Your Divine Light, and filled with gratitude, your steady Presence gives me the energy, clarity and empowerment needed to fulfill Your Divine Plan.

Gratefully, I say **And so it is, Dear Goddess! Amen!**

Integrating Soul Prayer

© Reverend Annie Bachelder 10/26/20

For the highest good of all, Great Creatress,

please, open my Spiritual Heart to full vibrancy.

Awaken me to your Divine Design.

By the power of your Spirit within me, I presence my Soul.

I embody Its Light and consciousness.

Oversee my Soul and physical experience as we become One.

Safe in Your embrace, my Soul's Light fills me to the brim.

Recognizing my Soul's Divinity and alliance with You,

I open to receive Its beneficial influence.

Embodying my Soul's Light, I am strengthened.

I am awakened to Its consciousness.

Like you, Great Creatress, my Soul embraces me kindly,

Guides me wisely,

Fills my heart with Its love,

Sweetens my thoughts, words, and deeds with compassion.

My Soul naturally forms my link with Thee, Great Creatress.

May all consciousness be of the Light.

And so, it is.

Amen

Exercise – How to Embody Your Soul's Light:

Close your eyes. Take 3 deep, cleansing breaths followed by complete exhalations to bring yourself fully into this moment.

1. Begin by becoming aware of a glowing sphere of radiant Light located 12 to 15 inches above your head. This is your 8th chakra (your Soul chakra). Let your sense of knowing tell you about the color, the shimmer, and the vibration in your Soul's Light. These qualities may change from time to time. Trust the changes. The Light is infinitely wise and knows what you need at every moment.

2. Observe as the Soul chakra pours its Light into the space between your Soul chakra and your crown chakra, creating a column of connecting Light.

3. Your crown chakra naturally opens to receive the Light of your Soul as it pours itself into your crown chakra.

4. Your Soul's Light fills your entire head, inside and out. Your Soul's Light fills your brain, scalp and hair, eyes, sinuses, jaw, and the atlas bone at the top of your spine. At any point in this process, you might feel a sense of your Soul's character.

5. Notice your Soul's Light as it fills your shoulders, arms, hands, and fingers.

6. Observe as your Soul's Light lovingly and affectionately touches all the organs and systems in the trunk of your body. Allow yourself to feel your Soul's love for this precious body It chose for you.

7. Observe your Soul's Light filling the entire trunk of your body, inside and out, including your skin. Your Soul's Light naturally pools in your pelvic cavity. It pauses in your hip sockets. Take a breath.

8. Follow your Soul's Light as it fills your thighs, knees, calves, ankles, and feet. Your Soul's Light fills the bones, muscles, tendons, and fascia tissues, as well as your blood system.

9. Take notice that very cell throughout your body contains a corresponding spark of Light reflecting your Soul's Light. Recognition in each of your cells of your Soul's Light generates a feeling of joyful reunion.

10. Remain focused on your Soul's Light and all your cells as they re-connect. Observe the interactions.

11. You might feel a click or a buzzing in your feet and legs as your body's connection with your Soul's Light is complete.

12. Ground your Soul's Light into the balance point of Mother Earth.

13. Now, send your consciousness up to the Great Creatress. Feel the sphere of Light that is the Great Creatress surrounding your Soul, you, and Mother Earth.

14. Spend as much time as you like here.

15. Create a memory file by placing the pointer finger of your right hand on the palm of your left hand so that you can fully embody your Soul's Light on command.

16. Easily and effortlessly, return to ordinary consciousness, wiggling your toes, rolling your shoulders, and enjoying a few relaxing breaths.

©Reverend Annie Bachelder 5-24-22

To heal the sense of separation, please use this exercise. We urge you to read this out loud every day for 30 days.

Affirmations: "I and My Soul Are One"
Channeled by Anubis

I and my Soul are One.

I and my Soul are inseparable.

I and my Soul belong together.

I and my Soul walk hand in hand on the path of enlightenment together.

I trust my inseparable Soul to love me no matter what transpires.

I trust my inseparable Soul to stand by me.

My Soul has never, and will never, reject me.

Consciously linked, my Soul and I are clearly directed to the highest and best outcomes for our mutual benefit.

My Soul and I safely grow, expand, and explore together.

My Soul is my best friend and the keeper of my innermost gifts, talents, and abilities.

My Soul assists me with solutions, insights, and inspiration.

My Soul never abandons me in times of trouble.

My Soul aids in my healing, maturation, and supplies the courage needed to progress on my path.

My Soul actively draws me toward uplifting opportunities and abundance.

The more I merge with my Soul the more healed and whole I am.

The more my Soul merges with me, the more we can accomplish together.

The more I identify as my Soul, the capabilities for achieving my aspirations increase.

The more I identify as my Soul, the fewer limitations, distractions, and obstacles I experience.

The more my Soul becomes my human identity, the more peace, inclusivity, and harmony I experience.

I now see through the loving eyes of my Soul.

I now experience through the expanded awareness of my Soul.

I now love with my Spiritual Heart, the heart of my Soul.

I now clearly hear and follow the wisdom and direction of my Soul.

I and my Soul are indivisible.

My Soul and I are One, we are One with the Great Creatress (the Divine).

Thank you, Soul. Thank you, Great Creatress.

Exercise: Interacting with the Space between the 7th and 8th Chakras

1. Close your eyes. Take three deep, cleansing breaths.

2. Inhale Light. Exhale grey energy.

3. Place your concerns in the lap of the Great Creatress while you focus on this exercise.

4. Become aware of your 8th chakra, the Soul chakra, about 12 or 15 inches above your head.

5. Embody your Soul's Light by witnessing your Soul chakra pouring Its exquisite Light into the space between your 7th and 8th chakras.

6. Notice that your Soul's Light forms a column of Light in this space, connecting the two chakras.

7. Allow your Soul's Light to entirely fill every part of your body until you vibrate in harmony with your Soul's Light.

8. When you are ready, return your attention to the space between the 7th and 8th chakras.

9. Zoom in on the column of Soul Light. Notice all you can about the quality of the Light. Notice the vibratory rate, colors, shapes, movement, or any vertical or horizontal frequency lines.

10. Energy is always changing. Simply observe the active energy inside the column of Soul Light.

11. Notice that there are no barriers to this column of Soul Light that delineate the space. You can test this by running your hand through the space like moving your hand through a hologram.

12. Choose a Soul quality such as peace, unconditional love, or kindness, that you would like to experience.

13. Get a sense of this quality as a word held just outside the column of Soul's Light and insert the word into the column.

14. Give yourself a moment to feel and assimilate this Soul quality.

15. Follow the Soul quality as it moves into and around your physical interior.

16. Notice how this quality affects different body parts. Notice where it lands and integrates itself into your body.

17. Let that go for now and return your attention to the space between your 7th and 8th chakras and the column of Soul Light.

18. Now, get a sense of a symbol representing the fulfillment of a desired event.

19. Insert the symbol into the column of Soul Light.

20. Observe the energy as the symbol is absorbed into the column of Soul Light.

21. Observe as the symbol enters and moves around your interior.

22. Relax and observe. Don't force anything.

23. Notice if there are particular body locations where the symbol most easily settles or affects.

24. Make a memory file of this process and how it feels, looks, and how it changes your energy.

25. Return to the column of Soul Light between your 7th and 8th chakras.

26. Let an embarrassing situation, or a moment you regret, come into your awareness.

27. Notice where in your body you have stored this memory.

28. Observe as your Soul's Light gently brings it into the column of light.

29. Allow the Akashic Beings of Light to gently and firmly remove the memory and the sensations associated with this experience.

30. When the removal is complete, the Akashic Beings of Light kiss your forehead.

31. Gently and easily, bring your attention back to your Soul chakra. Thank your Soul. Come fully back into the room and open your eyes.

Exercise: Feeling Your Soul's Light
in your Body

1) Close your eyes. Allow yourself to fully arrive in this moment. Yes, simply this moment.

2) Scan your body inside and out. Take it all in.

3) Feel the quality of this moment.

4) Ask your mind to stop rushing you.

5) Ask your mind to help you to focus on this moment as your total experience.

6) Now, take a few very deep, relaxing, and calming breaths to aid your centering.

7) Notice your inner screen on the inside of your eyelids.

8) Fully embody your Soul's Light.

9) You may be seeing, sensing, or "knowing" your Soul as beautiful Light that is illuminating your body.

10) Observe the color, or colors, of your Soul's Light.

11) Does your Souls Light have a misty outline? Or a crisp demarcation, a defined boundary?

12) Observe your Soul's Light deep inside your body.

13) How does your Soul's Light adjust to best harmonize with different organs?

14) Notice the wisdom of these adjustments, measured by the vibrance of the life-force energy these organs now exhibit.

15) Notice that your Soul delights in these excursions as you invite it to participate in unity with your blessed body and your consciousness.

16) Flowing between your physical body and your Soul's Light, is a mutual respect and adoration of your blessed body.

17) There is an intimacy between each individual cell and your Soul's Light as it flows gracefully through your blessed body.

18) In chapter 7, "How Your Soul is Constructed", we discussed how your Soul specifically and lovingly chose your body and your personality, as the perfect choice to be your Soul's expression on Earth.

19) Your Soul created you as it's experience module. This was done with respect and care. This is the bond between Soul, personality, and body.

This is the agreement between your Soul and your physical self.

20) Your Soul's Light is wise and knows exactly what you need at this moment.

21) Let your body absorb all the Light it needs. Revel in the peace and fulfillment of this moment.

22) Place your right pointer finger in the center of your left palm as a physical reminder of this experience.

23) You have the wisdom of the ages within. You know there is no other self that you need to be, to see, to feel, to know. The deeper you flow into your Soul, the more rarified and clarified are your perceptions, and the more connected to you are with the Great Creatress. And when you call out to your Soul, saying, "Come Soul, come Holy Light", you are calling all the Forces of Light to you. You are asking to be united with your blessed body, your Soul, and the Great Creatress.

24) You have everything you need, for the moment, for the day, and for continually improving life, don't you?

25) When you feel ready, return to reading the rest of the chapter.

Exercise: Becoming Conscious of All That is Holy

1. Take 7 deep, refreshing breaths. Inhale to your fullest point. Slowly and thoroughly exhale.

2. You can experience all that is Holy in your Permanent Atom of Light©. Locate it somewhere in the trunk of your body.

3. Place all of your consciousness inside of that very tiny yet powerful, brilliant spark of Light within you.

4. Sense the Holy energy within the exuberant Permanent Atom of Light. Sense the life packed within it ready to explode into your complete Soul.

5. You might find all that is Holy by embodying the Light of your Soul.

6. This too, was created in Holiness by the Great Creatress.

7. As you embody your Soul's Light you realize it is sustained in Holy Grace by the Great Creatress.

8. You might experience All that is Holy in the depths of your breath as you let yourself simply be.

9. No demands. No requirements. No effort. No muscling anything. No forcing.

10. Just breathe and be.

11. All that is Holy is within you. It is always there. Like an old friend.

12. Kind, patient, accepting. Yes. You know that Holiness, don't you?

13. Sense that Holiness in you. It is perfectly alive and well inside of you.

14. All that is Holy has you, and you have it.

15. The distinctions between you and Holiness are becoming quite blurred, aren't they?

16. Play with that blurriness. Put your attention where both you and all that is Holy reside, in peace, in comfort, in total ease. Rest there.

17. Breathe in that overlap of you and all that is Holy, and you find there really is no difference.

18. You belong to one another. Your essence is made of all that is Holy.

19. This is the strength of your heartbeat, the constancy of your blood flowing, the depth of your breath.

20. This overlap is the Spirit that lives within you that we are calling your Soul, that we are calling the Great Creatress, that we are calling all that is Holy.

21. There simply is no division. All is All. You are in it, part of it, filled with it, surrounded by it, enamored of it, and it is enamored with you.

22. By All That Is Holy, you are that. And that is you. By All That Is Holy. Created in pure innocence. Created divinely.

23. When you die, you transition from being encased in a body to being purely All That Is Holy. You become non-substance. You exist only as consciousness. Soul Consciousness. You transition into Holy peace. You leave the drama, exit stage left. No bow. No curtain call. No standing ovation. Simply released into peaceful All-ness. We are here to welcome you.

Exercise: Claiming Your Soul

1. Begin by embodying your Soul's Light, energy, and consciousness.

2. Become aware of your Soul chakra, the 8th chakra, about 12 to 15 inches above your head.

3. Sense the Light and energy in it.

4. Open your crown chakra and allow the Light of your Soul to enter your other chakras and your physical body.

5. Sense your Soul's Light as it fills every part of your body, even your toes.

6. Include your Soul's Light, energy, and consciousness in your physical experience.

7. Sense your Soul's Light as infusing with your body.

8. Wear your Soul as invisible clothing, as internal reckoning.

9. Orient your vision so that you are gazing through your Soul's eyes.

10. Listen with your Soul's hearing.

11. Feel your Soul's Light in your palms and fingers. Activate your Soul's sense of touch.

12. Activate your Spiritual Heart, your Soul's Heart.

13. From the deepest, tenderest part of the human you, send an invitation to Your Soul asking it to show you how it claims you.

14. Open your receiving as wide as you can and receive your Soul's connection, your Soul's claim of you.

15. Notice where it connects, and how. Notice Its gentle demeanor.

16. Perhaps there is an embrace. A deeper infusion of love.

17. Offer your Soul the best part of you, the part that is willing to grow, to play, to change.

18. Feel the acceptance, the partnership, the cooperation between you.

19. Silently claim your Soul.

20. Communicate with your Soul your willingness to see, hear, and know all that your Soul see's, hears, and knows.

21. Feel how secure you feel now.

22. Embody your partnership with your Soul often, while navigating even the simplest of moments. Do this regularly, and you will discover that this feels natural, and you can hardly remember a time when you did not feel the loving infusion and partnership of your Soul.

23. When this ends, bring your attention back into the room, and into ordinary reality.

Exercise: Receiving Light from Your Future Self

1. Begin by taking seven slow, deep inhalations followed by strong, complete exhalations.

2. With every inhalation you are bringing in your Soul's Light and Consciousness. 3) With every exhalation you are releasing density and complexity.

3. Inhale and feel your Soul's Light as it fills your whole beautiful body-servant.

4. Exhale, forcing all the old energy completely out of your lungs.

5. Inhale Soul Light. Exhale density.

6. Inhale Light and exhale overwhelm. Relax.

7. Inhale Soul Light. Exhale and relax.

8. Your Future Self stands in front of you. This is your Future Self of 2 months, 2 years, 20 years, even 2 lifetimes in the future.

9. Your Future Self looks kindly upon you. It is clear, calm, and composed.

10. Your Future Self emanates brilliant multicolored Light.

11. Your Future Self begins to direct its brilliance toward you.

12. This Light feels like a secure force for good.

13. Your Future Self is letting you know that everything is all right. Everything has worked out for your highest and best good.

14. Your Future Self makes clear that you have become stronger and clearer in the process. You become more your Soul Self in the process you are currently undergoing.

15. Your Future Self may have an important detail or message to share with you.

16. Your Future Self may simply be saying, "Relax. Everything is okay. The problem got solved. The dilemma got resolved for every ones highest good. You may now make peace with all your frustrations and all that has been bothering you."

17. Drink in your Future Self's Light. Soak up its presence. Fill yourself with your Future Self's peace. Soak up your Future Self's wisdom.

You easily trust your Future Self and know it is on your side, on your team, working for your highest good.

18. Now ask to be in the Light radiating from your Future Self of 2 lifetimes from now.

19. What is different about this Light? How have you grown?

20. What do you have to adjust in your present self to receive Light from this Future Self?

21. How does this Future Self deal with problems and dilemmas?

22. Ask if there is another message from this Future Self?

23. Thank your Future Selves, reserving a future opportunity to share your Future Self's bountiful Light and wisdom.

24. Bring to mind a problem that causes you fear and anxiety. Write out your responses as you apply the Akashic Transformation Process Master Questions©.

Exercise: Healing an Undesirable Past Life

(It is essential that your Akashic Records be open for this exercise so that you receive the Akashic perspective, the Soul perspective.)

1. Begin by embodying your Soul's Light and the consciousness within that Light.

2. Follow your Soul's Light as it pours into your body, filling every system, structure, and cell in your body.

3. Your Soul's Light spreads all the way down your toes and out the bottom of your feet.

4. Ground your Soul's Light in the center point, the balance point, of Mother Earth.

5. Your Soul's Light is so brilliant, so strong, that it glows beyond the confines of your physical body. It makes a cone of Light that both infuses you and surrounds you. It holds you steady.

6. Ask your Masters, Teachers, and Loved Ones to show you a past life that is ready to be released.

7. Your Masters, Teachers, and Loved Ones are directing your attention to a place in your body that holds an undesirable past life. Get a sense of this location and the energy of the past life in question.

8. Make your consciousness very small. Small enough that you can enter the interior of your body at the location where the past life has been stored.

9. It is as if you entered a room in another time, another place. Look around. See what is there for you to see. Trust your sense of knowing. Your Masters. Teachers, and Loved Ones may point out things, people, and circumstances that fill in the details.

10. Using your "sense of knowing", notice whether you are male or female, strong or weak, the clothing you are wearing, your social status, the time period, and your emotional state.

11. Who else is involved? What are their chief characteristics? How are they involved? Are they familiar to you?

12. Ask your Masters, Teachers, and Loved Ones why this past life is being shown to you?

13. Ask them what is the most important aspect of this past life for you to know?

14. Ask your Soul how this past life helps you evolve?

15. Ask your Soul why this past life is ready to be released?

16. Become aware of your Soul's Light melting, dissolving, and releasing any past life attachments to your body. The sticky, dense energy becomes light, misty, and effortlessly flows out of your energy field.

17. Confirm that your willingness matches the release of the unwanted effects of this past life.

18. Confirm also that the new neural pathways are established.

19. Your Masters, Teachers, and Loved Ones are supporting you, assisting in the evaporation of the past life and any residual energy is removed from you.

20. Thank your MTLO's for their love and support. Thank your Soul.

21. Let all that go. Gently bring your full attention easily and effortlessly back into ordinary reality. Make written notes about your experience.

Exercise: Release Yourself from Judgment Jail

1. Breathe deeply 7 times, inhaling into your low belly first, then filling your upper chest. Exhale forcefully and completely. You may have to push out the last bit of old air.

2. Now feel the relaxation that automatically follows.

3. Embody your Soul's Light. Notice that your consciousness changes from busy mind to relaxed, quiet mind.

4. Bring to mind a moment where you judged another person.

5. Without judging yourself for doing this, notice how fast your mind raced to judgment.

6. Know that your mind is designed to judge, to assess, to evaluate, as a preprogrammed survival mechanism.

7. Your mind is designed to name and classify dangers. That's its job.

8. Rather than resisting this programming, notice that you are choosing to have a different experience right now.

9. Ask yourself, "What are my options?"

10. The road to freedom is through acceptance, and through "expanding to include" that part of you which automatically judges.

11. Feel how your body relaxes when offered the option to accept your pre-programmed response to the other person. Now expand to include the whole scenario, judgment, and all.

12. Your Soul's Light gets brighter and larger in this state of relaxation. See if you can now feel, or sense, the presence of the Great Creatress.

13. Recall another occasion where you judged yourself intensely.

14. Feel the judgment in your body, your mind, and your heart.

15. In your inner mind you may be seeing, or feeling yourself trapped, as if in jail, the judgment jail.

16. Accept fully for this moment, that this is your experience when you judge yourself. Sit in this feeling for a moment. There will be a point where the sensations of judgment loosen and lift.

17. Stay with your experience.

18. Look at the bars that make up your judgment jail. You may feel the shackles around your wrists and ankles falling off.

19. The bars fold down or dissolve. You easily step out into freedom.

20. Take a moment to forgive yourself and anyone else involved.

21. Gently accept your new experience, accept the softening in your heart, and accept the friendly tone of your inner voice.

Thank your Soul. Thank the Great Creatress.

Exercise: Your Permanent Atom of Light©

1. Take several deep relaxing breaths. Breath deeply until your mind relaxes.

2. Let your body relax with each breath.

3. Release any tension in the body by breathing into the tension until it surrenders.

4. Now embody your Soul's Light.

5. Locate a spark of intensely bright Light somewhere in the trunk of your body.

6. This is your Permanent Atom of Light©. 7.Concentrate all your attention on Your Permanent Atom of Light©.

7. Let this spark of Light move in whatever direction and manner it chooses.

8. Simply follow it with your attention.

9. Notice how Your Permanent Atom of Light© increases in size or intensity as you focus intently on it.

10. Observe as Your Permanent Atom of Light© becomes larger, more powerful, more intense.

11. Notice how your body responds to your Permanent Atom of Light©.

12. Noticed the condition of your thoughts as you experience Your Permanent Atom of Light©

13. Your Permanent Atom of Light© is now as large as your body and becoming larger.

14. Your Permanent Atom of Light© finds its full size and brilliance and stabilizes there.

15. Allow yourself to bask in this Light.

16. Sense the peace of Your Permanent Atom of Light©.

17. Feel the constancy of Your Permanent Atom of Light©.

18. Notice how naturally connected you are to this Light.

19. Appreciate how connected you feel to your Soul and to the Great Creatress.

20. Sense the original power that is contained in your Permanent Atom of Light©.

21. This is the original spark of Divine Light from which you were created.

22. Allow yourself to experience the original Light and consciousness from which you are derived.

23. Get a sense of your belonging with this powerful, intense, brilliant Light.

24. Relax here for as long as you wish.

25. When you are ready, slowly and gently, allow your Permanent Atom of Light© to condense into the tiny spark that you first located.

26. Return to ordinary reality refreshed and renewed.

Exercise: Clearing Excessive Ancestral Influences

1. Take 5 deep cleansing breaths to refresh and organize your energy.

2. Embody your Soul's Light until your Light extends beyond your skin and you're ready to add in your connection with the Great Creatress.

3. Get a sense of two lines of ancestors forming behind you.

4. Notice whether the ancestral line behind your left shoulder are from your mother's or your father's line?

5. Converse with these ancestors, exploring the fear programming that began with them. Simply gather facts and examples of the kinds of fear that were promoted in the ancestral line.

6. What time in history did this pattern of fear begin?

7. Ask your ancestors, what was the original danger?

8. Which of your ancestors began this fearful reaction?

9. How did it personally serve this ancestor at the time?

10. How was a fearful reaction helpful to the ancestral line?

11. Why are they afraid for you now?

12. How are they trying to help you?

13. It's time to release the old energy pattern. Simply let the old energy leave your breath, your body, your consciousness.

14. Ask your MTLO's for assistance if you need it.

15. Notice how your energy shifts as your release the old programming.

16. Acknowledge that you accepted your ancestor's nomination to be the trail blazer leading the whole line to a better future.

17. Take a moment to form a new agreement with your ancestors so that you, and those who follow you, have greater freedom to explore, to grow, and to take big, confident steps forward, for the good of the whole ancestral line.

18. Show or describe to the ancestors the higher purpose of your intentions and activities.

19. Show them what your Soul wants for you.

20. You may need to take a firm leadership stand and tell them they are no

longer in charge of your spiritual growth. As agreed, when you designed this life, they are to follow your lead.

21. Ask for their cooperation and support in experiencing a life of achievement which the ancestors previously felt was too risky, daring, or beyond your capabilities.

22. Let this shift in energy settle into your consciousness and body.

23. When that feels complete, thank your ancestors, your Soul, and the Great Creatress for a job well done.

Exercise: Manifesting as Your Soul

You will want to take notes during and after this exercise. Make sure you have your pen and paper or laptop close by.

1. Take 7 deep, cleansing breaths. Exhale each one fully and completely. Take your time. You are oxygenating your brain and increasing your heartbeat.

2. Embody your Soul's Light. Sense the closeness of your Soul. Feel your Soul's love for you. Feel your heart area opening like a flower.

3. Get a sense of the Great Creatress' presence. Get a sense of Her love for you.

4. Focus on a heart's desire, something you need to experience during this lifetime. You may need to ask your Masters, Teachers, and Loved Ones to bring a heart's desire to your attention. Accept what they offer even if it different than what you planned.

5. Set your heart's desire on a table in front of you.

6. Silently, tell yourself the story of this heart's desire. What is it? What does it look like? How does this heart's desire make you feel? What does it do for you? What does it do for others? Why is this heart's desire so important to you? How does it fulfill a Soul purpose? Who else is involved?

7. Feel intensely the importance of this heart's desire. Pause here, if you need more time to really, really, really feel everything about this heart's desire.

8. Using your spiritual imagination, breathe life-force energy into your heart's desire. Do that again. And again.

9. Ask your Soul to help you. Observe what your Soul does to manifest your heart's desire.

10. Is your Soul bringing any energy out of your body and using it?

11. Or is your Soul removing something inside you that restricted the fulfillment of this heart's desire?

12. Ask your Masters, Teachers, and Loved Ones to assist in this process. Observe them closely.

13. Embodying, again, your Souls Light, and sense the Great Creatress' presence.

14. Ask her to demonstrate the next step in manifesting this heart's desire? Feel Her intention. Feel Her focus. Feel her single-minded attention.

15. Ask Her why she installed this heart's desire in you?

16. Ask Her how it serves Her Divine Plan for you?

17. Ask Her how it serves Her overall Divine Plan?

18. The Great Creatress now allows you to witness the benefit to humanity.

19. The Great Creatress now allows you to witness how this heart's desire plays out in your life, and in others' lives.

20. When this feels complete, thank the Great Creatress, thank your Masters, Teachers, and Loved Ones. Thank your Soul. Feel the rearrangement inside of you.

Exercise: Blessing Self-Doubt and Disappointment into Nothingness

1. Refresh your Akashic Records by repeating the whole prayer once.

2. Now, take three deep breaths, releasing them forcefully and completely.

3. Use your exhalations to aid in releasing old energy.

4. Embody your Soul's Light.

5. Surround yourself with your Masters, Teachers, and Loved Ones. Allow yourself to receive their loving support.

6. Expand your consciousness and connect with the love, authority, and power of the Great Creatress. She, too, is helping you in this process.

7. Ask your Masters, Teachers, and Loved Ones to help you to whole-heartedly bless and release your limiting history of self-doubt.

8. Whole-heartedly bless and release the unwanted effects of self-doubt throughout time.

9. Whole-heartedly bless and release any self-doubt that no longer serves you.

10. Whole-heartedly bless and release the lifetimes where self-doubt was the obstacle that defeated you.

11. Whole-heartedly bless and release every shred of unwanted self-doubt as it evaporates from you, like steam disappearing in the air.

12. Whole-heartedly bless and release all self-doubt that has been stored in your memory throughout the centuries.

13. Know that everything you bless and release is raw, unformed energy by the universe.

14. Take three deep cleansing inhalations followed by forceful, clearing exhalations. Notice how this refreshes your consciousness.

15. Whole-heartedly bless and release all memories of disappointment in this lifetime. Use your breath to aid this process.

16. Whole-heartedly bless and release all disappointment you experienced in past lifetimes.

17. Whole-heartedly bless and release all disappointment that you experienced while in your mother's womb.

18. Whole-heartedly bless and release all disappointment experienced by your mother, father, and your grandparents.

19. Whole-heartedly bless and release self-doubt and disappointment like steam dissipating in the air.

20. Whole-heartedly bless and release others misuse of your self-doubt for their selfish gain.

21. Whole-heartedly bless and release others misuse of your disappointment for their selfish gain.

22. Whole-heartedly bless and release all self-doubt or disappointment that may briefly appear through reading or seeing images depicting repression and control. These are not you.

23. Whole-heartedly bless and release your past until it is nothingness, until it is completely neutralized.

24. Whole-heartedly bless and release the past in service of your neighbors, your cities, your counties, your states, and all the countries everywhere on Earth.

25. Whole-heartedly bless and release the past in service of Mother Earth.

26. Whole-heartedly bless and release the past until you are no longer separate from the Great Creatress. Until you are neutral space. Pure consciousness. Until you are the Great Creatress.

27. Take three slow, deep, relaxed breaths as you calmly, gently, gracefully re-enter ordinary reality.

28. Thank the Great Creatress and your Masters, Teachers, and Loved Ones for their love and assistance. Thank your Soul, too.

29. Roll your shoulders and open your eyes.

Exercise: How to Align Your Self-will with Divine Will

1. Begin by taking 7 deep inhalations with forceful exhalations.

2. Notice how centered and stabilized you now feel.

3. Embody your Soul's Light, bringing it all the way down through your body from your 8th chakra down to the bottoms of your feet.

4. Your Soul's Light extends in a cone all around you.

5. Ground yourself up to the Great Creatress and down into the balance point of Mother Earth.

6. Allow yourself to receive the steadiness of this double grounding.

7. Become aware of your 3rd chakra, at the apex of your ribcage. This is the center of your self-will.

8. Your self-will extends out from your 3rd chakra like an energetic rope whose fibers seek connection with other humans and with the Great Creatress.

9. Imagine the Great Creatress' Divine Will as an energetic rope end dropping into your viewing screen from above.

10. She is extending Her Divine Will to you and your self-will for connection in the 3rd chakra.

11. Get a sense of Her Divine Will fibers opening and receiving your self-will fibers.

12. You may even feel the Divine Will fibers winding into and around your self-will fibers, blending together easily.

13. You are now connected to Her Divine Will like an infant in the womb is connected to the mother through the umbilical card.

14. Her Divine Will fibers tenderly enter your 3rd chakra blending the two ropes neatly into one woven energy rope.

15. Take a few deep refreshing breaths remaining connected.

16. Observe as Divine Will gently moves around the interior of your body.

17. Where inside your body does Divine Will go? What other parts of your body seem most receptive to blending with Divine Will?

18. Notice how Divine Will is interacting with your brain at the hippocampus and the amygdala..

Made in United States
Troutdale, OR
04/07/2024

19020963R10197